Psychology

in

Progress

General editor: Peter Herriot

Personality

Psychology in Progress

Already available

Philosophical Problems in Psychology
edited by Neil Bolton

Thinking in Perspective
Critical essays in the study of thought processes
edited by Andrew Burton and John Radford

The School Years
Current issues in the socialization of young people
edited by John C. Coleman

Applications of Conditioning Theory
edited by Graham Davey

Aspects of Memory
edited by Michael M. Gruneberg and Peter Morris

Issues in Childhood Social Development
edited by Harry McGurk

Brain, Behaviour and Evolution
edited by David A. Oakley and H. C. Plotkin

Small Groups and Personal Change
edited by Peter B. Smith

Personality

Theory, measurement
and research

edited by
FAY FRANSELLA

METHUEN

First published in 1981 by
Methuen & Co. Ltd
11 New Fetter Lane, London EC4P 4EE

Published in the USA by
Methuen & Co.
in association with Methuen, Inc.
733 Third Avenue, New York, NY 10017

This collection © 1981 Methuen & Co. Ltd
Individual chapters © 1981 the respective authors

Typeset by The Drawing Room
Printed in the United States of America

British Library Cataloguing in Publication Data

Personality. — (Psychology in progress)
1. Personality
I. Fransella, Fay   II. Series
155.2   BF698   80-41339

ISBN 0-416-72770-0
ISBN 0-416-72780-8 Pbk (University paperbacks; 719)

Contents

Notes on the contributors

J. Adams-Webber is Associate Professor of Psychology at Brock University, Ontario, Canada. Personality theory, social cognition and psychopathology are his main interests. His most recent publication is *Personal Construct Theory: Concepts and Applications* (Wiley, 1979).

Sheldon Blackman, Director of Evaluation and Program Development at the St Vincent's North Richmond Community Mental Health Center, is also an Adjunct Professor of Psychology at Long Island University. He is co-author with Kenneth M. Goldstein of *An Introduction to Data Management in the Behavioural and Social Sciences* (Wiley, 1971) and of *Advances and Applications in Cognitive Style* (Wiley, in press).

Christopher Dare is Child Psychiarist and Psychoanalyst working at the Bethlem Royal and Maudsley Hospitals. He is co-author with Joseph Sandler and Alex Holder of *The Patient and the Analyst* (Allen and Unwin, 1973), and of a long series of papers on 'Frames of reference in psychoanalytic psychology'. With Lily Pincus he is the author of *Secrets in the Family* (Faber, 1978). His main clinical interest is the integration of individual and family psychotherapies and he has research interests in this area also.

Peter Fonagy is Lecturer in Psychology at University College, London. His doctoral dissertation concerned the cognitive processes involved in dreaming, and he has presented several papers on the subject. Currently he is involved in establishing a dream laboratory in his department.

Fay Fransella is Reader in Clinical Psychology at the Royal Free Hospital School of Medicine, University of London. Her publications include papers on personal construct psychology and the relationship between cognitive and behaviour change and psychotherapy; among her books are *Personal Change and Reconstruction* (Academic Press, 1972), *Need to Change?* (Methuen, 1976) and, with D. Bannister, *Inquiring Man* (Penguin Books, 1971, 1980) and *A Manual for Repertory Grid Technique* (Academic Press, 1977). Her current research interest is the process of psychological change during psychotherapy.

Kenneth M. Goldstein, Director of Research and Program Development at the Staten Island Children's Community Mental Health Center, is also an Adjunct Professor of Psychology at Queens College of the City University of New York. He is co-author with Sheldon Blackman of *Cognitive Style: Five Approaches and Relevant Research* (Wiley, 1978) and of a chapter on cognitive style in McReynold's *Advances in Psychological Assessment*, vol. 4, (1977).

Paul Kline is Reader in Psychometrics in the Department of Psychology, University of Exeter. Among his many publications are *Fact and Fantasy in Freudian Theory* (Methuen, 1972), *Psychometrics and Psychology* (Academic Press, 1979) and, with R. B. Cattell, *The Scientific Analysis of Personality and Maturation* (Academic Press, 1978). His main interests are psychometrics, personality and the objective study of psychoanalytic theory.

Keith Oatley is Lecturer in Experimental Psychology at the University of Sussex where he has been since 1967, apart from a two-year break in Toronto. He is the author of two books, *Brain Mechanisms and Mind* (Thames and Hudson, 1972) and *Perceptions and Representations* (Methuen, 1978), and numerous articles on physiological and cognitive psychology. During the last five years his work has been on psychotherapy, groups and processes of personal change.

Joseph F. Rychlak is Professor of Psychological Sciences at Purdue University, West Lafayette, Indiana, USA. His major interests include personality theory, theory construction, the philosophy of science and the history of psychology. His approach to learning is the Logical Learning Theory. Recent publications include *The Psychology of Rigorous Humanism* (Wiley–Interscience, 1977) and *Discovering Free Will and Personal Responsibility* (Oxford University Press, 1979).

Boris Semeonoff is Reader in Psychology, University of Edinburgh. He is a former editor of the *British Journal of Psychology* and a past President of the British Psychological Society. His publications include *Personality Assessment: Selected Readings* (ed.) (Penguin, 1966, 1970), 'New Developments in Projective Testing' in P. Kline (ed.) *New Approaches in Psychological Measurement* (Wiley, 1973) and *Projective Techniques* (Wiley, 1976). Personality theory and assessment and psychometrics are his chief interests.

Peter B. Smith is Reader in Social Psychology at the University of Sussex. His principal interest is in the analysis of sensitivity training and allied group training methods, drawing primarily on theories derived from social psychology, having undertaken numerous empirical studies in this field. He is author of *Improving Skills in Working with People: The T-group* (HMSO, 1969), *Group Processes* (Penguin, 1970), *Groups within Organizations* (Harper and Row, 1973), *Group Processes and Personal Change* (Harper and Row, 1980) and *Small Groups and Personal Change* (Methuen, 1980), as well as many other articles and papers.

Editor's introduction

Thoughts on and investigations into the concept of personality have been bedevilled by a lack of agreement on what 'it' really is. Yet 'it' does not exist, any more than do intelligence or motivation. Their only reality is in the minds of those seeking to understand people as individuals and as groups of individuals. It is because so many theorists strive toward a better total understanding of his or her fellow human beings that such a vast range of approaches to the study of 'personality' is to be found in psychology today. This book is concerned with a sample from this pool of approaches.

Uncertainty about how best to describe and understand personality is not the only problem with which one is faced. The evolution of the discipline of psychology, with its roots in nineteenth-century physics, has led to the rather extraordinary situation in which the study of the whole person is set apart from the rest of psychology. If psychology had sprung from the 'new' physics things might well have been very different. We might have had a conception of the person as an entity in action, intimately bound up with the environment in which we all exist. This might well have led to the study of the person becoming the very basis of the whole discipline of psychology rather than, as at present, being only one of its many 'areas' of study.

Yet psychology is continuing to evolve and now finds itself in hot debate over this very issue of action. Evidence of this is provided by Neil Bolton's editorial comment (in the book in this series *Philosophical Problems in Psychology*) that one preoccupation to emerge from the contributors 'is an emphasis on the importance of the concept of action'. He also stated that psychologists rarely make reference to philosophical analysis, and few would disagree with him. Both these points are relevant to this volume. First, personality theory has evolved along with psychology, culminating in the action-centred theories represented here by those of Kelly, Rogers and Laing. Second, the philosophical issues underlying personality theories are taken as this volume's starting point. The past lack of interest in philosophical analysis seems particularly strange when considering the study of personality, since all its theories are about you and me and all these theories must have some at least implicit notion of the sort of creatures we humans are – are we pulled or pushed into action or are we in the driving seat? Are we largely determined or are we free? Are we moulded by the events that happen in our lives or are we self-creating? And so on. It is such issues that Joseph Rychlak examines in the first chapter.

Part II considers the first and profoundly the most influential theory of Freud. His model of the person is implicit as indeed it is in most of the theories covered in this book, but it is these implicit philosophical strands that Rychlak makes explicit. Christopher Dare's chapter on the Freudian psychoanalytic theory of personality is unusual in some respects. His perspective differs from that of many other authors of psychology introductory texts on this topic in that it is the view of a practising analyst. Dare takes the position that all psychoanalysis is a theory of the person and as such has no single component that can be labelled a 'Theory of Personality'. He therefore offers the reader a broad review of the development of the psychoanalytic model of the person, or rather the mind of the person, as well as describing the data base of psychoanalytic theory – the psychoanalytic situation. The reader is certain to gain more insight into ongoing psychoanalytic thinking from this perspective than he would from a review of Freud's developmental theory and of particular personality types which, as Dare points out, have been abandoned almost completely by analysts but, paradoxically, have been the focus of many previous reviews.

Dare's chapter is followed by that of Boris Semeonoff on some methods of measurement associated with the psychodynamic approach; the third chapter concerns research. It is often said that one of the main problems with Freudian theory is that it is scientifically untestable. Peter Fonagy addresses himself to this issue and cites experimental literature to indicate whether or not this commonly held view is substantiated.

This format of chapters on theory followed by measurement and research has been adopted where relevant in each part of this book. Measurement and research, particularly the latter, are so often given only passing mention in personality texts, yet a theory's usefulness in generating ideas is arguably one of the major criteria of its validity. Each part has thus been divided into separate chapters, even if written by the same author. This will enable the reader to unearth the point of interest in, say personality questionnaires, without having to spend time digging. The risk of providing this aid to reading is a disjointed appearance. I hope this will not prove to be the case.

What follows in Part III has its roots more firmly in modern times. The development of sophisticated statistical procedures, notably factor analysis, has largely gone hand in hand with the approaches to personality of Cattell and Eysenck. These factor analytic theories, the questionnaires with which they are intimately associated and the massive amount of research which they have stimulated, are outlined and described by Paul Kline. To facilitate a more complete understanding of these theories, he has included a very clear and succinct summary of the factor analytic procedure in Chapter 5.

In more recent years, there has been an increasing focus in psychology on the relationship between cognitive variables and behaviour and this is also the case in the field of personality. In Part IV Sheldon Blackman and Kenneth Goldstein discuss how our thought processes, or cognitive styles, influence our behaviour and hence 'personality'. Because of its concern with cognitive structure, some overlap occurs between this Part on cognitive style and Chapter 12 in Part V by Jack Adams-Webber. It has so happened that the idea of cognitive complexity arose directly out of George Kelly's personal construct theory but has become a distant area of research now generally classified under cognitive style. This is a good example of the inevitability of overlap in a book on personality, since each theorist is viewing the same event – 'us' – and each is standing in a different place.

It is often argued that George Kelly indeed proposed a 'cognitive' theory and, if so, it should be in Part IV of this volume. However, it is suggested in Chapter 10 that this argument is based on a misunderstanding of Kelly's view of the person. It is more than thought processes that make us the sort of people we are. Just as Kelly is often categorized as a cognitive theorist, so he is sometimes called a 'humanist'. If so, he might well have been included in Part VI along with discussions on the work of Rogers, Laing and Maslow. He and the humanists do indeed focus on the qualities of being human, such as the experience of 'me' and the purposes we ourselves put into action – we are self-creating. All are also reactions against the behaviourist tradition, seeing it more productive to increase our understanding of ourselves and others by looking upon ourselves as if we were actors on the world scene rather than reactors to it. However, Kelly differs from Rogers and Laing in thinking it important to go beyond the study of personal experience in our search for understanding. His theory also has a much wider range of convenience in being able, potentially at least, to increase our understanding of those without language – be they human or non-human. In fact, the range of convenience of Kelly's theory is the whole realm of the psychology of the person and is not just limited to what is traditionally called 'personality'. Because of these differences from the cognitive theorists on the one hand and the humanists on the other, Kelly's theory stands on its own as Part V.

Of all areas of study in psychology, personality is arguably the most exciting. Increasing our understanding of each other has profound implications not only for our personal lives, and our personal interactions, but also for the fields of politics, law, religion and, in fact, for any situation in which human beings interact. It also becomes of crucial significance in the field of psychological disorder. If we accept that the medical model is not necessarily the best one for psychologists to work within, then it is to the personality theorist that many look for guidance. In most of the approaches discussed in this volume, attention has been paid to the contribution each has made, and is making, to our understanding of those in distress. Whether or not there are 'facts' about personality to be discovered, at the present time we can say that psychologists are actively and energetically striving towards the goal of understanding the quirks of human nature.

FAY FRANSELLA

Part I
Personality and philosophy

1 Philosophical bases of personality theories

Joseph F. Rychlak

As we begin our study of personality there are certain issues which we must consider of a 'philosophical' nature. Historically, psychology has tried to divorce itself from philosophy by stressing the importance of scientific proof in the discovery of observable knowledge. Most psychologists today look at philosophy as the examination of unprovable questions, such as whether there is a true 'reality' existing independent of our senses (how can we ever know?), or the effect of a non-material 'mind' (which can never be measured directly) on matter. Issues like these seem naturally to focus on the area of personality study, and they cannot be dismissed as irrelevant even though we would prefer to avoid them. When we describe people we just have to recognize that everything we say is not easily captured in the same language we use to talk about the workings of inanimate 'nature', such as the paths of the stars, or the shifts in weather patterns.

The first thing we must do is define what we mean by philosophy, and then the implications for personality study will be easier to see. The word philosophy tends to frighten people needlessly, because they assume that there is 'a' body of philosophical knowledge all worked out and that the only people who really understand it are philosophers. Surely undergraduate students in a personality course cannot be expected to deal with this body of philosophical knowledge, particularly since it is probably very abstract, making it difficult to understand and, above all, deadly dull! This is a fairly common attitude held by undergraduate students, and we must begin now by stressing that in its most general phrasing, philosophy is *not* 'a' uniform body of knowledge waiting to be memorized. Though there are certain historical questions which philosophy as a scholarly discipline has addressed over the centuries, in its most basic sense, philosophy is merely the study of *assumptions* made by a human reasoner.

Human beings *must* begin making certain assumptions in order to reason, and whether they are aware of it or not, these assumptions influence what can and will then be learned, discovered, or 'known' about that which interests them. Philosophy merely helps spell out for us what we *already know* in our assumptions *before* we bring these assumptions to bear in understanding (knowing more!) about whatever it is that we take an interest in. The word philosophy is often defined as the 'pursuit of wisdom', but in this pursuit we do not always 'go forward' to learn only that which is yet to be known ('new things'). We can also 'turn around' and look at the assumptions we make in going forward – just as we have now been looking at the assumptions made about what philosophy means. In the present chapter we are going to look at five major assumptions from which those men and women who study personality are likely to choose in 'going forward' to work out their unique approaches. If we can gain an appreciation for these basic assumptions we will have practised a little philosophy and also prepared ourselves for the study of the various personality approaches taken up in this volume.

Organic assumptions

One of the first assumptions which occurs to us as we set about explaining anything is to suggest a substance of some kind which possibly 'makes it up'. We mentioned above the effect of mind on 'matter'. What is matter? The assumption here is that this is a basic substance of some kind, and that if we want to understand why some things behave one way and other things behave differently, we might look into the kinds of substances which go to make them up. Some of the earliest theories of ancient Egypt and Greece were oriented to such explanations, in which everything was seen as being made up of materials such as water, earth, fire, air and so on. In 380 BC Hippocrates, the father of medicine, proposed that human beings were made healthy or ill depending upon the mixture of such organic substances as black and yellow biles (body fluids) that combined in various ways to strike a certain balance in the body's 'chemistry' (as we would say today). Too much black bile relative to the other biles in the body and the person would be pessimistic and depressed in mood.

This kind of explanation of behaviour became very popular in the rise of medicine over the centuries and today psychologists often refer to it as the 'medical model'. Medical models thus seek to explain not only physical health but all behaviour by finding some underlying organic cause including body fluids, hereditary substances such as genes, and even micro-organisms that might infect the body and cause various forms of illness.

The medical model favours a point of view which philosophers call *realism*. Realism holds that our knowledge of the world is based upon what is 'really there', in the hard facts of observed experience. Our minds copy an order in reality which is truly existing, independent of our minds. Philosophical explanations which place emphasis on the contribution which mind makes to knowledge are called *idealisms*. A completely idealistic account would hold that there is *no* reality; that is, everything known experientially is mental and the fact that we happen to believe in an independent reality is itself merely an idea about something rather than a 'real fact' that must be accepted.

Freud and his followers were confronted with the traditional realistic, medical-model style of explanation in accounting for mental illness. Freud once joked to Jung, a friend and colleague who later broke with him to found a rival school of psychoanalysis, that their medical colleagues seemed to be waiting for the discovery of a micro-organism to explain mental illness 'as if for the messiah who must after all come some day to all true believers' (McGuire, 1974, p.116).

Freud began finding reasons for mental illness other than weak heredity, infections or bodily decline. He began to describe the causes of mental illness in terms of 'wishes' and 'counter-wishes', and in so doing introduced an idealistic theme into the realisms of his day. Even so, he retained enough of his medical education to keep a central idea of the organic medical model in psychoanalysis. He always believed that an explanation of behaviour was more thorough if it were put in terms of the balancing of underlying forces in the personality system. Thus, Freud turned a strictly physical concept of energy into what he called *libido*. Freud considered libido to be the energy of sexual instincts, and Jung thought of it more broadly as a desire to live and to extend behaviour into every facet of life's possibilities.

This style of trying to explain observable behaviour in terms of some kind of underlying force that is balancing or imbalancing, being used up, and so on, is called *reductionism*. The reductive explanation tries to account for what is observed by breaking down (reducing) the overt and apparent to the uniform material or energic foundation for everything that exists. In physical science this was done through the so-called principle of the *conservation of energy*. Wood burns to create a fixed amount of heat per unit of wood-substance, which in turn heats water to a certain degree Fahrenheit, before it turns into steam to drive a steam engine for exactly 'so' long, which can, in turn, move a railway carriage down the line for a precise distance, and so on. In each successive instance, the energy which was 'there' as a potential in the wood is transformed but also conserved as it serves different functions. In time, due to the loss of efficiency and the friction involved in moving railway carriages along lines this energy gets used up, but we can explain the motion of a train by understanding the principles of a steam boiler.

In similar fashion, we find personality theories which try to explain behaviour by reducing it to the consumption of underlying (reductive) needs. The concept of *motivation* enters here, for to be in need is essentially to have a high level of motivation. Need-gratifications such as obtaining food when hungry or sexual release when under a drive for sexual intercourse is said to reduce motivation. Some theories of learning have relied on this 'drive-reduction' idea to suggest that learning occurs thanks to the fact that certain behaviours end in the lowering of a drive level. The ideal state of motivation is that of *homeostasis* or 'balance' and the personality is said to take on those behavioural styles which will ensure such a well-balanced (satisfied, actualized, and so forth) level. It is always possible on the organic assumption to tie need level to heredity, suggesting, for example, that some people are born with a greater need for this or that physical satisfaction than other people.

Hereditary theories and the medical model have come under attack in the rise of modern psychology. Although many modern theorists accept the likelihood of some inborn influence on behaviour, as well as the organic substrate of needs, the trend in modern psychology has been to stress learning over simply innate predispositions or biological involvements. If people become abnormal in behaviour it is because of what happened to them *after* birth, and in interpersonal relations, rather than what they were physically predestined to do. Freud never really clarified the distinctions between what are his more biologically-sounding conceptions (realism) and what are his clearly non-organic conceptions (idealism) of people making themselves ill entirely at a psychological level.

Evolutionary assumptions

Closely related to the organic explanations of history, and in one sense growing out of them, we have a second major assumption made in personality description having to do with the idea of an evolution or a development taking place. An essential suggestion here is the idea of a progress or advance. To evolve is to grow, to become more effective, hence to improve in some fashion. We tend to accept this notion of a progressive development today, but history teaches that it actually took centuries for western philosophy to accept this notion of progress (Becker and Barnes, 1952). In early Grecian times (BC) it was believed that humanity had descended from a Golden Age, and that rather than becoming better and better the course of civilization was 'down hill'. The Renaissance period in western history helped foster the idea that humanity could improve, and doubtless the rise of scientific knowledge in the seventeenth century was taken as evidence that there was a progression in the knowledge and life-style of so-called 'advanced' societies. In the nineteenth century we witness the introduction of the immensely influential theory of Charles Darwin — that an organic evolution has been under way in the course of animal life and that *homosapiens* is the highest form achieved in this progression to date.

There were other evolutionary theories in modern times, based more on historical than biological conceptions of advance. The dialectical theory of Hegel, which held that history moved according to a thesis–antithesis and synthesis of opposites and/or contradictions, was also influential in the rise of the idea of progress. As adapted by Marx into the communistic theory, we see large segments of humanity accepting the view today that there is an oppositional march of civilization through the contradictions of the class struggle.

Communism holds that some day in the future a much better society will evolve in which all class-consciousness will end. Whether or not we believe this theory or the evolutionary theory of Darwin, we cannot deny the historical fact that the drift to a view of progress took place and that it has had its impact on personality theory.

In psychoanalytical theory we find many Darwinian themes, such as the assumption that children are like 'primitive' human beings, re-enacting in many ways the origins of society. The Oedipal complex is supposedly a re-creation in each of our early lives of the way primitive human beings formed a family unit. This theory is based on an analogy to the fact that while developing *in utero* we 're-enact' our organic histories in the sense of having gills at one point, a tail-formation at another, and so on. Freud, and then many of his followers, also made use of developmental stages through which we supposedly move in maturing to adulthood.

In recent times an important developmental theory has been proposed by Piaget (1967), who sees all human beings as passing through four stages of cognitive function, each stage representing a further degree of abstraction and freedom from sensori-motor experience. Piaget also views the progression of development in a dialectical manner, as occurring in terms of an opposition between internal and external events which then reach a higher level of equilibrium. Children first assimilate or 'take into' mind an understanding of their thumbs by sucking them as if they were nipples. In time, a differentiation is made and the child's level of understanding increases through the working out of an inside–thesis (knowledge of nipple) and an outside–antithesis (sight of thumb), leading in time to a new internal synthesis (nipple v. thumb), and so on.

Evolutionary themes are also prominent in the writing of Maslow (1954) (see Chapter 13), which emphasize that our very needs in motivation are ordered according to the survival value of organic evolution. We are all fundamentally animals, in need of certain basics such as food, water, sexual release and the like. Once these more basic satisfactions have been realized, we witness the emergence of higher-order needs. Maslow teaches us that though the basic needs of life are important, they do not really tell us much about our higher motivations. It is not really possible to 'reduce' our highest aspirations to our base, animalistic promptings, as the organic theorists suggest. Maslowian theory has fostered what is sometimes called a Third Force in personality study, because it rejects aspects of both the psychoanalytical tradition (Force One) and the behaviour-istic tradition (Force Two). The details of this Third Force movement will be taken up in Chapters 13 and 14.

Another very important theme reflected in Maslow and other personality theories such as those of Rogers and the existentialists (Chapter 13) is that of *actualization* or *self-realization*. One of the things which the latter theorists dislike about psychoanalytical or behaviour-istic theories is that they seem to 'fix' the personality structure early in life. For example, both Freud and another early collaborator who later founded his own theory, Alfred Adler, had the personality structure pretty well 'set' by the age of five years. Children who had passed their fifth birthday were not viewed as under continual development, change, or growth. Of course, if events came up demanding that changes be made neither Freud nor Adler would say this was impossible. Indeed, the very idea of entering psychotherapy implies that changes in behaviour can occur. But it was not the usual course of psychological 'development' to be constantly changing throughout life. Those personality theorists who reacted against this non-developmental conception were basing their arguments on the image of human behaviour suggested by evolutionary theory. There is a related issue here, one which takes us into our next assumption, and fixes our interest on the *source* of this development. Is the person under evolutionary advance a mere pawn in the evolutionary game? Or does he or she have a hand in what will be advanced or improved upon?

Agency assumptions

If we do things to alter the chemistry of underlying drives – 'lower' them in some way – then how much actual control do we have over what we *believe* we are intending to do? If a person says 'When I get hungry I choose to eat only what I have decided tastes good to me', this suggests that he or she is 'in control' of eating behaviour. This would mean that the person is an 'agent' of his or her behaviour. Philosophically speaking, agency refers to the source of control as being the *person* himself or herself. Usually, the term *self* is used in personality to describe agency. Self means that an identifiable style, a 'sameness', is to be seen in the person's behaviour because he or she does indeed develop consistent preferences to do one thing rather than another. The self chooses, and the observed behaviour that follows is an 'effect' of this preliminary choice.

Now, the explanations of natural science which Freud had to face specifically detracted from the concept of agency in human behaviour. The point of the medical model is to suggest that a disease's symptoms are the *effects* of underlying organic causes ('bad' genes or germs, etc.). The patterns of measles which break out on a child's body are not agents of anything. They merely reflect what is going on organically underneath, where the foreign organisms (germs) are at work 'causing' the illness in the first place.

If we extend such reductive explanations to 'abnormal behaviour' in general, which now becomes like the symptoms of a disease, then it follows that there is no self-identity acting as agency in this behaviour. The psychotic person who 'sees' what is not there (hallucinates) is under direction from below, from his or her organic breakdown of some kind. The same would apply to a more normal person who just happens to fear enclosed places (claustrophobia). Such people do not choose to see what is not there or to experience terror in certain situations. Their symptoms, like the child's measles, simply 'turn up' thanks to organic reasons.

Well, maybe the same holds for *all* behaviour, which is *never* a question of true agency. Maybe there are underlying organic causes in everything we do, and our sense of agency is merely an illusion. As this style of explanation was to be worked out in academic psychology – which took its lead from natural science rather than from the medical model *per se* (see Rychlak, 1977) – the concept of *drive* as a stimulus (cause) of behaviour (response) began to take over the role of agency.

Behaviouristic psychology has since its beginnings in the writings of John Watson (1913) specifically tried to account for behaviour *without* agency. According to behaviourism, the person's responses are always 'effects' and that is true even when the responses made are verbal statements like 'when I get hungry I choose to eat only what I have decided tastes good to me.' A person who said this would doubtless make the agency assumption and believe that he or she could, in fact, make a self-selection which would act as a 'cause' of the eating behaviour to follow. Behaviourism denies that this takes place, because the person is not an agent of behaviour. What this person will select to eat is itself an 'effect', a behavioural tendency without choice which has been shaped through drive-reductions into him or her in the past.

In fact, the very language used to express this so-çalled preference has been shaped into the person's behaviour without his or her agency being involved. As a child, this person was born with an hereditary need for food. When hungry, this need was reflected in a rising drive level (organic assumption). Then, certain foods were introduced by parents which, in turn, resulted in a drive-reduction of this hunger motivation (satisfied hunger drive). Certain foods have implicit drive-stimulus value (such as sugars), but in the main what the person comes to 'choose' in the present is what has typically lowered his or her drive level in the past. There is no real choice being made here. According to the behaviourist, agency is an illusion (we shall see another type of argument like this below, having to do with environmental rather than biological controls on behaviour). In taking this position behaviourism has endorsed a long-standing philosophical position. Philosophers have for centuries debated this question of whether or not human beings can really control their own destiny, under such topics as freedom of the will, determinism, and above all, *teleology*. The latter term is based on the Greek word *telos*, which refers to the 'end' for the sake of which behaviour is being intended. For example, the Greek philosopher Socrates (Plato, 1952, p.262) once pointed out how people can put up with something negative in order ultimately to gain something positive as an end. Thus a businessman might put up with an annoying and potentially dangerous sea voyage in order to turn a profit in some distant land. Socrates made the agency assumption here, believing that we can indeed decide on the ends which we wish to pursue. By and large, those philosophers who have accepted agency in behaviour tended to idealism. Their oppponents took a realistic thesis and tried to show how what we 'think' is itself merely an 'effect of what is really going on in the hard facts of our biology'. Behaviourism is, of course, a decidedly realistic psychological theory.

It would not be extreme to suggest that much of what we call 'personality' study in psychology has to do with this fundamental question – whether or not there is really agency in behaviour. This was the first real challenge facing Freud and the other analysts, who were working in face-to-face contact with human beings and taking what these people had to say seriously. The theories which issued from such contact are often called 'psychodynamic' today (see Part II). As we noted above, when he began speaking about wishes and counter-wishes as somehow influencing behaviour, Freud was departing from exclusive reliance on the organic assumption and moving in the direction of the agency assumption. A wish is simply another way of talking about hoped-for intentions. There is one major change he made in agency theories such as those of Socrates' businessman: Freud proposed that it was possible to have *more* than one end or 'intention' in mind at the same time. People are more complex than we give them credit for. Also, Freud argued that there are many wishes which people have as desires that they would prefer to deny having. Wishes that mother die or father be made sick reflect such hoped-for ends which the child would not like to admit having. Sexual wishes in relation to a parent were also frequent 'ends' that a person might have yet not admit having, even to himself or herself. What person would want to admit that he or she desires a parent sexually (Oedipal Complex)?

Due to such objectionable intentions, Freud suggested that there is a tendency to censor what will be admitted into conscious awareness and what will be 'kept out'. This keeping out of certain intentions (wishes) from consciousness Freud called *repression*, and the fact that there is a portion of mind in which these inadmissible ideas are 'housed' he called the *unconscious*. Philosophers like Schopenhauer had talked about the unconscious before Freud, and they had even suggested that one could express wilful control over one's behaviour from out of this 'unknown' realm of mind. This is one of the key issues with which personality study is still wrestling: *can a person be an unconscious agent of his or her behaviour?* Though he found it an embarrassment in trying to account for such unconscious agency, Freud (1923, p.593) did, in fact, answer 'yes' to this question, and the other analysts followed his lead. One of the most frequent errors made by students of personality is to equate the Freudian unconscious direction of behaviour with the control of behaviour directed by underlying organic factors. It is easy to reason as follows: 'Behaviourism holds that we are not really determining our conscious behaviour. Psychoanalysis holds that we are not really determining our conscious behaviour. Hence: behaviourism and psychoanalysis have the same position on behavioural determination.' This is false. Freud has an unconscious agency in his theory whereas behaviourism does not make room for agency at all.

The non-analytical and non-behaviouristic theories of personality which have developed since Freud have not been so willing to place great emphasis on the unconscious direction of behaviour. Rogerian (1951) theory, for example, tends to borrow terminology from the

Gestalt psychology movement, which opposed behaviourism early in the present century. The Gestalt theorists emphasized the fact that whatever we know consciously is only so because of a frame of reference within which we understand that which is 'known'. For example, if we see a tree in the distance, or, think of a goal in the future, these items in our understanding are framed in by a background which gives them meaning as much as the 'thing' itself. The tree is merely a *figure* on the surrounding *ground*. We forget about the ground and are not conscious of it, but it is always 'there' in the sense of a potential. Figure and ground together constitute a kind of field, a totality of (dialectically) interdependent relations which make up our understanding. Now, according to Rogerian theory and several of the existentialist theories of personality, what Freud meant by unconscious behaviour is 'really' a matter of the ground factors involved in behaviour. Even so, the Rogerian and existentialistic theorists are prone to make the agency assumption. The basic theme in these views is that the person can and should assume responsibility for his or her own life.

Kelly's (1955) personal construct theory (see Chapter 10) also has the person as agent in behaviour, conceptualizing or construing events according to personal controls. Kelly felt that the analysts had *reified* the unconscious mind (transformed a theoretical idea into a 'real thing'). For his part, most of the so-called unconscious mental contents are personal constructs of a visual nature; that is, they are pre-verbal notions that people have framed about life in infancy and childhood, so that they were not put into words. Although not expressible in words, such early constructs show up in dreams and they influence behaviour daily, not from out of some unconscious region but rather out of the same place whence all our ideas come. Note that this is still a *telic* or *teleological* view of behaviour. That is, Kelly assumed that the person freely selected the visual material on the basis of which he or she framed personal constructs and behaved 'for the sake of' – or some alternative that could also be freely construed. We next turn to another assumption which has countered such teleological description in behaviour.

Environmental assumptions

Everyone knows that human behaviour occurs within a complex set of circumstances. What we 'do' in life depends upon what is open to us. We cannot throw snowballs in summer, and few people spend a day at the beach in the winter. We have to be quiet in church and are expected to cheer loudly at athletic contests. Our level of income and education predicts well where we will live, the size of our family, our political outlooks and recreational pursuits, and many other things as well. National heritage and religious affiliation add further complexities into our life-styles. When we think of such climatic, cultural, and socio-economic factors all funnelling down to us through our family influences – the teachings of our parents, siblings, grandparents, uncles, aunts and others – it is easy to see how a case can be made for the view that what we 'are' as personalities is what our environment has made us out to be.

We have already discussed the organic assumption, which draws its rationale from built-in physical needs, hereditary influences and the like, but now we are adding to this the claim that through environmental learnings of one sort or another, such as the direct instruction of our elders or our own efforts to copy and imitate the behaviours of our peers, we come to behave as our environment directs (determines) us to behave. Sometimes this argument is made at a broader level, bringing in socio-historical explanations. Some of these arguments are Marxian or neo-Hegelian suggesting, for example, that in the class struggle there are ideas being presented out of a vested interest – reflecting class biases.

Harking back to the previous sections, we arrive at the question: if all these factors enter in to give us our life-style, our attitudes and world opinions, why do we need to flatter ourselves into thinking that we are agents of our behaviour? In other words, even if we have some slight 'say-so' over what we will eat today or the kind of work we might follow, does not our socio-economic and socio-political background shape us to value in a fixed way, and will not these values in turn determine our food and occupational choices? The environmental assumption thus presumes that, organic considerations aside, human beings are social organisms set in an historical period and living within a given class structure, and that what they 'think' is as much a 'society thinking' as it is a 'person thinking'.

Not every theorist who emphasizes the effects of society and history on behaviour would deny agency in behaviour. That is, someone like Socrates might appreciate the bias which a professional identity gives the person so committed. The dentist notices things about people's teeth which the minister would overlook completely in judging them by their morality. But Socrates would view these unique biases as framed by the person as grounds 'for the sake of which' they behaved quite intentionally. Simply because all dentists look at a person's smile whereas ministers look at their morals does not mean that the human beings known as dentists or ministers are not in control of their own behaviour.

In psychology, a vigorous position in opposition to this agency assumption has been put forward by Skinner (1971), who argues in effect that personal control is an illusion. There may be some counter-control in everyone's behaviour, so that we are not mere pawns in the flow of events, but Skinner makes it clear that the human person is *never* an originating source of control. Nor is it possible for the person *ever* to be autonomous – that is, completely arbitrary and free from environmental direction. Behaviour is itself a matter of 'coming at' life, or emitting so-called *operant* responses. These responses 'operate' on the environment and often effect it in some way, yet they are *not* the controlling agencies that we humans fancy them to be.

Drawing an analogy with Darwinian natural selection, Skinner observes:

> The environment not only prods or lashes, it *selects*. Its role is similar to that in natural selection, though on a very different time scale, and was overlooked for the same reason. (Skinner, 1971, p.18)

In other words, we first emit a response, and if the environment provides us with a reinforcement of some sort leading to our automatically emitting more of the same type of operants on succeeding occasions, we are shaped into being what we 'are' completely without intention – that is, without self-direction or so-called agency.

One might think that a reinforcement following operant behaviour would necessarily be an organic drive-reduction of some sort, but Skinner insists that he does not care and indeed can never be certain what a reinforcement will be for the person. It is easy to guess that a piece of candy given a child following the child's operant responses of picking up his or her toys suggests a drive-reduction of some biological sort. But psychologists have no way of measuring this reinforcement directly. They merely infer it. And supposing the mother merely hugged the child to obtain the same result? What drive do we infer is reduced in this case? Why does candy work with one child and a hug with another? Skinner rejects all such physical drive theories in preference to a purely empirical determination of what seems to 'work' in behavioural manipulation. If we can empirically demonstrate that a level of operant behaviour is maintained or possibly increased due to some set of circumstances following its emission, we have determined empirically that reinforcement has taken place. Knowing what reinforcements 'work' on the person we can shape his or her behaviour accordingly.

Skinnerian conditioning is conceived differently from the drive-reduction theories which were once predominant in psychology. Some theorists attempt to combine both the classical drive-reduction explanation and the Skinnerian view of behaviour, and even to bring a modicum of agency into the explanation (see, for example, Bandura, 1969, p.26). There is much theoretical turmoil in modern learning theories, and they have been moving to *cognitive* psychological explanations in recent years. Cognitive psychology (see Chapter 8) borrows from the fields of cybernetics and information processing. This style of explanation meshes better with classical behaviouristic theory except that a drive-reduction explanation is not necessary. Behaviour is seen as a matter of processing information, which is put in, stored, retrieved, and put out (or fed back) in certain predictable ways. Now 'information' is a concept which nicely meshes with the environmental assumption. People 'are' what their environments over their past lives programmed them 'to be'. Here again, no agency is specifically called for. A self-identity would become just another input programming from the past, as the person is told that he or she is responsible for this or that, and must choose this or that, and so forth, without ever really being free of the environmental 'forces' shaping behaviour.

Most personality theorists who employ the environmental assumption today either fail to confront the issue of agency, or they specifically deny that agency occurs in human behaviour. There is a tradition in psychology dating back to its founders which has kept theoretical descriptions clear of any vitalistic or anthropomorphic colouring (see Boring, 1950). This may be changing, as today we are becoming more understanding of how science is created by the scientist as actor – or agent. Many of the leading scientists of history in the physical sciences were more open to telic description than were our leading psychologists (see Rychlak, 1977).

Assessment assumptions

To assess personality is to measure it in some way, capturing the total pattern at once, or possibly focusing on certain distinctive features of the person's behavioural tendencies. Not every psychologist believes that it is possible to capture something so unique and potentially elusive as personality in a measurement (test, scale, or questionnaire) and even those who believe that it can be so assessed disagree on the manner in which this is to be done. We also see the other assumptions about personality being mixed into the question of assessment, such as the realism–idealism issue. The realist would assume that in measuring the effects of personality we would be sampling something that really exists, an underlying genetically determined trait of some type which brings about the observed behavioural regularities we call 'personality'. The idealists, on the other hand, would hold that the testing instrument used to measure personality may sample behavioural preferences of the person as an agent, preferences which are not necessarily tied to anything substantial ('real') at all.

In the factor analytic theories of Eysenck and Cattell (see Chapter 5) we see a decidedly realistic emphasis, with the suggestion being advanced that some combination of hereditary – constitutional and early environmental habits are being sampled by the testing procedures followed. In the personal construct approach of Kelly (see Chapter 10) we find a more idealistic emphasis, in which the repertory grid identifies the uniquely held and personally generated construct system of the person under study.

Still other psychologists dislike the use of tests altogether. Rogers and the existentialists (see Chapter 13) are wary of tests, because they seem always to press the person's behaviour into the preconceived terminology of the test builder. That is, a test is 'made up' by a test giver, who has it in his or her mind what will be measured by this test. Subjects are put in the position of answering questions which may or may not have relevance to their actual behaviour. Just because a question can be asked does not mean it is fair to the person's actual behaviour, as in the old joke 'Have you stopped beating your wife?' Critics of standard tests argue that they always press the person into the preconceived ideas of the test givers.

One of the oldest issues in the measurement of personality was taken from the philosophical writings of Windelband (1904) by the psychologist Allport (1937). Windelband analysed the different approaches to data collection which sciences like physics and history take, but his arguments were easily adapted to the problems of personality study. A science like physics or biology employed what Windelband called a *nomothetic* form of study, because in this case large numbers (*nomo* = number) of sampled items are used to get an average or typical finding. For example, we might study the hearts of many animals (of the same or related species) and then form a generalization of what hearts are, how they work, and so on.

But the scientific study of history itself *cannot* be accomplished in the same nomothetic way that biology and physics are studied. In order to understand how the peoples of Great Britain behave, and to appreciate why they value what they do, we must have a picture of their unique course of historical life-style over the centuries. This is made even more important if we wish to contrast the people of Britain with those of France. In this case we cannot expect to take a sample of French people and a sample of British people, give both groups tests of some sort, and come up with an explanation. We are forced to study the unique histories of France and Britain quite without regard for the sampling of large numbers. Windelband called this form of study *idiographic* (*idio* = one's own, personal). Idiographic study does not result in general laws, applicable to everything in nature as the law of gravity does. Idiographic study results in distinctive and often non-generalizable descriptions of unique but meaningful events and outcomes.

When he transferred Windelband's terminology to the study of personality, Allport highlighted the fact that some psychologists think of their task as a nomothetic sampling and cataloguing of personality concepts which refer to everyone, whereas others take their job to be the idiographic understanding of what is unique about the individual person. In general, when we try to capture a total personality in all its uniqueness we speak of the construct employed as the *personality type*. When we try to frame a number of individual dimensions along which everyone can be studied, these constructs are called *personality traits*. To call someone a 'leader' implies a total quality of personality style, whereas to speak of the person's capacity for 'leadership' implies a personality trait. One of the first major efforts to assess personality was that of the global, personality-style type of assessment. This is how Freud approached his study of clients, and Rorschach proposed that we could come to understand the total personality based on how people uniquely organized their perceptions of an amorphous stimulus like an inkblot. Rorschach's inkblot test (1942) was the result, and a new theme in the history of personality study was launched called *projective* testing (see Chapter 3).

Projective tests are in the main idiographic instruments, in which it is assumed that the person is assessed by 'putting himself or herself' into the results through unconsciously ordering the contents according to unknown motives. Other projective testing instruments were to follow, with the major alternative to the Rorschach being the Thematic Apperception Test, usually called the TAT (Morgan and Murray, 1935). Whereas in the Rorschach the person looks at a series of inkblots and tells the examiner what he or she 'sees' in the blots, in the TAT a subject makes up stories to pictures of different types (see Chapter 3). Projective testing remains an important aspect of personality study, but in recent decades (since about 1950) its importance to the scientific study of personality has steadily given ground to the so-called *objective* tests or questionnaires (see Chapter 6). Objective tests are based on nomothetic assumptions, and they rarely presume to be capturing the total personality type, but have well-defined statistical procedures for identifying traits or other so-called 'dimensions of personality'.

What is personality? Can we agree on a single view?

We have only scratched the surface of a philosophical analysis of personality study, but already it is obvious that this is a complex area. Agreement on what personality 'is' depends upon the assumptions made in putting it to study, and it can now perhaps be appreciated that there are diverse and basically irreconcilable differences in these assumptions. It does not seem likely that we will ever see total agreement. About the most general statement that can be made regarding a definition of the area is that personality places emphasis on the *style* of behaviour. All animals 'behave' in the sense of moving about, eating, sleeping, and so on. But the higher we go in the scale of animals and the more complex this behaviour becomes – including the verbal behaviours of language – the more does its style or pattern begin to attract our interest rather than its sheer motility. Three people move along a path, chatting between themselves. They have comparable bodily structures and speak in a common language, but it is the *style* of their walking and talking, the content of what they say, or avoid saying altogether, which attracts our interest as students of personality. How did they get the way they are and what is their future likely to hold, given their unique combination of personality tendencies?

In the final analysis, this interest is what philosophers of all ages have wondered about. They spoke of human nature and today we speak of personality. But it is all the same. We are studying ourselves, wondering why we do what we do and how it is that not everyone does precisely the same thing even though there is much in common across all people. It is in answering these quesions that our real differences arise. Philosophy helps us understand our differences by spelling out our diverse assumptions. What we should hope to do is, rather than finding agreement in a single personality theory, agree upon the diversity in assumptions which we make and, understanding our differences in light of this agreement, pursue a multiplicity of approaches to personality study. In the long run, this will prove most beneficial to the understanding of human behaviour.

Suggested further reading

Bakan, D. (1966) *The Duality of Human Existence*. Chicago: Rand McNally.

Chein, I. (1972) *The Science of Behavior and the Image of Man*. New York: Basic Books.

Kuhn, T. S. (1970) *The Structure of Scientific Revolutions* (2nd edn). Chicago: The University of Chicago Press.

Langer, S. K. (1948) *Philosophy in a New Key*. New York: Penguin.

Part II
Psychodynamic approach

2 Psychoanalytic theories of the personality

Christopher Dare

The practice of psychoanalysis

Psychoanalytic theory and practice have some peculiarities as subjects which differentiate them from related topics and tend to render their style and methodology confusing and obscure. In fact, it is difficult to describe the nature of the field of psychoanalysis. In an autobiographical essay, Freud (1925) describes how he started his adult professional life thinking of himself as a pure scientist and yet he ended up writing papers whose content resembled more the art of biography or short story writing than the science of neurophysiology from whence he had come. At the end of his life Freud was the recipient both of the Goethe prize for Literature and the honorary fellowship of the Royal Society. That he should receive high awards in both science and literature demonstrates the ambiguity of Freud's subject to his contemporaries. It also shows the impression of profundity which his work gave even though its essential nature was uncertain.

The ambiguity of psychoanalysis stems from a number of sources. Firstly, it comes from the nature of the clinical task of psychoanalysis which is psychotherapy. The process of psychotherapy, whereby the clinician attempts to help his patient change during the clinical encounter, purely by the conversation which goes on between the therapist and the patient, seems to have many connotations. For example, the psychotherapist has seemed reminiscent of the confessional, the Guru, the counsellor, of personal friendship, of the shaman and, at times, of a quasi-political leader. All these are qualities of the non-specific element of many psychotherapies, and take no account of the particular and, hopefully effective, worked-out elements. The ambiguities of psychotherapeutic practice, with the greater or lesser importance of these non-specific elements, contributes to the ambiguities of psychoanalysis as a whole.

Secondly, psychoanalysis gains ambiguity by its chosen subject matter. Unlike other psychotherapies, such as those practised within the framework of behavioural psychology, psychoanalysis does not take as its prime interest the pattern of overt acts and communications of the patient. Instead, its field of study is the subjective experiences of the person. Clearly, subjective experience can only be induced from the outward expression of the person. However, psychoanalysis is, at its centre, concerned with the functioning of hypothetical entity, namely that of the mind. The chosen subject matter gains complications by the philosophical difficulties of the mind–body problem. This compounds the ambiguities that psychoanalysis has from the nature of the practice of psychotherapy.

The third source of potential ambiguity in psychoanalysis may, for many of its students, be the foremost. This is to do with its scientific status. Freud and most of his followers have clearly identified themselves as scientists. The basis for their claim comes in part from the tradition of their academic training in medicine which is the major discipline of origin of psychoanalysts. The achievements of nineteenth-century medical science came, not from the practice of formally conducted, statistically analysed experiments, but from detailed and systematic observation. Distinguished critics of psychoanalysis in Britain tend to attack, and attempt to dismiss, psychoanalysis because the subject has not moved from a descriptive conceptualization of science to an experimental one. For example, Medawar (1967) criticizes psychoanalysis because it does not use a scientific methodology in which hypotheses are chosen because of their potential disprovability, and Eysenck (1957) because of its lack of adherence to statistically manipulable experimental techniques.

Psychoanalysis indeed does not comply with the two requirements of these particular exponents of twentieth-century science.

Sympathetic critics (for example, Rycroft, 1966 and Ricoeur, 1970) have urged that psychoanalysis give up its claim to scientific status. If it is not a science, however, it is difficult to find a category within which to put the subject. Its most devastating critics have suggested that it is a religion, a secret society, a confidence trick, a collection of archaic mumbo-jumbo, a series of insubstantial arm-chair beliefs, or a dangerous form of personal indoctrination, threatening the mental stability of patients but having no possibility of contributing to their mental health.

Although it is difficult to state the category of human activity to which psychoanalysis, as a whole, belongs, it is not an impossible activity to describe. The following will be a brief description from which the discussion of psychoanalytic theories of the personality can be derived.

Psychoanalysis can be described by the activities of its practitioners. This is to examine the intuitive understanding of the communications to the analyst by the patient whether they be children or adults in individual psychotherapy, members of a psychotherapy group or patients in an in-patient milieu. The analyst observes what the person says and does, what the body posture is, and above all, attempts to identify what sort of relationships the person attempts to establish with the analyst or with others present. From these observations, the analyst attempts to make intuitive propositions about the patterns of the data, above all trying to understand the communications of the patient to the analyst or to the others present, as expressions of fundamental ways of functioning of the person (i.e. of the personality).

To help him construe his patient, the analyst has a number of general models of human functioning, which will be described later. These models have a number of basic assumptions in common (Sandler et al., 1974). For example, there is an assumption that the activities of the person can be understood in terms of the functioning of the hypothetical apparatus, the mind. Secondly, there is an assumption of meaning or determinism. By this it is implied that whatever a person is doing can be understood to have a meaning and is never purely random or accidental. Thirdly, there is an assumption that at all times a person is attempting to make adaptation so as to balance a number of inner-derived drive demands with external contingencies. The assumption that there are inwardly derived trends of the person, which are likely to come into conflict with the exigencies of the outside world, is also a fundamental proposition of psychoanalysis. Fourthly, there is a general assumption, in psycho-analysis, that human beings are historical. How a person is, in the present, can only be understood, in any complete way, by reference to past patterns as well as to those of current life. The personality in the present in part expresses trends to go on solving problems, that derive from past patterns of experience, especially experiences in personal relationships.

Having come to some conclusions about the general and particular meaning of the patient or patients' activities in his presence, the analyst proceeds by making interventions. These are intended to draw the patient's attention to important features whilst at the same time working in the general direction of helping bring about change, in relation to the problems which originally initiated the analysis. The assumption that the person meeting them is seeking some sort of help for underlying problems is one reason why it is difficult for analysts to engage in experimentally controlled activities. In the way that the patient or patients respond to the interventions, structured to focus their attention on the underlying pattern the therapist has noticed, the psychoanalyst hope to be able to confirm, amplify, modify or reject the preliminary understanding.

This process of making detailed observations leads to communi-cations concerning the observations in the form of interventions of an interpretative nature. Following the interpretation, the analyst, by carefully observing the patient's response, attempts to assess the accuracy of the interpretation. This process of 'hypothesis testing' forms the basis of the analyst's claim to be engaged in a scientific activity. Although it is in no way a scientific experiment, a psycho-analytic psychotherapeutic encounter does have the form described so far and accounts for the changes and amplification in the psychoanalytic understanding of mental life over time.

Psychoanalysts, therefore, do a great deal of hypothesis and theory construction but, unlike armchair philosophers, the analyst is forced to check his thoughts and theories against observations of patients. There is always an inclination to find that what one believes one will observe, but the clinical demands on psychoanalysts require that, in some way or other, they demonstrate usefulness both to their patients and to their colleagues. The necessity of maintaining credibility as a therapist and as a thinker, to patients and colleagues, does not give psychoanalysts scientific qualification but it does contribute to the nature of the subject.

In essence, therefore, the psychoanalyst sees the task as helping patients understand the workings of their mind. In particular, the psychoanalyst interests himself in helping the patient understand the unconscious aspects of mental life, especially as it is governing the patient's attitudes and relationships with other people.

In the early years of the subject, psychoanalysts had been mostly concerned with the relationship of the person to the self. That is to say, with models which stress the mind as being an agency to control the multiple instinctual drives which Freud tried to define. Subsequently this stress changed to an emphasis on the mind as an intermediary apparatus between intrinsically derived impulses of the person, the drives, and the outside world of people. In the first years of psychoanalysis, practitioners used a nosology of mental disturbance like that of their psychiatric colleagues. Freud attempted to understand different classes of mental functioning which distinguished one category of patient from another. Unlike their medically orientated colleagues, however, psychoanalysts have, in time, become rather uninterested in making precise differentiations between categories or classes of patient. Psychoanalysts continue to use a nosology whose nomenclature includes categories of neurosis, different forms of neurosis; psychosis, different forms of psychosis; personality disorders and so on. However, psychoanalytic understanding of disorder is not essentially different from psychoanalytic understanding of normality. Psychoanalysts are interested in the causation of the sorts of disturbances which are categorized by classical psychiatry or are identified by more psychologically measured categories. However, they are much more inclined to establish the links between normality and disturbance and disturbance and normality, rather than emphasizing their differences.

Because of the preoccupation with the relationship between subjective experience and presentation of the self to the outside world, psychoanalysis can be considered to be primarily interested in the subject of personality. Perhaps, because of this central orientation of psychoanalysis, the concept of personality is not used in a technical way. In a sense, the whole of psychoanalysis is about personality and so a separate subject heading for personality is redundant. We shall mention in this chapter some more technically used conceptualizations which are relevant to our topic. For example, we will mention character, identity, the self, and above all the ego, but none of these is coterminous with personality, although all are certainly, in the psychoanalytic view, closely linked to it. In this list of words used in psychoanalysis relevant to the topic of personality, the absence of the word temperament is striking. Unlike most subsequent psychoanalysts, Freud makes a number of references to innate predispositions which give a tendency to a particular neurosis but above all to a particular personality. These innate qualities which might be representative in temperamental differences between people, are very little considered in psychoanalysis. The concept of character, with its derivation from a linguistic route meaning that which is carved on stone, might be expected to refer to fundamental aspects of the personality which relate to temperament. Although Freud did try to describe some basic character types, for example that of the anal character (Freud, 1908) which might have led psychoanalysts in the direction of identifying temperamentally different personalities, the word has come to have a particular and peculiar meaning. The word is used in psychoanalysis to refer to what are technically called ego-syntonic qualities of the personality. That is to say, character is understood to be those aspects of the person of which the person is aware but accepts willingly and does not resist, attempt to change or feel uncomfortable about (cf., Schafer, 1979).

When patients come to a psychoanalyst the motivation which brings them may be that they seek symptomatic relief from particularly defined problems. Alternatively patients may be expressing a more general dissatisfaction with themselves, for example, complaining that they do not seem to get on very well with people or cannot make satisfactory love relationships, or that they do not feel that they can fulfil themselves fully in their work. Other people come into analysis because they wish to know more about themselves. Whether or not the person is asking for psychoanalytic help because of symptoms, of which might be described as a psychiatric disorder, or they are seeking openly to know more about themselves, or are expressing unease with aspects of themselves which could be straightforwardly defined as their personality, the psychoanalyst will not encourage them to expect a focus on relief of symptoms. Instead, the psychoanalyst will encourage the patient to talk about themselves in a very free way; and then respond to this in a manner that may encourage the development of the patients' interests in self-exploration and self-understanding.

If the patients' requests or needs for symptomatic relief are too urgent they are unlikely to be able to use psychoanalytic treatment. Similarly, if they do not have any sort of capacity of self-observation and cannot develop any interest in self-understanding then they will not stay in psychoanalytic treatment. This must not be taken to imply that psychoanalysts are uninterested in relieving their patients of unpleasant and troublesome symptoms or that psychoanalysts do not vary their techniques from person to person. The psychoanalyst, in his early encounters with his patients, tries to demonstrate to them the nature of the task they would be undertaking with him, so that they, in coming to be committed to the treatment, do so knowing what it is about. The psychoanalyst conceives his task as being essentially one of facilitating change in some of the fundamental relationships that the person has with self and the outside world. Through these changes in personality there will be a discovery of ways of being which do not require recourse to symptom formation and which enhance the capacity to enjoy satisfactory relationships and fulfilment in other life activities. This process is one in which the patient understands much more fully the way he or she works as a person and is aimed at giving the patient the opportunity of being able to change aspects of personality which cause dissatisfaction.

Psychoanalysis and personality function

So far, this chapter has been mainly concerned with demonstrating the nature of psychoanalysis and with showing that the concept of personality is so central to it that the therapeutic practice and the theoretical models of psychoanalysis can be said to be almost exclusively concerned with personality. Having established this, the rest of the chapter will be used to describe some of the basic ways of understanding personality function that are available within psychoanalysis. In order to explain the way the rest of this chapter will be constructed, the reader must realize that because of the way psychoanalysis develops and in particular because of the absence of a method for the disposal of redundant and unfashionable ways of thinking, present day psychoanalytic writings often show evidence of multiple, overlapping and to some extent contradictory, models of the mind and personality. Over time the basic preoccupations of psychoanalysis tend to change and appropriate models for understanding and describing these preoccupations are developed. Unfortunately, moreover, the language that is used to describe the new preoccupations and to develop the new models is often heavily in debt to preceding phases of psychoanalysis. Sandler (1969) has put it succinctly when he says that psychoanalysis used new words for old concepts and the same words for changing concepts.

To cope with this problem, any exposition of psychoanalytic theory must give some sort of historical account of itself. Therefore the rest of this chapter will be concerned with describing the way psychoanalysis, in its unfolding history, has come to describe certain basic aspects of the workings of the mind which are, in fact, basic descriptions of personality functioning. What will follow has been much more extensively described in a series of papers as part of an effort to discern the basic outlines of the various models of the personality available within psychoanalysis (There are eleven papers by Sandler et al. published between 1972 and 1978 in the *British Journal of Medical Psychology*). These papers attempt to show that within contemporary psychoanalysis are found practitioners using descriptions of psychological functioning which demonstrate a number of different models of the mind being used simultaneously.

It can be argued that the psychoanalytic models of the mind are not really models in the sense that the word is usually employed in contemporary mathematical sciences. This topic is extensively discussed in Bowlby (1969) and by Miller et al. (1960). In order to avoid these ambiguities, in the series of papers referred to above we use the notion of 'frame of reference' rather than that of model. Gedo and Goldberg (1973) do use the Freudian versions of personality structure as models. Other critics of psychoanalysis, however, have implied that what the psychoanalyst calls the model of the mind is more a mythology. Although this view is sometimes raised as a fundamental objection to the method and content of psychoanalytic theory, the conceptualization of the cultural importance of myths in stabilizing society, propounded by Levi-Strauss (1963) would not substantiate this as a demolitional criticism.

The psychoanalytic models

The affect-trauma model

Freud's first observations on neurotic patients were in the direction of appreciating that neurotic, especially hysteric, symptoms had a meaning. However, the meaning was obscured from the patient's conscious knowledge by an active process of keeping unwelcome or socially unacceptable thoughts out of conscious awareness. He believed, as did a number of his contemporaries (Breuer and Freud, 1895) that patients suffering from mental disorder had a general defect of the brain related to motions of degeneracy. Freud thought that this 'weakness' of the mind enabled such patients easily to forget the origins which explained and gave meaning to their neurotic symptoms. He thought, in particular, that hysterical symptoms in young adulthood were an expression of traumatic experiences, usually of the nature of sexual seductions, in childhood or young adolescence. The symptoms were understood as symbolic expressions of the feelings aroused in the traumatic experience.

In summary then, the idea was that the traumatic experience aroused feelings in the young person which could not be fully expressed and resolved at the time of the trauma. Later in life, when the young person was more grown-up and more likely to have other sexual encounters, the traumatic experience was revived. However, because of the social unacceptability of the nature of the earlier experiences, for example a sexual encounter with a relative, the person had to repress the detailed memories and yet still had to cope with the unresolved emotion. Freud considered that the quantity of emotion ('affect-charge') constituted a pressure for expression of the feeling in some form of discharge. Symptoms were understood as physically symbolic expressions of the affect or displaced versions of the trauma in the form of obsessions or phobic anxieties.

This model, which was essentially for the explanation of neuroses in young people, had few implications for personality theory at the time it was being described.

However the notion that the personality had a function to cope with strong emotion, and will have characteristic ways of dealing with or expressing the various emotions, remains part of the general psychoanalytic theory of personality. This model has been described in Sandler et al. (1972c).

The topographical model

Towards the end of the nineteenth century Freud's views as to the nature of the causation of the neuroses underwent a fundamental change. In the course of this change, he introduced two very important ways of thinking into psychoanalysis which have remained basic aspects of the subject. Firstly, and surprisingly, in a study of dreams (1900), Freud developed a clear model of the mind. This model encapsulated the importance of the idea of unconscious mental processes being *forcibly* held out of consciousness. A major distinction was made of the sorts of logical thinking that are characteristic of the usual language and descriptions that people give in thought-out discourse. This style of logical, reality-orientated, socially respectful thinking was ascribed to a system of the mind called 'the system Conscious' (and the form of thinking was called 'secondary process thinking'). Another style of thinking that Freud thought was most clearly shown in dream processes was given the name 'primary process thinking'. This was thought of as the particular quality of mental processes within the system Unconscious. Thinking in dreams, as Freud saw it, showed a heavy emphasis on symbolic expression of basic human urges of sexuality, angry and greedy strivings and so on. Thoughts could easily jump from one subject to another without regard to logic or the demands of the real world. Such thinking was dominated by wishes to find urgent expression of the basic human drives, and showed no trace, in the purest form, of socialization.

The mind was thought to be layered. The deepest layers consisted of the system Unconscious. The most superficial layers were of the system Conscious and had access to control of the motor and perceptual apparatus and could also call upon memory consciously. In between these two layers Freud hypothesized a third element, namely the system Pre-conscious. In this third system thinking was of the logical, reality-orientated sort, that is it was a secondary process in nature. However, the contents of this system were thought to be momentarily out of consciousness. They were not subjected to a process of active repression; but rather were not currently being attended to.

The second major development in Freud's thinking in this phase of psychoanalysis was to construct a view of human life being determined by basic sexual drives which had to be mastered in the course of development in order to conform to social demands. Sexual drives were thought to originate throughout childhood in the forms which, if expressed in adulthood, would be considered perverse. That is, they would have excessively oral, anal, or exhibitionistic elements, and so had to forcibly kept out of consciousness. Access to the system Conscious was blocked by the forceful process of repression which was conceptualized as occurring on the boundary between the system Unconscious and system Pre-conscious. At this point there was hypothesized a 'Censor'. In this theory, neuroses were seen as the manifestations of a combined wish; on the one hand ('a compromise formation') to express a certain sort of sexual desire which, if openly acknowledged, would look like a perversion and, on the other hand, the struggle to prevent the expression of that desire. Thus hysterical neuroses were seen, essentially, as the outcome of expressions of wishes pertaining to anality, leading to excessive preoccupations with cleanliness and orderliness rather than to the messiness and love of messing which were characteristic of the anal child.

Although, like the affect-trauma model, the topographical model was originally designed, in part, to explain neurotic phenomena, it in fact is a worked-out model of the mind. Because it emphasizes the mind as mediating between the inner, drive-dominated wishes of the person and the outer, socially conforming aspects of the person, it is a rather full model of the personality. The distinction between normality and pathology was extensively diminished by the introduction of this model and the major difference between people with an obsessional or phobic personality and an obsessional or phobic neurosis is merely the degree to which the symptoms are felt to be unacceptable or are believed to be tolerable parts of the personality.

Contemporary psychoanalysis continues to use, in certain aspects of its discourse, parts of the topographical model. The major distinction between conscious and unconscious thinking processes and the idea of forceful repression forcing from consciousness certain aspects of the wishful life of the person continue to be very much part of the thinking of psychoanalysis. Instinctual-drive theory, which has been amplified by the introduction of the notion of an aggressive drive, remains an essential part of the thinking of some analysts although, in general, the importance of different sorts of instinctual drives leading to different sorts of personality types is given much less emphasis.

The structural model

In the second decade of the twentieth century, Freud's thinking underwent a further major transformation. He had become impressed by aspects of mental functioning, such as the unconscious sense of guilt (1917), of the distinctions between self-love and love of the other (1914), and with the place of the conscience in mental life. In response to these considerations he produced a new model of the mind (1923). Here, instead of making the differentiating elements of the mind the unconscious or conscious qualities of their contents, he proposed that the drive-dominated, wishfully urgent aspect of the mind should be called the Id. Impulses deriving from the Id would, in this new model, be expressed only after being 'processed' within the Ego. This structure in some ways comes nearest to a psychoanalytic formulation of what, in common parlance, is referred to as 'the personality'. The Ego is seen as controlling a large number of mechanisms, such as the ability to think, synthesize, organize, to control physical activity and to mobilize the various defence mechanisms. These are employed as the ego functions both to control the basic urges of the person and yet at the same time to find methods of giving some satisfaction for instinctual-drives. The Ego was thought of by Freud as having also to pay heed to the ideals and rules (conscience) that the person adopted from the parental figures and from society in general. So important were these considerations that Freud embodied ideals and conscience in a separate structure, namely the Superego.

Outward functioning of the person was now considered to be, essentially, the business of the Ego. In balancing the demands of the instinctual drives, on the one hand, the rules and regulations of the Superego on the other, and the exigencies of the outside world, the Ego gave a predictability and regularity to mental life and the qualities of its function were the qualities of the personality.

Most psychoanalysts in the contemporary world express dissatisfaction with the structural model as well as with the topographical model. None the less the conceptualization summarized in this account still features strongly in the psychoanalytic literature.

Object-relationship theory

As mentioned in the previous paragraph, instinctual-drive theory has not been totally demolished within psychoanalysis and yet preoccupations with different sorts of drives and their exact nature and their colouring of the personality have been waning in the last half-century. Increasingly psychoanalysts, in their therapeutic work, have been concerned with identifying the nature of the relationship that the patient develops with them. In this work (the analysis of the transference) the psychoanalyst tends to see repetitions of experiences that represent problems of relationships and which derive from the person's early life experiences with the family of origin. In these conceptualizations, personality is dominated by personal relationships.

In the course of time, the person develops a sort of model or picture of himself, the 'self-representation', which is partly conscious and partly unconscious. It represents a large number of patterns and plans based on past experiences and it structures, in turn, future experiences. It is set alongside an internal model of other people, 'object-representations'. These consist of internalized versions of the people who have been important in the life of the individual. Personality is seen to be dominated by the attempt to achieve certain sorts of sequential, organized, self-object relationships. The pattern of adult life is governed by attempts to work through, repeating and transforming, earlier important and structuring life experiences in the family of origin relationship pattern. Erikson (1950, 1959) has integrated a version of Freud's theory of development, and the pressures that characteristic patterns of culture transmit, through the family, to the child. He regards these different stages of life as representing way stations for personality development. Erikson summarizes phases of life as 'crises' which leave their mark on the personality in the form of the 'identity'. The works of Bowlby (1969, 1973, 1980) and Winnicott (1957, 1958, 1965) have been important, in their own ways, in introducing to psychoanalysis particular ways of linking the earliest experiences of the person with the mother to later personality development.

Summary

This short excursion through the history of psychoanalysis, in the context of an attempt to define the nature of the psychoanalyst's work and the subject matter, is necessary in order to give an understanding of the multiple ideas that are contained within the contemporary psychoanalytic approach to personality. An organized or coherent theory of the personality is not available within psychoanalysis, because the whole subject is essentially to do with personality development, formation, structure and contribution to disturbance. Indeed, so close is the connection between the psychoanalytic theory of the personality and that of disturbance that it is best to conceptualize the psychoanalytic theory of abnormality and its presentation in psychological disorder as being one of personality variation.

Suggested further reading

Sandler, J., Dare, C. and Holder, A. (1973) *The Patient and the Analyst.* London: Allen & Unwin. This provides an exposition of the psychoanalytic situation.
For details of the Sandler, Dare and Holder 'Frames of Reference' papers, the reader should consult the Bibliography at the end of this volume.

3 Projective techniques

Boris Semeonoff

That a chapter on projective techniques should immediately follow one on psychoanalytic theory is simultaneously appropriate and, to some extent, misleading. Introductory texts in psychology usually define the projective approach to personality as that based on the assumption that the individual 'will project much of his own personality, his conflicts and his motivations into his response' (Marx, 1976) to a test stimulus. Some writers are also at pains to distinguish between this use of the term 'projection' and Freud's use of the word to denote a 'defence mechanism' whereby the ego protects itself against anxiety; viewed in this sense, according to Rycroft (1968) it is 'the process by which specific impulses, wishes, aspects of the self, or internal objects are imagined to be located in some object external to oneself'. Such a distinction, however, is more apparent than real. Freud himself, as Rabin (1968) points out, wrote in *Totem and Taboo*:

> But projection is not specially created for the purpose of defence, it also comes into being when there are no conflicts. The projection of inner perceptions to the outside is a primitive mechanism which, for instance, also influences our sense-perceptions so that it normally has the greatest share in shaping our outer world. (Rabin, 1968, p.10).

The origins of projective techniques

Although projective techniques, designated as such, had not yet come into existence, Freud may be said here, as well as in a still earlier passage (1911), to have formulated what is now often labelled 'the projective hypothesis'. But while projective techniques are most likely to be used by psychodynamically oriented psychologists in a clinical setting, others, for example McClelland and his colleagues (1953) in their work on achievement motivation, have exploited the projective hypothesis from a non-psychoanalytic standpoint. Indeed, in one of the introductory texts referred to above (Davidoff, 1976), projective techniques are mentioned only in this context. And this may be seen as illustrating the anomaly implicit in the opening sentence of this chapter: not everyone endorses the whole of psychoanalytic theory, but even those who find it basically unacceptable may find that – perhaps unwittingly – they make use of its concepts.

A further direct link between projective testing and psychoanalysis exists in the fact that the first strictly projective study to be published was Jung's paper 'The association method', which appeared in the *American Journal of Psychology* in 1910. It is customary these days to dissociate Jung's teaching from Freud's, but Jung's use of 'word association' represents an application of a principle common – indeed fundamental – to both: the belief that circumstances of which one is unaware may influence one's behaviour, adjustment or life-style. This is of course yet another alternative formulation of the projective hypothesis.

The year 1910 also saw the publication of another, similar but contrasted, study of word association, that of Kent and Rosanoff. As the present writer has noted elsewhere (Semeonoff, 1973), the two papers may be seen as representing opposed views of the nature and function of projective inquiry. To amplify: in the pattern of a patient's responses to a standard list of 100 stimulus words Jung claimed to identify the existence of a set of 'complex indicators' – evidence, in other words, of problem areas in the patient's adjustment to his or her life situation. The nature of the problem might, to varying degrees, be apparent, but such indications would be taken as a starting point for further inquiry, such exploration constituting, at least to some extent, the process of psychoanalysis.

The Kent–Rosanoff 'Free Association Test' also makes use of a standard list of 100 stimulus words, but evaluation is basically in terms of 'commonality', that is, the observed frequency of specific responses obtained in a standardization population. The authors had hoped that the test would serve as an objective aid to psychiatric diagnosis but, although valuable in research with clinical groups, it proved – perhaps not surprisingly – relatively insensitive in the study of the individual. In this respect the Kent–Rosanoff test provides an early examplar of the 'actuarial' or psychometric use of projective techniques, an approach which some might categorize as only marginally projective. Nevertheless, the following comment by one of its authors is worth noting:

> In cases in which it is desired to use the association test for the purpose of detecting pathogenic subconscious ideas of complexes that may be suspected to exist, the examiner's familiarity with the case will suggest to him special stimulus words adapted to the particular case; these stimulus words may be given together with those regularly employed... (Rosanoff, 1927, pp.546-7)

What we have here is an expression of readiness to adapt a standard instrument to specific requirements, or to allow the individual to communicate information not assessable within the normal framework of the technique in question. This, it could be maintained, is in fact the essence of the projective approach to personality study: the provision of a channel of communication using a special language, in the sense that any highly specialized form of human activity may be said to have a language of its own.

The reader will have noted that both applications of the word association method were developed in a clinical context. Nevertheless, as evidenced by the still earlier use of word association as a traditional laboratory exercise, the method can throw light on the life history of the 'normal' individual. A parallel can perhaps be seen in the claim that even an ostensibly well-adjusted person can benefit, through increased self-knowledge, from undergoing psychoanalysis. So it is with projective techniques. Some writers appear to suggest that they are used *only* in a clinical setting. Thus Peck and Whitlow (1975) write of projective techniques: 'Responses are not taken at face value, but are valuable only in so far as they provide clues to underlying conflicts and defences.' It could be argued that no human being is entirely without conflicts; be that as it may, projective psychology is concerned with much else besides.

This point can best be illustrated through a consideration of some specific techniques. For a fuller discussion of a wide range of projective techniques the reader is referred to the present writer's book (Semeonoff, 1976) and to the various handbooks listed in the Appendix to that volume. In connection with each of those described here, the reader is strongly urged to have the test materials at hand, or at least a book or article in which they are illustrated. Francis-Williams' *Rorschach with Children* (1968) contains, among other things, beautiful reproductions of the Rorschach inkblots. Materials for most of the other techniques dealt with are illustrated in Semeonoff (1976).

The Rorschach

Description. 'The Rorschach' must be unique among psychological tests in having no 'official' designation, yet being so well known as not to require one. It is the archetypal projective device, and much of the controversy – pro and con – generated in relation to projective techniques applies mainly, either by implication or explicitly, to the Rorschach. Yet many descriptions of it, especially the brief ones, contain errors or misapprehensions. Thus, it is commonly said that the Rorschach is a method of personality assessment based on 'what one sees in a series of inkblots'. This is true to the extent that *content* is one of the recognized scoring categories, and indeed one of the current trends in Rorschach practice is to stress the importance of content. The orthodox approach, however, emphasizes the more formal aspects of the perceptual process. Rorschach himself (1921/1942) asks 'Is the answer determined only by the form of the blot, or is there also appreciation of movement or colour?' And 'Is the figure conceived and interpreted as a whole or in parts? Which are the parts interpreted?' These questions refer to the scoring categories that have come to be known in English as *determinants* and *location*.

Procedure. The Rorschach test material consists of ten inkblots, symmetrical, apart from very minor deviations, about a vertical axis. Five are shaded black on white, two (the second and third in the series) contain red as well as black and three (the last three) are multichromatic. The subject is asked to say what he sees in each blot in turn. This part of the procedure (during which the tester must not intervene) is sometimes called the 'free association period' – a misnomer, since Rorschach makes it clear that the subject is being asked to report what he *perceives*, not what the blots make him think of. This 'performance proper' – the term preferred by Klopfer and colleagues (1954), Alcock (1963) and others – is followed by an 'inquiry', a question and answer period in which the subject has an opportunity to clarify and amplify his responses. Accuracy in scoring depends to a large extent on information obtained in the inquiry. The use of the inquiry also epitomizes the nature of the Rorschach test situation as a communicative process or interaction, in which both subject and tester are – perhaps to differing extents at different times – jointly 'in control'. Furthermore, as Schachtel (1967) points out, the subject's perception of the test situation itself may influence his response to the inquiry. Sensitivity to all these things is included among the skills of the projective psychologist.

It is not possible here to go into full details of Rorschach scoring. Rorschach himself died very soon after launching his 'experiment' (as he called it), and his ideas about interpretation of inkblot response have been modified and extended by a number of authorities who vary in the details of their usage. A brief survey must also be misleading to the extent that it appears to assign uniform 'meanings' to individual scoring categories. All Rorschach writers, however, agree that a Rorschach 'protocol' must be interpreted *as a whole*, paying due regard to relationships among the categories, sometimes expressed as ratios, but sometimes involving consideration of what is present and what is not.

Scoring. Location scoring is mainly associated with intellectual functioning: Rorschach uses the term *Erfassungstyp* (Ger. *erfassen*: to comprehend) to denote the distribution of responses over the various location categories as defined below. As already noted, Rorschach 'systematizers' (a term coined by Exner, 1974) tend to differ in their scoring, but all make use of the response categories 'whole' (W), 'normal (or 'large usual') detail' (D), 'infrequently used detail' (usually Dd) and 'space' (S). In so far as S responses involve something in the nature of figure–ground reversal the rationale for their association with 'oppositional tendency' becomes apparent. The other location categories can be interpreted in terms of how carefully one examines the stimulus material, one's responsiveness to a global impression, processes of analysis and synthesis, and so on.

Determinants scoring as compared with location scoring, covers a wider range of variation in both perception and interpretation. Only the most important aspects are covered in the following summary.

What one sees in an inkblot is undoubtedly 'determined', first and foremost, by recognition of a familiar shape or *form* (F). It is virtually impossible to imagine a Rorschach protocol in which form perception plays no part; almost equally unimaginable, however, is a protocol in which nothing beyond recognition of form was operating. The first of Rorschach's 'questions' quoted above referred to 'appreciation of movement and colour'. Colour (C) is of course an objective stimulus quality actually present in the blot material, whereas movement (M) is something inferred, or 'supplied', by the observer. Rorschach insisted rather strongly that to be scored M a response had to involve kinaesthetic imagery; that being so, the M scoring was normally restricted to 'human' movement. Later writers have adhered to the latter proviso more closely than to the former.

Broadly speaking, however, the M response is related to 'inner resources', interpreted in a variety of senses. Chief among these is its contribution to what Rorschach called the *Erlebnistyp*, commonly rendered in English as 'experience balance'. The other element in this 'balance' is the colour response, representing reactivity to external stimulation. According to whether the number of M responses is greater or less than a 'weighted colour sum', the individual is said to be *predominantly* 'introversive' or 'extratensive'. Much has been written about whether this distinction is or is not the same as Jung's introversion–extraversion dichotomy. Whatever the answer, the important fact to recognize is that for Rorschach these terms represented separate modes of experience rather than opposite poles on a continuum. Thus for Rorschach it is possible to score high (or low) on both variables, so that an intermediate position, in terms of the 'balance', may have sharply contrasted meanings. Beck (1960) developed this idea in his formulation of the *experience actual* (EA) – a summation of movement (M) and colour (C) response – to indicate breadth of experience or to 'uncover a fuller measure of how that person glows outwardly and fantasizes within' (Beck, 1978).

Returning to determinants scoring, two outstanding points remain for comment: first, *shading* is a variable on the scoring and interpretation of which the systematizers diverge rather widely, but there is general agreement that response to shading, particularly dark shading, is related to the handling of anxiety. Second, all systems recognize that a high proportion of responses are based on a combination of form (F) with some other determinant, the relevant scoring conventions taking account of whether the additional determinant plays a major or minor role. While recognizing the dangers in so doing, one may hazard the generalization that form dominant indicates adequate handling of the affective elements represented by the other determinant.

Content.   Comment has already been made on the minor importance traditionally attached to content and its scoring; indeed it may be said that the choice of content categories is largely optional, except that attention is always paid to responses involving living creatures, human (H) or animal (A), or parts thereof (Hd, Ad). Most systems also recognize *popular* (P) and *original* (O) content responses, these being variously defined according to explicitly stated criteria. Such consensual or idiosyncratic perception, as well as the total number of responses (R), has varying implications both for intellectual functioning and for personal illness.

The 'sign' approach to interpretation extends the concept of 'diagnosis' based on a combination of indicators. This, however, is 'holism' of a different sort: not the patterning of response so much as the isolation of factors that are 'consistent with, though not pathognomonic of', a particular condition. The phrase in quotation marks – borrowed from Alcock (1963) – is also a pointer towards projective practice in general: on the basis of the evidence a given technique will yield, hypotheses are formulated for which confirmation will be sought elsewhere. The area that has attracted most interest is probably that of brain damage, the earliest and best known work being that of Piotrowski (1937), whose 'organic signs have' – to quote Alcock again – 'stood the test of time to a remarkable extent'. Other areas studied have included neurosis, homosexuality, suicide risk (a comprehensive survey will be found in Goldfried et al., 1971). Somewhat similar, although limited in the manner its title (*Rorschach Content Interpretation*) implies, is a more recent book by Aronow and Reznikoff (1976). One can perhaps sum up the sign approach by saying that its adoption tends to make projective inquiry an *examination*, rather than a shared process of exploration.

Derivatives of the Rorschach

While the systematizers who took over after Rorschach's early death have added a good deal to his groundwork, one element they have neglected is Rorschach's explicit statement that in order to make re-testing possible more than one series of 'plates' must be available; he goes on to list some of the circumstances in which 'the test must be repeated with the same subject'. It will be seen that for Rorschach the concept of test–retest reliability was doubly meaningless: change in the pattern of responses was to be expected, and he takes it for granted that the same instrument cannot be administered twice.

'Parallel' series.   It is doubtful whether the creation of fully interchangeable forms of a test is a realistic aim, even in the cognitive field. When the criterion of 'correct answers' is absent the aim becomes even more illusory. It is not known to what extent Rorschach actually used the parallel series to which he refers, but which have not survived. Of two devised by his close associates, one, the Behn–Rorschach (Zulliger, 1956), is closely similar in all essential features, but has definable differences in stimulus quality. The other, the Zulliger Test (Zulliger, 1962, 1969), is a three-card series which the present writer (Semeonoff, 1968) has found useful in a selection context. Experience there gained has shown that while a 'shortened Rorschach' can yield, in general terms, much the same information, the range of insight is restricted, and that the quantitative aspects of the data would require radical restandardization.

The Holtzman Inkblot Technique.   Psychometric sophistication has rarely been a main concern of users of the Rorschach. When the authors of another of the introductory texts alluded to at the outset (Baron et al., 1977) refer to projective techniques as 'a series of measuring devices' they would seem to be ascribing to them a function that few projectivists would consider relevant. Psychologists who had criticized the Rorschach on the ground that it lacked psychometric 'respectability' welcomed the Holtzman Inkblot Technique (HIT) (Holtzman et al., 1961; Hill, 1972) as remedying this lack, and for its increased 'objectivity'.

The HIT represents a complete reworking of inkblot perception, more so than is commonly realized. Once again an introductory text (Wheeler et al., 1974) errs, in saying apropos of Holtzman: 'More recently some new inkblots have been standardized, so that Rorschach's set is now extended.' The main innovations are that parallel series, each of forty-five blots, are provided, and that only one response to each card is recorded. In addition, not all the figures are symmetrical and a wider range of single colours and colour combinations is provided. Scoring is on twenty-three variables, some traditional, others innovative; in some cases placement on a point scale is required. Interpretation is almost entirely based on empirically established associations; apart from a few self-defining categories, no interpretative hypotheses are attached to single or derived 'scores'.

The most obvious departure from Rorschach ethos is of course the limitation of responses to one per card. This is claimed to 'control for R' (the total number of responses), and so to simplify computations. But the orthodox Rorschacher will maintain that it is of a person's nature to give many or few responses, and that such restriction 'controls' in the sense that it impedes freedom of expression. Hayslip and Darbes (1974) have indeed shown that 'intra-subject response consistency' can be affected. All in all, it seems unlikely that the HIT will ever *replace* the Rorschach, at any rate as a clinical instrument. As a research tool, on the other hand, its merits are evident.

Attempts have also been made to adapt the Rorschach test to group administration. If provision is made for free response, the Rorschach test situation may be said to be approximated, however distantly. If, on the other hand, a forced choice technique is adopted, the essentials of the Rorschach method are lost.

The Thematic Apperception Test

Murray's Thematic Apperception Test (TAT), the second of the two major projective techniques, in some ways comes closer than the Rorschach to 'non-technical' conceptions of what projection means. Thus Fernald and Fernald (1978) state that 'When a person perceives his or her own characteristics in another stimulus, animate or inanimate, we generally say that *projection* has occurred.' Others have noted that such perception may not be entirely conscious, as when one identifies with or 'feels for' a character in a play or book. The 'stimulus' in the TAT is a series of pictures, and the subject is invited to make up a story about each, or, in some variants of the technique, simply to say 'what is happening here'.

Murray first described the TAT at length in *Explorations in Personality* (Murray, 1938), as part of an intensive study of a college student population, and in conjunction with an exposition of his 'proposals for a theory of personality'. Briefly, Murray's system postulates two elements: *need*, a force or process in the organism, activated by the perception of *press* in the environment, press being defined simply as the potential for the arousal of a need. *Thema*, which gives the technique its name, is the interaction of press and need variables, *apperception* or recognition of which constitues the story the subject tells. The extent to which empathy is involved in this apperception is a matter of controversy. Projection in the sense of a defence mechanism, however, is not generally believed to take place, so that Haber and Fried (1975) would, in this context, be wrong when they say that 'the clinician hopes to tap aspects of the subject's personality that the subject himself deems unacceptable and therefore must not be aware that he is revealing.'

Whereas materials and conditions for the administration of the Rorschach are carefully specified, the TAT is a flexible instrument which can be adapted to individual circumstances and requirements. The standard series consists of twenty pictures administered individually in two sessions. The subject speaks his or her stories, which are recorded verbatim, and a certain amount of prompting and encouragement is provided for. The origins of the test in a male college setting are still apparent, but for some of the items attempts have been made to provide 'alternative' pictures more suitable for female subjects; there are also a few specifically 'children's' pictures. However, practice has hallowed the use of group administration, with written response, shorter series, and even the introduction of 'new' pictures. Thus Semeonoff (1976, 1976a) has experimented with coloured pictures, which have a number of advantages over the rather sombre standard series.

Murray's own method of interpreting the TAT data is basically in terms of the relative frequency of need and press variables as evinced in the actions of the focal figure or figures in the stories. What can be reckoned 'high' or 'low' (or 'usual' or 'unusual' in a more qualitative sense) must of course depend on the nature of the population in relation to which a given person is being assessed. 'Norms', if used, will therefore be highly specific to the context of a given investigation. They will also 'date', a phenomenon that affects the stimulus material itself. Again, while the Rorschach is relatively culture-free, TAT response will be affected by cultural factors, and many attempts have been made to produce TAT material appropriate to a particular culture (see Murstein, 1963; Semeonoff, 1976). On the cognate problem of effect of racial differences between subject and tester the evidence is conflicting. Some writers (e.g. Schwartz et al., 1951) have found that black subjects produced more, rather than less, ideas when tested by a white examiner, a possible explanation being that the situation was seen as more task-oriented. It may be supposed, in general, that anything that allows TAT figures to be perceived more 'as real people' will facilitate response and provide for added insight. And again, unwillingness or inability to treat a TAT stimulus as anything but a picture may itself be an important indication of defensiveness.

Murray's system of analysis may be said to contain at least rudimentary 'scoring', in the Rorschach sense. Other writers on the TAT have proposed other scoring systems; these, however, diverge much more radically from the 'original' and from one another. Both Murstein (1963) and Semeonoff (1976) describe a number of systems in some detail; Murstein also calls attention to varying emphasis on form and content. But since the TAT is principally concerned with adjustment to or perception of specific life-situations it follows that content variables are the more likely to be informative. From this it follows, in turn, that stimulus material must be appropriate to the investigation in hand: an outstanding example is the different requirements of a clinical and of a vocational context. On the other hand, a plea has been made (e.g. Hartman, 1970) for agreement on a 'basic' set of TAT pictures, adoption of which, supplemented as required, would facilitate research. A position combining both points of view is that of Arnold (1962), who, while finding some of Murray's pictures more useful than others, claims that 'any general kind of pictures can be used' – adding, indeed, that equally valuable TAT material may be obtained using 'short descriptive sentences' as stimuli, in place of pictures.

Arnold's standpoint rests on the use to which she puts the TAT and her method of analysis. From each story she extracts an 'import', a brief generalized restatement of the theme of the story, rather like the 'moral' of a fable. Imports are scored on a point scale ranging from

+ 2 to − 2, representing the amount of positive action or resolution shown by the characters in the way in which they handle the situations in which they are involved. Arnold quotes research showing a summed 'Motivation Index' to be positively related to vocational effectiveness in a variety of spheres, a finding corroborated by Sneddon (1971) in a study of selection of marriage guidance counsellors.

Derivatives of the TAT

Children's Apperception Test (CAT). While some of the variations described perhaps depart sufficiently in practice from Murray's original formulation to be classifiable as 'derivatives', there are numerous other techniques based on the interpretation of pictures that diverge still further.

A rather direct derivative is the adaptation of the method for use with children. The best known example is Bellak's Children's Apperception Test (Bellak, 1954), a series of pictures showing animals in (mainly) anthropomorphic situations. Children are interested in animals, and it has ever been claimed that animals 'mean more' to children than do human beings; Bellak and Adelman (1960) discuss this topic at some length. It was therefore assumed − probably wrongly, it later seemed, following experience with a 'human' CAT (CAT–H) (Bellak and Hurvich, 1966) − that children would empathize more readily to animal pictures. Be that as it may, one can say with some degree of confidence that in general children empathize easily − even inevitably. Show a child a picture of a family situation, or ask a child a question about a hypothetical family, and the answer will be in terms of the child's own family, understandably so since that is the only family of which the child has had experience.

A further feature of the CAT is that a good deal of its content is explicitly 'psychoanalytic' in character, that is, it is assumed that it will evoke themes associated with the traditional preoccupations of depth psychology. If one's view of human behaviour in general is based on psychoanalytic concepts, one will of course interpret thematic apperception response along those lines irrespective of the detail of the stimulus material. But it has to be borne in mind that Murray, himself a psychoanalyst, wrote of 'depth interpretation' in the TAT: 'inferences of this sort can be validated only by data derived from some kind of psychoanalysis' (Murray, 1943, p.18). (Similarly Rorschach (1921) said 'The test cannot be considered as a means of delving into the unconscious.')

Object Relations Technique (ORT).   A more explicit commitment to a specific psychodynamic orientation is seen in the Object Relations Technique (Phillipson, 1955, 1973). The ORT uses the traditional thematic apperception method, but systematically varies the stimulus material in terms of perceptual variables analogous to Rorschach determinants. There are three 'series' of cards: A, characterized by light diffuse shading, designed to evoke themes related to early dependence; B, darker and more definite in outline, commonly associated with perception of threat; C, introducing colour in an almost intrusive manner, presenting strong emotional challenge. Based principally on Fairbairn's teaching on 'object relations' (Fairbairn, 1952), the ORT lays particular stress on the test situation as itself an exemplar of object relations, with a therapeutic as well as an exploratory function. Perhaps more than any other technique it illustrates the tenets of projective psychology as set out earlier in this chapter. Understandably, therefore, expertise in the ORT cannot be acquired without commitment to the standpoint it represents.

Object relationships, interpreted on a more superficial level, may also be said to be studied through various family relations techniques (e.g. Jackson, 1950, 1966; Howells and Lickorish, 1967). These are almost self-explanatory: pictures showing children in family situations have to be interpreted, the amount of fantasy production varying with the technique. Projection, as already suggested, is mainly direct and 'near the surface'; deeper problems can be more effectively studied by other methods, notably structured play.

Other techniques

Discussions of projective techniques usually concentrate on the Rorschach and the TAT, often to the exclusion of all else. Behaviourally the two have much in common, each entailing verbal response to visual stimuli. Yet Frank (1939), to whom credit for formally introducing the concept of projection is usually accorded and whose classification of projective techniques is frequently quoted, would place them in different categories. The TAT is classed as 'interpretive', and the Rorschach as 'constitutive', meaning that the subject 'imposes structure' on amorphous substance or a 'semi-organized field'.

The present writer has suggested an alternative taxonomy (Semeonoff, 1973), in which particular stress is laid on the distinction between verbal response and manipulative activity.

Structured play

Mention of play, above, provides a useful link to techniques falling within the latter category. 'Sand-tray' equipment has long been familiar in child guidance and child psychiatry settings; its systematization by Lowenfeld (1939) is the subject of a book by Bowyer (1970), in which a number of variants of the method, mainly of continental European origin, are also discussed. The aim is of course primarily therapeutic, using the principle of abreaction, or what is sometimes called 'acting out' a problem, through symbolic activity. Opinions differ about the degree to which a child patient can benefit from interpretation. Thus, Pickford (1963), author of the Pickford Projective Pictures, basically a TAT variant, claims to have 'treated many children successfully without using verbal interpretation at all', adding that sometimes 'more resistance is excited by interpretation than by simply listening with insight'.

The Lowenfeld Mosaic Test

Lowenfeld's name is also associated with the Lowenfeld Mosaic Test. Although the standard test did not appear until 1954, many British psychologists were familiar with the Mosaic in the 1930s, a time when the Rorschach had yet to make a substantial impact. It is essentially an 'activity' technique, and reflects its author's interest in integrating personality study with educational method. This does not, of course, imply any sort of constraint on the subject's production, the task being to construct a 'design' using a set of flat wooden or plastic pieces, in five shapes and six colours. The material is very attractive, and lends itself to a rich variety of possibilities, both for creative production, at all levels, and for systematic classification.

However, attempts to 'psychometrize' the technique have not been very successful, perhaps because Lowenfeld herself was unsympathetic to this approach. The most extensive normative study has been that of Ames and Ilg (1962) on developmental trends: these would seem to have been well established. A recent paper by Mahmood (1978) describes the construction of a set of 'criteria', scoring on which was shown to discriminate within a group of psychiatric patients undergoing rehabilitation treatment. But in general the Lowenfeld Mosaic is most useful as a vehicle for patient – clinician interaction of the type described earlier in this chapter.

The Colour Pyramid Test (CPT)

The CPT of Schaie and Heiss (1964) shows both similarities to and differences from the Mosaic Test. The material consists of one-inch squares or 'chips' which have to be arranged to form a five-layer pyramid outlined on paper. The standard set consists of ten 'colours', variants of which make up a total of twenty-four 'hues'; it is possible, however, to use a more restricted range. Current practice requires the subject to make, successively, three 'pretty' and three 'ugly' pyramids. The rationale for the latter task is unclear, but it seems to be that the 'ugly' pyramids represent, in some way, latent (possibly even repressed?) elements in personality structure.

A similar assumption is made in the now usually discredited Szondi Test (Deri, 1949) and in the Lüscher Colour Test (Lüscher, 1969, 1970), also often dismissed as trivial. Both these involve statements of preference, in the one case for photographs or faces, in the other for colours. In both 'negative choices' (i.e. dislike or low rankings) are presumed to relate to rejected tendencies in the person's own personality. While validity of such an assumption would repay investigation, its importance for the CPT is minimal, since most of the recommended analysis can be carried out on the 'pretty' pyramids alone. Attention is paid to consideration of form, 'mainly amount of structure in each of the pyramids', breadth and consistency of colour choice, frequency of use of individual colours and certain combinations of the latter to form so-called 'syndromes'. Form, on the analogy of Rorschach location, is clearly related to cognitive functioning; the remainder of the analysis is concerned with the subject's affective life. The insight offered is perhaps limited, but the CPT makes for a genuinely projective situation, while scoring is fully objective. Recent work by Semeonoff (1980) indicates validity of at least the basic assumptions of the method, and points the way towards extension of its scope.

Human figure drawing

No account of projective techniques could be complete without some mention of human figure drawing. For most children drawing is a form of play, particularly – but not only – when the child is free to draw whatever he or she chooses. Some work has been done (e.g. Elkisch, 1960) on the projective use of 'free art expression', but in general attention has been concentrated on 'Draw-a-Person' and similarly named techniques, of which there are many competing variants. Children's drawings of the human figure were first systematically exploited by Burt (1921) and Goodenough (1926), in both cases from a psychometric standpoint; interest in their diagnostic possibilities came later. This is a field in which people seem to feel that the production '*must* have projective implications' (Semeonoff, 1971), and much of the early work appears to have been uncritically based on *a priori* assumptions. Harris (1963), who revised and extended the Goodenough test, came to the conclusion that 'drawings are not generally useful as diagnostic devices for personality study'. He adds:

> Children may use many and ingenious devices to portray their ideas, limited only by the medium or by their lack of practical skill. What appears to the naive adult analyst as a 'bizarre' feature may have a straightforward and perfectly sensible explanation in light of the child's thought and intention. (Harris, 1963, p.148)

The closing phrase gives the key to the aim of the genuinely projective approach to children's drawings – understanding rather than 'objective' uniform evaluation of specific definable elements.

Psychometric considerations

Rather little has been said in this discussion about the psychometric aspects of projective testing.

Key concepts in all psychological testing, according to the elementary texts, are to be found in the terms *standardization, reliability* and *validity* (see also Chapter 6). How far are the requirements met in the application of projective techniques? The answer will depend on the extent to which quantitative information is sought – that is, how far measurement is seen to be involved.

Standardization implies the setting up of norms, and this depends in turn on the establishment of standard conditions of administration. What then *is* 'standard'? All projectivists recognize the importance of rapport (see, e.g. Alcock, 1963). This, to be adequate, depends on the perception of a common purpose, and that will not be achieved through adherence to a uniform introductory formula. As already indicated, few projectivists see measurement as a primary aim of projective inquiry, but nearly all users of the Rorschach, for example, subscribe to the concept of the popular response (P), and what is 'popular' is of course determined by a normative procedure. Similarly with the recognition of common themes in the TAT.

With reliability one is on less sure ground. Comment has already been offered on 'alternative form' reliability. In the Rorschach, at least, split-half reliability between, say odd- and even-numbered cards is not really feasible, in view of the carefully designed sequence of stimulus qualities in the separate cards of the standard set, and of the impossibility of distributing the coloured cards equally. Surprisingly, however, it has been shown (Hertz, 1934) that split-half reliabilities for certain variables do hold up at acceptable significance levels, suggesting that the changing response of a subject to successive cards in the Rorschach series can be interpreted as the same basic personality, functioning somewhat differently, yet consistently, in differing circumstances.

However, projective response is more than a set of numbers derived from a set of variables; so consistency, or change, in projective data from the same person on different occasions must be regarded as something more than what is encompassed in the term psychometric reliability. The writer's experience (Semeonoff, 1958) with marriage guidance counsellor candidates who have reappeared for selection – possibly some years after initial rejection – has shown that their TAT material is recognizably that of the same person, responding to a new situation. Psychoanalysis is sometimes stigmatized as pessimistic, on the grounds that it teaches that personality is immutably laid down in the first five years of life. This represents a misunderstanding of Freud's 'psychological determinism'. The very term 'psychodynamic', often equated with the psychoanalytic standpoint, indicates the possibility for change – if not of the personality, as such, at least in adjustment and behaviour. Projective techniques are sensitive to such change, which may accompany psychotherapy, or other modifications of one's life situation. As such they cannot exhibit statistical reliablity in the narrow sense.

Validity presents still further problems. To ask whether the Rorschach or the TAT is 'valid', in general terms, is meaningless. Validity, as English and English (1958) say, 'is always validity for the measurement of a particular variable', and if a projective technique is to be of any value the associations it claims to exist between certain forms of response and other psychological phenomena must be shown to rest on fact. How public, in the sense of being accessible to the outside observer, such phenomena need to be is another matter. Of the 'experience type' Rorschach wrote (p.87): 'It indicates how the person experiences, but not how he lives, or toward what he is striving.' Again, in the CPT there is reason to believe (Semeonoff, 1980) that what the 'Drive syndrome' (total use of yellow, green and brown) is measuring is not drive level but drive potential.

In both these instances, the information obtained is about the subject's experience rather than his behaviour. Schwartz and Lazar (1979) make a similar point when they say that projective interpretation is not probabilistic but semantic. To serve as an adequate basis for prediction, projective response would have to be regarded as 'sampling at random from a finite universe' of behaviour. No such sampling takes place in clinical inquiry, be it projective or otherwise. Rather, as Schwartz and Lazar go on to point out, 'once patterns of meaning (in test response) are established the clinician goes beyond the tests, mapping his observations against a nosological scheme.' Blatt (1975) develops a similar theme, concluding with a plea for 'conceptualizing diagnostic assessment as a more integral part of the therapeutic process'. Viewed in this light, the recent trend in the clinical psychology profession *towards* therapy and away from assessment, often explicitly endorsed as a mark of progress, seems both misguided and impracticable. Without understanding there can be no therapy.

The above discussion may appear to have ducked the problem of criteria for validity. For an overview of the present status of projective techniques, which must ultimately rest on demonstration of validity from some point of view, the reader is referred to a survey of the major techniques by Klopfer and Taulbee (1976). Although admittedly declining in popularity, these techniques emerge remarkably well, even by conventional psychometric standards. The paper opens with the question 'Will this be the last time a chapter on projective tests appears in the *Annual Review of Psychology?*' Time alone will tell, but if the answer is 'yes', followed by a withering of interest, psychology will be the poorer and a source of insight will have been lost.

Suggested further reading

Buros, O. K. (ed.) (1970) *Personality Tests and Reviews*. Highland Park: Gryphon Press. This work reprints the Personality sections of the first six *Mental Measurements Yearbooks*, affording a complete overview of projective techniques and opinions about them, up to the mid-1960s. Subsequent events are covered in the *Seventh* (1972) and *Eighth* (1978) *Yearbooks*.

Rickers-Oviankina, M. A. (ed.) (1960) *Rorschach Psychology*. New York and London: Wiley.

Zubin, J., Eron, L. D. and Schumer, F. (1965) *An Experimental Approach to Projective Techniques*. New York and London: Wiley.

4 Research on psychoanalytic concepts

Peter Fonagy

There are numerous instances of authors questioning the validity of psychoanalysis on the grounds of inadequate scientific rigour (e.g. Ellis, 1963; Eysenck, 1965). The criticisms concern both the nature of the *evidence* used in psychoanalytic expositions and the quality of psychoanalytic *theorization*.

The shortcomings of the clinically based evidence used as data in support of psychoanalytic theory have been well reviewed (Wolpe and Rachman, 1963; Eysenck and Wilson, 1973; Jurjevich, 1974). These authors stress that the nature of the evidence used in psychoanalytic expositions is either private data or evidence drawn from non-scientific fields (e.g. folklore, mythology, etc.) and that evidence provided by the patient in analysis is inconclusive as it might be attributable to suggestion through the analyst's interpretations. A second area of criticism concerns the quality of theorization in psycho-analysis. Attacks have recently been made from both within and outside the psychoanalytic camp, and some of these will be briefly discussed.

The identity crises of psychoanalysis

Psychoanalytic theory (as outlined in Chapter 2) is formulated in a body of knowledge that Freud (1937) termed 'metapsychology'. This deals in concepts such as instincts, the system unconscious, the superego and so on. There have been many critiques of metapsychology by analysts (e.g. Peterfreund, 1975; Gill, 1976; Klein, 1976; Rosenblatt and Thickstun, 1977) but perhaps the most thorough has been provided by Schafer (1976). Scientific critiques of Freud's energy and structural model have always claimed that concepts such as 'libido' or 'id' are no more than bad metaphors as they correspond to no aspect of psychology, neurophysiology, embryology or endocrinology, and they have questioned whether any correspondence between the theory and reality is possible. Schafer outlined how its 'pseudo-scientific', metaphorical terms have led psychoanalysis into intolerable conceptual and logical confusion.

He has attacked the language of psychoanalysis on the grounds that it encourages reification (the treating of metaphoric terms as entities). For example, as ideas and thoughts are non-substantial they cannot be said to be *in* the unconscious, especially since the latter, not being a location, could not contain these anyway. Similarly there can be no real barrier in the brain with which to restrain thoughts and emotions. According to Schafer, psychoanalytic language also encourages anthropomorphism (the description of a part of a person using terms which can only be applied to the whole individual). Thus the ego cannot be said to experience helplessness. The id cannot be said to feel frustrated. The use of reification and anthropomorphism lead inevitably to paradoxes like the following one described by Fingarette (1974): how can the censor discern that an impulse needs to be repressed without being conscious of it, but if it is conscious of it anyway why does the impulse need to disguise itself?

Schafer's solution involves a revised system of terminology in which verb–adverb constructions substitute for the reified, mechanistic, anthropomorphic noun–adjective constructs of metapsychology. In this way the mental apparatus is not split anthropomorphically into components and the only agency is that of the person who acts. For example, 'his aggression was finally released' becomes 'he finally acted angrily after all this time'; 'resistence to the process of analysis' becomes 'engaging in actions contrary to analysis whilst also engaging in analysis itself'.

Spiro (1979) has objected to Schafer's approach on the grounds that dispositional properties (e.g. an angry woman) are not reducible to simple behavioural dispositions (her acting angrily). As Meissner

(1979) pointed out, the experiential element (the sense of frustration and paralysis in resistence) is lost from the description. Others have questioned the clinical usefulness of Schafer's long and sometimes tedious retranslations of metapsychological concepts (Rawn, 1979; Frank, 1979).

Alternative solutions of the problems of metapsychology involve the transposing of psychoanalysis into a framework similar to that of semantics or literary criticism, where the sole criterion of a valid interpretation is its intelligibility (Rycroft, 1966; Ricoeur, 1970; Steele, 1979). Other analysts recommend discarding the claim of psychoanalysis to provide a model of the mechanisms of the mind and concentrating on its clinical investigation of why people behave in particular ways (Home, 1966; Klein, 1973, 1976). However, Freud's contribution would have been a great deal less if he had abandoned either of the above pursuits (Jahoda, 1977) for, as Sandler and Joffe (1966) have pointed out, it is important to examine the interdependence of the experiential and non-experiential levels of psychological processes. The experience of a fantasy cannot be understood fully without reference to the nature of the process of fantasizing.

The solution proposed by Peterfreund (1971, 1975), Noy (1973), Basch (1976) and Rosenblatt and Thickstun (1977) avoids the alienation of psychoanalysis from empirical psychology. These workers have attempted to integrate metapsychology into an information-processing framework and have thus demonstrated that the possibility of a common language between the two disciplines exists. However, as Wurmser (1977) has correctly pointed out, this solution is no less metaphorical than the metapsychological model it attempts to replace.

The relevance of experiments for psychoanalytic theory

The problem with metapsychology appears to be that the psychoanalytic situation does not provide sufficient information concerning psychological processes to avoid recourse to metaphorical and anthropomorphic statements. A careful examination of Fingarette's paradox cited above reveals that more information concerning the complexities of the process of thinking would avoid the absurdity of having to conceive of the mind thinking that it should not think a particular thought. There might very well be a number of different processes of thought, one of which could inhibit further processing of the other and thus prevent it from reaching consciousness.

Research relevant to psychoanalytic theory from alternative scientific loci has not tackled this problem. Research on the therapeutic effectiveness of psychoanalysis may help to validate it as a treatment method, but the relevance of therapeutic success to the validity of the theory is analogous to the relevance of the effectiveness of aspirin to a theory of headaches (Schmidl, 1955; Kline, 1972). Observational techniques, especially during the past twenty-five years, have been useful in drawing analysts' attention to phenomena not normally encountered in the clinical setting; for example, Freedman's (1977, 1979) studies of deaf and blind children and Bowlby's (1969, 1973) studies of separation are particularly instructive, but have not illuminated the psychological processes underlying these phenomena.

Experimental investigations reviewed in detail by Kline (1972) and Fisher and Greenberg (1977) have set out to validate psychoanalytic observations by recreating them in laboratory settings and thus provide a public verification of psychoanalytic assertions. Many however question whether there is any connection between psychoanalytic theory and research purporting to be its empirical examination. Most studies ignore the function and falsify the content of psychoanalytic concepts, which in any case could no more be confirmed or disconfirmed by laboratory investigations than the observations of a naturalist could be falsified in the artifically created environment of a greenhouse. At the same time they fail to describe or elucidate the psychological processes underlying clinical phenomena and thus give little aid to analysts attempting to reduce the conceptual difficulties facing their discipline. A review of the research on the psychoanalytic theory of personality will illustrate these points.

Review of experimental work related to the psychoanalytic theory of personality

The following review of the experimental work which relates to the psychoanalytic theory of personality will be divided into two sections. Firstly, studies which have adopted a 'naive' validational approach will be reviewed and evaluated. Secondly, studies which are not direct tests of psychoanalytic theory, but which nevertheless cast some light on the nature of the psychological processes which may underlie phenomena described by analysts will be considered.

The validational approach

Three questions have regularly been asked in empirical studies of psychoanalytic personality types: (1) Is there a correlated set of personality traits which matches the psychoanalytic description of the oral, anal or phallic character? (2) Is there support for the psychoanalytic hypothesis related to the ontogeny (development) of these character types? (3) Is there evidence to show that particular personality traits are associated with the instinctual concerns which are supposed to underlie them? (For example does an excessively tidy person also overemphasize his toilet routines?). Each of these questions will be examined in relation to the psychoanalytic character types.

The oral personality.   Freud's theory of personality (see Chapter 2) implies that the nature of a person's resolution of problems arising at a particular stage of libidinal development will determine his or her character, defences and neurotic symptoms.

In his 'Three Essays on Sexuality' published in 1905 Freud divides early sexual development into three stages according to the zone of the body through which the sexual drive manifests itself. The oral, anal and phallic stages face the child with different tyes of conflicts. The child develops or acquires a cluster of traits that help him to master especially troublesome conflicts (caused by a combination of constitutional and environmental factors). Thus permanent character traits are regarded either as unchanging perpetrations of original childhood erotism or as defences against this.

The oral character as described by Abraham (1927) and also by Glover (1924) comprises a list of at times contradictory features. The incompatibility of the traits is to some extent accounted for by the subdivision of the oral stage into the passive, receptive, sucking and the active, aggressive, biting subphases. Following this distinction a number of studies differentiate two types of oral personality, one dominated by passive, dependent attitudes, and the other by active, aggressive ones. Furthermore, conflicts of exceptional magnitude (fixations) may be caused by either excessive indulgence of a child, or by his continuous frustrations. The oral character is summarized by Fisher and Greenberg (1977) as being preoccupied with issues of giving and taking, concerns about independence and dependence, extremes of optimism and pessimism, unusual ambivalence, impatience and the continued use of the oral channel for gratification, (e.g. talkativeness, tooth-grinding, chewing).

Several studies have examined whether these traits do indeed hang together in a single factor of orality or perhaps two factors reflecting the oral passive (sucking) and the oral aggressive (biting) subphases of the oral stage. (See Chapter 5 for a description of the statistical procedure of factor analysis.) Kline and Storey (1977) have recently reviewed these investigations. Strongest support for the oral character is provided by Goldman-Eisler's (1948) studies where a single bipolar factor on which traits of pessimism, passivity, aloofness, oral verbal aggression and autonomy loaded highly on one pole of the factor, and the opposites of these traits loaded at the other end. Unfortunately, she did not provide evidence for the validity of the scales she used other than face validity. The factor analytic study of Lazare et al. (1966) provided similar results which is hardly surprising since Goldman-Eisler's items were adopted for their questionnaires. Other studies have either found no satisfactory matches between psychoanalytic theory and the results of factor analysis, or their implication is severely restricted by inadequate methodology (e.g. lack of control for social desirability or low inter-item correlations).

Kline and Storey's own attempt at validating the oral character was more successful. They were able to demonstrate that a scale of oral optimism associated with the first subphase of the oral stage (including the qualities of dependency, fluency, sociability, liking of novelty and relaxation) and one of oral pessimism associated with the second subphase of the oral stage (including the qualities of independence, verbal aggression, envy, coldness and hostility, malice, ambition and impatience) both had high inter-item correlations, suggesting that they were homogeneous traits. A factor analytic study of these scales, designed to validate the questionnaires, also produced meaningful results. Although this is methodologically the best demonstration of the existence of an 'oral character' to date, no evidence is offered which might link either of these scales with psychoanalytic conceptions of the development of orality.

A second series of studies has investigated the relationship between personality variables and early oral experiences. Fisher and

Greenberg (1977) review no less than twenty-five of them.

Investigations of the relationship between feeding practices and later behaviour have produced equivocal findings. Goldman-Eisler (1951) succeeded in relating her orality factor to length of breast feeding, and Sears et al. (1953, 1965) related the severity of weaning to dependency. Authors of other studies, however, have found no relationship between duration of breast feeding and traits such as jealousy (Peterson and Spano, 1941) and dependency (Thurstone and Mussen, 1951). However the indices of feeding styles used in these studies in no way do justice to the complexities of a mother's interaction with her infant.

Studies which have examined the effect of early maternal behaviour on personality by and large favour psychoanalytic theory. Kagan and Moss (1962) observed that protective ('warm') mothering produced *dependency* in the male child although this relationship disappeared when the child passed the age of ten. Hernstein (1963) in an eighteen-year longitudinal study, found that 'warm' ('protective') mothers tended to have children who were less food-finicky and on the whole more independent than children with 'cold' mothers. The finding of greater dependence as well as greater independence in children with warm and protective mothers may be considered problematic for psychoanalytic theory. The fact that both the findings are fully consistent with the supposed effects of fixation at the oral stage is unlikely to surprise critics of Freudian theory.

Some studies have observed feeding practices in different societies and have attempted to relate these to personality variables. For example, Whiting and Child (1953) demonstrated that in cultures where there was a high degree of concern about the feeding of the baby, this was reflected in the frequency of irrational beliefs concerning the involvement of the oral region in the causation of illness. Unfortunately the validity of the dependent variable (attitudes to disease) was assumed rather than demonstrated.

The experimental behaviour of orally fixated individuals has been examined in a number of studies. The extent of a person's orality has been found to correlate positively with responsivity to verbal reinforcement (Timmons and Noblin, 1963), to advice (Tribich and Messer, 1974) and to social support in stress (Sarnoff and Zimbardo, 1961) confirming the notion that oral characters are rather dependent. However the various measures of orality used in these and other studies are so diverse that perhaps the only quality they have in common is their lack of validity. Measures such as responses to the Blacky pictures (Blacky is a dog whose activities are designed to arouse and measure oral, anal and phallic anxieties) or behavioural indices such as number of mouth movements or ice-creams consumed, have no more than face validity. They may or may not be measuring what psychoanalysts call the investment of libido in the oral phase, and until such time as these measures are validated, we are forced to limit our conclusions to the predictive significance of ice-cream consumption and avoid making statements concerning psychoanalytic theory.

The anal character.   Freud (1908) suggested that the characteristics of orderliness, parsimony and obstinacy as well as the traits of intellectualization of problems and indecisiveness might often be used together by an individual in order to reduce anxiety created by conflicts around the age two or three over an unusually intense erogeneity of the anal zone. The type of personality which combined these traits was termed the anal or obsessive–compulsive personality.

A number of studies have attempted to verify that anal character traits do cluster together. In a recent review Pollak (1979) cites no less than twenty-four correlational and factor analytic studies which have affirmed that traits consistent with the clinical description of the obsessive–compulsive personality frequently emerge together, usually as a single factor. Lazare et al. (1966) found, for example, in their factor analysis of a 140-item questionnaire that the following traits loaded highly on their third factor, which strikingly resembles the anal personality: orderliness, severe superego, perseverance, obstinacy, rigidity, rejection of others, parsimony, emotional constriction and self-doubt.

Three major reviews of the area (Kline, 1972; Fisher and Greenberg, 1977; Pollak, 1979) agree that the major qualities which Freud ascribed to the anally oriented personality do hang together. Hill (1976) however, in a methodological review of six of the studies considered by Kline to be good ones, revealed major methodological weaknesses in each. He pointed out, for example, that the impressive consistency of anal traits in the Lazare study could be almost totally attributed to the high correlation of all the traits listed above with the trait of orderliness. If this trait were partialled out, the factor disappeared. He concluded that in view of bad sampling techniques, high residual correlations, illegitimate use of combined scores and factoring techniques and biased factor interpretations, none of the studies had demonstrated the Freudian concept of anal character.

Better support for the anal personality may be obtained from studies in which questionnaire and behavioural measures of anal anxiety have been correlated with specific behavioural measures of orderliness, obstinacy and parsimony. Rosenwald (1972) for example demonstrated that the amount of anxiety experienced by persons about anal matters predicted how carefully they arranged magazines when requested to do so by the experimenter. The obstinacy of a subject in shifting his opinion was predicted by the difficulty he experienced in solving a puzzle which involved immersing his hand in a faecal-like substance. Furthermore, Noblin et al. (1966) have demonstrated that anal orientation, as revealed by the Blacky test, predicted susceptibility to monetary rewards. Fisher (1978) has illustrated that racial prejudice based on skin colour is predicted by an individual's attitudes to cleanliness and thrift, implying that colour prejudice is at least partially the unfortunate consequence of an unconscious connection between skin colour and faeces. These findings and those of several similar investigations, provide convincing evidence solely because the predictions they make are highly counterintuitive and seem difficult to account for in any context other than the psychoanalytic.

The libidinal fixation of the obsessive–compulsive character at the anal stage of development is thought to reflect unusual, extreme parental behaviours at the time of toilet training. A series of studies has failed to verify that the anal personality differs from other types in the age of initiation or completion of toilet training, or in the severity of training procedures (Finney, 1963; Hetherington and Brackbill, 1963; Sears et al., 1965). Several investigations have however identified a relationship between mother's and child's anality (Beloff, 1957; Finney, 1963) and Pollak (1979) regards these as support for a social learning theory alternative to the psychoanalytic hypothesis concerning the aetiology of the anal character. This explanation however would not account for the counterintuitive findings reviewed above linking obsessive – compulsive behaviour with anxiety concerning anal impulses.

The phallic personality.   The author's search of the literature has revealed no empirical work on this personality type which is worth reporting.

Conclusion from research on character types.   We have seen that although there is evidence indicating that personality types corresponding to the psychoanalytic descriptions of the oral and anal character do exist, most studies have major problems concerning validity, and there is no evidence to link these character types with psychosexual aetiologies. Some studies have related individual personality traits to pregenital fixations. These studies however rely for their validity on the counterintuitive nature of their findings which tend to preclude alternative interpretations.

A crucial problem of this research is that the formulations of the three character types, which these studies were aimed at validating, are far from being crucial components of psychoanalytic theory, which since the early 1920s has turned away from relatively simple formulations of instinctual development, and has taken more note of the development of the ego.

Other components of personality structure.   The present day psychoanalytic theory of personality could be more appropriately termed a theory or model of the person as it involves all aspects of the theory, not just a single component of it. The notion of personality encompasses not just the idea of eroticism, fixations, and regressions, but also notions of conflict, of defensive structures, of the ego, of unconscious processes, and so forth. These are necessary components of the overall theory and require empirical study in their own right.

Empirical studies of children's attitudes to their parents aimed at validating the *Oedipus complex* have not borne out the shift in feeling from mother to father predicted to occur around the age of five or six by Freud (Kagan and Lemkin, 1960). Studies of *castration anxiety* have confirmed that boys are more concerned about physical injury than girls (Pitcher and Prelinger, 1963) and that adult males respond to sexual stimuli by displaced expressions of castration anxiety, for example, fear of death (Sarnoff and Corwin, 1959). Investigations of *penis envy* have found no evidence that women assess their bodies as in any way inferior to those of men (Fisher, 1973). Studies of the defence mechanism of *repression* have illustrated that emotional material is more easily forgotten than neutral material (Wilkinson and Cargill, 1955; Levinger and Clark, 1961). *Displacement* and *sublimation* have also been demonstrated to occur under controlled conditions (Miller and Bugelski, 1948; Wallach and Greenberg, 1960). Halpern (1977) demonstrated that subjects who denied being aroused by pornography *projected* more lust onto a disliked person than a less defensive group. It is unfortunate that few of the studies reviewed above may be considered to be investigating processes analogous to those described by psychoanalysts, as most of the experiments involved conscious rather than unconscious thinking and emotion. Freud's concept of repression, for example, refers to the loss from consciousness of ideas with associational links to unconscious material; such links were not demonstrated to exist in the laboratory studies of this mechanism of defence. Children's Oedipal feelings are similarly supposed to be unconscious attitudes and hence not measurable on a questionnaire which taps the conscious emotions.

Evaluation of studies considered so far.   Evidence has been reviewed from investigations aimed at validating the psychoanalytic conceptions of personality. Some findings were found to be consistent with the theory and others were opposed to it, but what relevance do these findings have? The short answer is: none. Neither the positive nor the negative findings can either prove or disprove the theory. That penis envy is not detectable in women's responses to questionnaires does not imply that Freud was incorrect in detecting it in his female patients. It similarly does not follow from the observation that the oral personality type is detectable on the basis of questionnaires, that the analysts concerned had described their patients fully and accurately. The questionnaire is one source of data about people, the couch is another. Data from these discrepant sources need correspond no more closely than the observations of an ethologist concerning the mating behaviour of a rodent correspond to the performance of the same animal in the laboratory. Psychoanalytic theory may only be considered to be verified if the observations of individual analysts match those of independent colleagues. That is if, on the basis of publicly available evidence, any person who shares the community of experience will conclude that it is true (McIntosh, 1979).

Few of the experiments reviewed above may be of either practical or theoretical use to clinicians. At best they illustrate that some psychological processes pinpointed by analysts are also arguably observable in the laboratory. A number of clinicians, frustrated with the small yield of laboratory research, decided to turn their consulting room into a laboratory. Luborsky (1973), for example, investigated the process of momentary forgetting in his patients and found that such incidents tended to follow immediately the expression of a conflict-related thought. These findings are, of course, in line with a 'repression-based' model of the phenomenon but further suggest that repression is an undifferentiated process which, once activated, interferes with memory processes in a general way. Experimental studies which go beyond the point of inadequately replicating clinical phenomena do however exist, and it is to these that we shall now turn.

Psychological investigations of unconscious processes

Unconscious perception.   The assumption of a dynamic unconscious sets psychoanalysis apart from all other schools of psychology. The concept of unconscious motives, affects, and attitudes plays a large part in the psychoanalytic theory of personality. The exploration of these processes might be of considerable relevance to analysts.

Several studies reviewed by Dixon (1971) have demonstrated that verbal stimuli which are either too quick or too dim for the subject to be aware of, will nevertheless affect his associative processes. Marcel and Patterson (1978) reported that associations following the subliminal presentation of a word were linked to it in meaning. The relevance of this finding to psychoanalytic theory lies in the demonstration that thoughts in the form of associations may occur in the absence of awareness. Freudian theory also postulates that conscious emotions are often responses to unconscious internal stimuli. Tyrer, Lewis and Lee (1978) showed that a subject's self-rated anxiety was increased following the subliminal tachistoscopic presentation of unpleasant words (e.g. cancer). Similarly, O'Grady (1977) demonstrated increased GSRs to subliminally presented emotive picture stimuli (e.g. breast). Thus a process whereby emotions may be elicited from subjects without awareness of their source can be observed in the laboratory. These findings lead to the development of a view of the human information-processing system in which consciousness is not essential to cognition and it only periodically samples the ongoing processing of information. This model would be highly consistent with psychoanalytic theory.

The phenomenon of perceptual defence, closely related to subliminal perception, casts some light on the functioning of defence mechanisms. Worthington (1964) in a demonstration of this phenomenon, asked light-adapted subjects to sit in a dark room and indicate when they achieved sufficient dark-adaptation to perceive a dim white light. Unknown to the subjects the light source they were asked to report was a white disc with either obscene or neutral words written on it in black letters. In spite of the fact that the subjects were not even able to identify the disc, let alone small patterns on it, dark-adaptation took a great deal longer when the word was of an emotional kind. A similar, defensive increase of perceptual threshold was observed by Dixon and Haider (1961), who found that if an emotive word was presented to one eye at subliminal intensity the threshold of the other eye to a small dim light changed. Shevrin (1973) demonstrated that the cortical responses of subjects 'defending' against subliminal stimuli became distinctive after only 40 msecs of stimulus presentation. This implies that processing for meaning at a preconscious level is much faster than its conscious counterpart.

These findings have important implications for the psychoanalytic model of the mind. In these experiments the subjects must perceive the word at some level in order to recognize its threatening nature, and then make a decision not to perceive it after all. The apparent paradox is easily resolved if we accept Dixon's (1971) model of two mutually inhibitory information-processing systems functioning at different speeds, only the slower of which is linked to consciousness. Many psychoanalytic notions considered by Schafer and others to lead inevitably to similar paradoxes will probably be resolvable in similar ways. The question of agency (of who the person is that acts) will not be decided by philosophers but by research in the areas of normal and abnormal psychology.

If studies using subthreshold stimuli are tapping those unobservable psychological processes which were postulated by psychoanalytic models on the basis of clinical data, then using these stimuli should significantly reduce the problems of demonstrating unconscious conflicts experimentally. This is indeed the case. In a series of truly remarkable experiments Silverman and his colleagues (1976) demonstrated that 4 msecs subliminal tachistoscopic exposure of stimuli related to important unconscious conflicts either increased or decreased psychopathology, depending on whether the stimulus had conflict-intensifying or conflict-alleviating connotations. Silverman demonstrated that stimuli designed to enhance the conflict over incest which is thought to be central to homosexuality led to increased homosexual orientation for men. In a similar study, Silverman and colleagues (1978) used stimuli aimed at enhancing Oedipal conflicts thought by Freud to underly problems over competition in all males. They observed a drop in performance of students in a competitive dart-throwing task following the stimulus 'Beating Daddy is OK!'

Silverman's group have performed over thirty similar studies. Using subliminal methodology, they were able to explore specific dynamic hypotheses related to a number of conditions. Subliminal conflict-enhancing stimuli with oral aggressive content caused thought disorder in schizophrenics, whereas stutterers responded to anal conflict-enhancing stimuli with increased speech disorder. The effectiveness of the technique is limited to non-conscious presentations, confirming the psychoanalytic notion that unconscious thought processes are qualitatively different from their conscious counterparts and further underlining the inadequacy of laboratory approaches to psychoanalytic theory which limit their focus to the conscious processes of their subjects.

Explorations in neuropsychology. Psychoanalysis aims to provide a complete view of man's psychological world. It is therefore legitimate for us to search for neural processes which might provide potential mechanisms for the psychological functions described by psychoanalytic theory.

(1) Unconscious processes and the brain. Assuming that the existence of unconscious processes has been successfully demonstrated in the laboratory, can we isolate such processes at the level of the brain? Weiskrantz (1977) summarized studies which demonstrated that subjects with lesions in the visual cortex who experienced blindness in a portion of their visual field could correctly guess the position of lights and the shape of objects in their supposedly blind field. Weiskrantz (1980) reported on thirty-six patients with occipital lesions who experienced blindness but nevertheless to their own great surprise guessed with over 70 per cent accuracy. Weiskrantz and Warrington (1979) demonstrated that amnesics who claimed to remember nothing acquired eye-blink conditioning without

having been aware of doing so. Clearly, both the external stimulus in the case of cortical blindness and the memory of the task in the case of amnesia are outside the patient's awareness, but this does not appear to hinder the efficiency of task performance, which is not distinguishable from a normal level. Weiskrantz (1977) has suggested that such unconscious processing goes on in subcortical centres. John (1976) has suggested that when an area specialized for a particular function is removed from the cortex, other areas in the cortex which perform this function take over, but output from these areas is too weak to reach consciousness. In this model then, the whole of the cortex, not just subcortical structures, may underly non-conscious information processing (cf., Hilgard, 1980). Thus consciousness appears to be just one specialized form of neural activity. This is highly consistent with the psychoanalytic hypothesis.

(2) Unconscious memories. Penfield (1958) when directly stimulating the temporal cortex of patients found that they reported phenomenal experiences of 'bygone days' including the entire spectrum of emotional content as well as visual and acoustic components. Thus the central nervous system appears to preserve a record of past experiences and perceptions of astonishing detail which is not normally available to consciousness. It is possible that these percepts encoded as memories form the basis of the preconscious and unconscious systems.

(3) The death instinct. The destructive or death instinct (Freud, 1920) has been the most controversial concept within psychoanalytic literature, perhaps as a result of its intuitively improbable function – self-destruction. Heilbrunn (1979) drew attention to the relevance of recent endocrinological discoveries for this area. Denckla (1974, 1975a, b) found that the declining responsivity of ageing tissues to thyroid products (which leads to a slowing down of metabolism) is not a natural process, but the result of the release of a substance he called the 'death' hormone which blocks the breakdown of thyroxin. Denckla (1977) claimed that mammals' life-span is regulated by a biological clock which acts on the endocrine glands to produce a failure of the immune and circulatory systems. Whether this hormone relates to psychological processes described by Freud in connection with the self-destructive instinct will be an important issue for future investigations.

(4) Primary and secondary processes. Freud (1900) distinguished two modes of cognitive functioning: the primary and the secondary

processes. The former is associated with dreams, contains no logic, no respect for time, sequence of negation, is dominated by the visual modality and condenses, displaces and symbolically represents its contents in such a way as to make them bizarre and incomprehensible for rational thought. The secondary process is analogous to our everyday thinking. A number of authors have recently equated the functioning of the dominant hemisphere with secondary processes, whereas the visually–spatially oriented minor hemisphere has been linked with primary process type thinking (Bogen, 1969; Galin, 1974; McKinnon, 1979).

Hoppe (1977) and Dimond (1979) have supported this contention with data from split-brain patients. In these patients the complete bisection of the pathways connecting the right and left hemispheres results in an isolation of the experiences of these two halves of the brain. As the ability to speak is localized in the left half, all phenomenal experiences reported by these patients refer to the left hemisphere (Zaidel, 1978). The dreams reported by these patients are free from primary process distortions and bizarreness and lie much closer to the ordinary modes of thinking of awake adults. Studies with non-brain-damaged patients indicate that the left side of the face and body is more likely to show signs of emotion (Sackheim and Gur, 1978) and emotional conflict in terms of hypochondriacal complaints and conversion symptoms (Kenyon, 1976; Galin et al., 1977). These findings are consistent with the notion that the emotion-dominated primary processes are localized in the right hemisphere.

The implications of these results are encouraging. From the viewpoint of personality theory two points may be made: (1) The conscious self of split-brain patients seems to be firmly associated with the secondary process left hemisphere which asserts itself over the right hemisphere (these subjects often sit on their left hand in order to allow their right hand to perform a task without interference). Moreover, split-brain patients do not report that their memories of themselves are very different from their present selves, implying that consciousness of their own consciousness is also located in the left side of the brain; (Eccles, 1979; Dimond, 1979; Oakley, 1979). (2) If primary process functioning is linked to the right hemisphere it is no longer possible to assume that it represents some sort of childlike, archaic process. After all why should half the brain stop developing? It is more probable that the primary processes, in their interaction with the secondary processes, with the aid of highly developed underlying neural structures, play a more adaptive and creative role than the one normally ascribed to this mode of functioning by psychoanalytic theory (McLaughlin, 1978).

Conclusion

Some psychoanalytic personality types and some isolated components of the psychoanalytic theory of personality have been demonstrated in the laboratory. However, it would be misguided to regard these as confirmatory evidence for psychoanalytic concepts since the equivalence between laboratory and clinical observations has not been demonstrated. More promising are studies which make use of preconscious stimulation in an attempt to cast some light upon psychological processes underlying unconscious phenomena. The neuropsychological investigations reviewed imply that neural mechanisms corresponding to psychoanalytic postulates do exist. These studies do not validate psychoanalytic theory but they strongly indicate that, far from being an outdated model, Freud's theories are by and large consistent with many findings from diverse areas of present-day laboratory investigations. Much more psychological research however remains to be done on the information processing mechanisms which mediate phenomena such as regression, fixation, repression, reaction-formation and so forth before psychologists may be said to contribute usefully to the development of psychoanalytic theory.

Suggested further reading

Fisher and Greenberg (1977) offer a comprehensive, somewhat uncritical account of validational studies; Kline's (1972) review provides a more evaluative text.

There is as yet no text available which selectively summarizes empirical work aimed, not at validating psychoanalytic concepts, but at offering information concerning psychological processes which might be involved in these. A good source for these studies are the journals *Psychoanalysis and Contemporary Science* and *Psychoanalysis and Contemporary Thought*.

Part III
Factor analytic approach

5 The work of Eysenck and Cattell

Paul Kline

Introduction

H. J. Eysenck and R. B. Cattell are two outstanding figures in the
modern study of personality. Both have developed elaborate theories
based upon the factor analysis of measures of personality (largely, but
not exclusively, questionnaires) and have produced, since the war, a
huge number of research papers and books. They can be considered
together not only on account of the similarity of their approach but
because they are perhaps the last active workers of the London school
of psychology. Both have also been heavily influenced by Spearman, the virtual inventor of factor analysis, to whom Cattell was a
research assistant, and by Cyril Burt, an egregious exponent of factor
analysis. Eysenck is based at the Institute of Psychiatry at the
Maudsley Hospital, London, while Cattell emigrated to America and
worked until the last few years at the University of Illinois. He is now
at Hawaii.

Plan of the chapter

To understand their work it is essential to grasp the fundamentals of
factor analysis. Thus in this chapter we shall explicate its essentials,

concentrating on the underlying rationale and logic. We shall then examine some of the objections to the technique, frequently raised by psychologists, especially the problem of the infinity of possible factor analytic solutions, a problem at the heart of the differences between Eysenck and Cattell. We shall then describe and critically evaluate first the work of Eysenck and then that of Cattell. Finally, we shall briefly look at some other factor analytic findings and propose a solution to account for the apparently disparate results.

Factor analysis

As a first step to understanding factor analysis, which is a statistical technique aimed at simplifying complex data, it is helpful to define the various terms.

Definition of a factor

Nunnally (1978) has provided an excellent and succinct definition. 'Any linear combination of the variables in a data matrix is said to be a factor of that matrix.' Thus, for example, a factor could be formed by combining the scores on four variables, say, numerical ability, verbal ability, spatial ability and abstract reasoning, and these could be differentially weighted in this combination. This precise definition has been elaborated by Eysenck (1953). He argues that a factor is a condensed statement of the linear relationships obtaining between a set of variables, and that factor analysis can be used in three ways.

Factors as descriptors. Suppose we factorize the intercorrelations between 100 variables and 10 factors emerge accounting for all the variance. As they stand (without rotation which we shall discuss later) these 10 factors may not be interpretable. However, mathematically, because they account for all the variance, we can describe the data in terms of 10 factors rather than 100 variables, a more parsimonious description. This descriptive use of factor analysis is legitimate although, obviously, of little value in the study of personality since uninterpretable factors can hardly be thought of as useful knowledge.

Factors suggesting hypotheses. Suppose again that we have factored a battery of personality tests and a factor emerges loading on all our tests of obsessional traits, that is, related to such tests (factor loadings are also discussed later). This suggests that there is a general factor or dimension of obsessional traits. This hypothesis could then be tested experimentally. This is the main use of factor analysis in the study of personality and is essentially the method utilized by Cattell and Eysenck and other leading factor analysts.

Factors refuting or supporting a hypothesis.   In this case we might expect from clinical evidence or psychological theory that among a particular set of tests, a factor would appear. The resulting factor analysis can thus refute or support the theory. Kline and Storey (1977), for example, hypothesized that an oral factor would emerge loading on dependency, generosity and optimism, based on a study of psychoanalytic developmental theory. In this instance the factor analysis supported the hypothesis. This use is also important in the study of personality, but most psychological theories are insufficiently precise to allow clear hypotheses concerning factors to be made.

To some readers, even given the examples of the three different uses of factor analysis, the notion of a linear combination of variables may not seem especially meaningful. Royce (1963) examined in detail the nature and meaning of factors. He discovered that factors had been variously described as dimensions, determinants, functional unities and taxonomic categories. Royce's own definition seems to us, however, perhaps the most comprehensive and illuminating – 'a construct operationally defined by its factor loadings (correlations with variables)'. Or this may be combined with Nunnally's (1978) definition to obtain a linear combination of variables defined by its factor loadings.

Before we can go any further in understanding factor analysis, a few further terms must be defined and discussed.

Factor loadings

These are the correlations of the factors with the variables. Thus, if a factor loads 0.2 on neuroticism and 0.45 on state anxiety, it means that the construct correlates 0.2 with neuroticism and 0.45 with state anxiety. It must also be pointed out that the cross-multiplication of factor loadings enables one to reproduce the original correlations between the variables. The power of factor analysis should now be clear. We can by reference to a small number of factors, reproduce an original matrix of correlations. Factors are, therefore, an elegant way of summarizing data. Furthermore, as Royce argues, each factor is a construct defined by its factor loadings. It is not a vague term arbitrarily defined by clever word play, but a construct or dimension mathematically defined and able by definition to account for the observed correlations between variables.

Interpretation of factors

In our discussion of the descriptive use of factors, we pointed out that their value for the study of personality was low because their factors were not interpretable. This brings us to the question of the basis for their interpretation. The interpretation or labelling of factors depends on their factor loadings. Thus, if a factor loads, for example, on measures of anxiety, psychogalvanic reflex, and general fearfulness, it could clearly be labelled as 'neuroticism'. To interpret a construct which correlates with such measures, we have to conceive a variable which would, as it were, fit, and neuroticism fits the bill.

Two points are to be noted concerning the interpretation of factors from their factor loadings. First, in the best of psychometric work factor identification does not rest on the loadings alone. The factor loadings are used to develop a hypothesis concerning the identification or interpretation. This hypothesis is then put to the experimental test. To take our previous example: if we thought that a neuroticism factor had been found we would obtain the scores of neurotics and non-neurotic controls on the factor and correlate our factor with other tests of neuroticism, thus putting it to experimental test. Finally, perhaps, we would correlate the factor with factors claimed to be independent of neuroticism. In this way the factor can be externally verified.

The second point is fundamental – critical to the whole use of factor analysis as a technique for the study of personality. It concerns the interpretability of factors. In our discussion of descriptive factors we said that the factors might be uninterpretable. This means that an examination of the factor loadings of each factor fails to reveal what the factors, as constructs, are. In this case the factor analysis is not abandoned but is *rotated to simple structure*. These terms rotation and simple structure must now be explained because rotation to simple structure as we have argued (Cattell and Kline, 1977) is a *sine qua non* of adequate factor analytic work.

Factor rotation

An objection to factor analysis is that there is no unique factor analytic solution: indeed there is an infinity of possible solutions. Heim (1975) regards this as a reason for not using the technique at all. Certainly in the field of personality there is considerable disagreement over factor analytic results with almost as many solutions as factorists. However, Thurstone (1947) argued that rotation to simple structure could overcome this difficulty and this view has been strongly supported by Cattell (1966) and Cattell and Kline (1977).

Factors as vectors.   Factors can be regarded as vectors in factor space. The infinity of possible solutions derives from the fact that there is no *a priori* method of fixing the position of these axes in factor space relative to each other. The only constraint is that cross multiplication of the factors can reproduce the original correlations.

Simple structure, as defined by Thurstone (1947), aimed to rotate the vectors relative to each other to the position that resulted in each factor having a few high loadings and a large number of low or nil loadings. This makes each factor simple to interpret, hence the name. How this is done in principle, and some of the problems involved, will be discussed later. Here it is sufficient to say that the rationale of simple structure is the law of parsimony, Occam's razor, for each factor analytic solution can be regarded as a hypothesis accounting for the correlations and thus the most simple is to be preferred. Cattell (1966) has strongly adopted this position and has devoted much research effort to the proper attainment of simple structure – failure to attain it being the weakness, in his view, of much factor analytic research in personality. Cattell, indeed, places so great an importance on simple structure, for it is only these simple factors that tend to be replicable, that we must now examine the problem of how simple structure is to be reached.

Rotation to simple structure.   To grasp the problems of rotation to simple structure a few further technical terms must be defined.

(1) Orthogonal factors and orthogonal rotation. If the factors in the rotation are kept at right angles (orthogonal) to each other, then the factors are themselves uncorrelated, for the cosine of the angle between the vectors indicates the correlation between the factors. Cattell (e.g. Cattell and Kline, 1977) has always argued that orthogonal rotation almost inevitably prevents the attainment of simple structure, for in the real and complex world, basic fundamental dimensions, such as factors, are likely to be correlated. This argument seems exceedingly powerful and the present writer is in full agreement with Cattell on this point. However, Guilford (e.g. 1959) whose work has been an important influence on Eysenck argues that a set of uncorrelated factors is *per se* more simple than a set of correlated factors, even if the individual uncorrelated factors are not so clear. Guilford, therefore, persists in working with orthogonal rotations. Most factor analysts aim for correlated or oblique rotations.

(2) Oblique factors and oblique rotations. In oblique rotation the angles between the vectors can be of any size so that they can take up the position yielding the most simple structure as defined by Thurstone. Since the cosine of the angle between the vectors indicates the correlation between them, oblique factors are correlated.

In any large scale study with a considerable number of oblique factors, it is possible to factor analyse the correlations between the factors: resulting in second-order factors. The correlations between these second-order factors can be factored resulting in third-orders and so on until at last only one or two orthogonal factors finally emerge. Thus primary factors load on the original test variables, second-orders load on primary factors and third-orders on second-orders. These higher-order factors are thus likely to be very broad, fundamental concepts.

(3) Attaining simple structure. Cattell (1966) has long made the point that the best way to attain simple structure is to adopt a rotation procedure which maximizes what he calls the hyperplane count – essentially the number of nil loadings. Although there is a variety of methods for reaching simple structure (see Harman, 1976), this criterion seems generally accepted. So it is arguable that the old objection to factor analysis, that there is an infinity of solutions, can now be answered. Modern oblique rotation computer programmes can reach simple structure with reasonable agreement in most cases between the results.

So far then we have seen that factor analysis is a technique which reveals mathematically defined constructs accounting for observed correlations between variables. Where simple structure has been revealed, then we have the most elegant, parsimonious, and replicable account of the data.

Some practical rules for factor analyses

When we come to evaluate the work of Cattell and Eysenck in the following sections of this chapter, we shall be forced to consider the adequacy of their factor analytic techniques. Many published factor analyses are full of technical flaws which render their findings dubious or, in some cases, worthless. This is not always due to ignorance on the part of the researcher, but to the simple practical problems in obtaining large enough samples and of the large computational problems involved in obtaining simple structure.

Cattell (1973) and Cattell and Kline (1977) together with Nunnally (1978) have summarized the practical necessities for adequate factor analysis and the following rules are based upon their suggestions.

Sampling variables.   If we are trying to map out the most important variables in some areas of psychology (a task for which factor analysis is especially suited), then it is essential that we fully sample the universe of variables. Unless we can be sure we have done this, as is obvious, certain factors may never emerge. Thus, for example, in the field of personality, if we insert no measures of anxiety, then no anxiety factor will be found. Clearly, therefore, adequate factor analytic studies attempting to define personality must demonstrate that the full universe of variables has been sampled or, at least, that the variables in the analysis are samples from a properly defined population.

Sampling subjects.   There is less agreement among factorists concerning the problems of subject sampling. Guilford (1956) recommends that samples should be homogeneous and that different samples should not be combined into one. However, homogeneity tends to lower correlations and thus factors become less clearly defined. In addition to this, samples should reflect populations and these may well be heterogeneous. The solution is to have factorization among heterogeneous samples and among the sub-groups making up the samples.

Sample size.   This is a critical variable for the quality of factor analysis. Guilford (1956) has argued that 200 is a minimum number of subjects for a reliable factor analysis because this reduces the standard error of the correlations to a negligible amount. With samples smaller than this factor structures should be replicated in different studies.

Ratio of subjects to variables.   This is also a critical variable. For reasons of matrix algebra there should always be at least twice as many subjects as variables in a factor analysis. Below this ratio, results can be statistical artefacts. While Guilford (1956) advocates this ratio, Nunnally (1978) is far more stringent and suggests ten times the number of subjects to variables. This criterion makes large scale mapping studies of the area hard to carry out, for simple practical reasons. What is, therefore, clear is that adequate factor analysis (unless replicated) should involve a minimum of two times subjects to variables.

Other rules.   There are various other rules suggested by Cattell (1973) and Nunnally (1978) of a more technical kind, aimed at producing simple structure, which we cannot here comment upon, of which the most important is that the right number of factors should go into the rotation. Cattell (1973) suggests that the Scree test (Cattell, 1966a) should be used to establish the significance of factors, although this is only one of a number of possible methods.

R, Q and P analyses

Before examining the work of Eysenck and Cattell, we must mention that the standard factor analysis of variables (R analysis) is not the only kind available. People can be factored (Q analysis) resulting in groups of subjects, a useful technique in clinical psychology. P analysis is also useful where the scores of one subject (over time) are factored thus showing fluctuations of mood and state. There are yet other designs (see Cattell and Kline, 1977) but they are little used in the study of personality and will not be discussed here.

Conclusions

Generally if we can see that variables have been properly sampled, that there is a large number of subjects, that the ratio of subjects to variables is large, that simple structure has been reached by oblique rotation and that the results have been replicated, then we feel *some* confidence in the results.

The work of Eysenck

The empirical base

Eysenck's studies of personality began in the 1940s and are still continuing. The original investigation in which he identified the two personality factors, extraversion (E) and neuroticism (N) was a rating-scale study of 700 psychiatric patients who had been screened so that those suffering from organic brain damage or physical illness were excluded from them. Thirty-nine rating scales were completed by psychiatrists for each patient and subjected to factor analysis. Two factors emerged accounting for the variance in this psychiatric sample (Eysenck, 1944): (1) Neuroticism loading on items such as badly organized personality, abnormal before illness, little energy and narrow interests. (2) Extraversion, a bipolar factor loading at the extraverted end on sexual anomalies and conversion symptoms, and at the introverted end on depression, obsessional traits and apathy. This work was quickly followed up (Eysenck, 1947) and it was shown that these two factors were normally distributed among 1000 male and 1000 female neurotics. Two points need to be noted. First, these findings are clearly limited to neurotic samples and second with thirty-nine variables there can be no confidence that these are the only factors of any importance. Furthermore, at this point in the work there were no external criteria for the identification of the factors.

Extension of the research and factor identification

Over the years a prodigious research effort resulting in around fifty books and more than 300 papers, not including the work of independent investigators, has established the nature of these factors and their psychological meaning and implications. Here we shall attempt to summarize the current position indicating briefly the research basis of the claims.

The tests.   Although E and N were originally found in ratings, a number of personality questionnaires have been developed at the Maudsley Hospital; the Maudsley Medical Questionnaire (MMQ) which measured N; the Maudsley Personality Inventory (MPI) which measured both E and N and had a lie scale to help identify subjects trying to create a good impression; the Eysenck Personality Inventory (EPI) measuring E, N and L (the lie scale) and most recently the Eysenck Personality Questionnaire (EPQ) measuring E, N, L and P, the new psychoticism factor. All these tests can be regarded as essentially equivalent, In addition, for developmental studies, junior versions of the MPI, EPI and EPQ have been developed suitable for children from about 9 years of age and upwards. There is also a simplified adult version for subject of low intelligence, the Eysenck–Withers Inventory.

The MMQ is concerned largely with psychiatric symptoms and is thus not suitable for normals, and was quickly replaced by the MPI. However, the other tests constitute the empirical basis of the results we shall discuss. They consist of items of the Yes/No format, of which a typical example (not in the tests) is 'Do you sometimes feel just dispirited?' All these tests are highly reliable and there is good evidence concerning their validity (although this is less so in the case of the EPQ, partly because it is still new and the evidence has not yet accumulated).

Description of the factors.   Each of the three factors can be regarded as a syndrome of traits or behaviours which cluster together. They are independent of each other and are orthogonal, higher-order factors.

(1) Extraversion. This is characterized by: sociability, friendliness, enjoyment of excitement, talkativeness, impulsiveness, cheerfulness, activity and spontaneity. The extravert is stimulus-hungry and expressive. The introvert is the opposite of this: aloof and inhibited.

(2) Neuroticism. This is characterized by: worrying, moodiness,

tension and nervousness. Physical symptoms of anxiety are associated with it, butterflies in the stomach, sweating, turning pale and even, in extremes, fainting.

(3) Psychoticism. This involves feelings of persecution, irrational mysticism, a liking for very strong physical sensations, inhumane cruelty and lack of empathy. Not surprisingly, it is high in violent criminals; most normals score low on this factor P, whereas on N and E they score around the mid-point. It can be seen as tough-mindedness.

The factors as dimensions.   In Eysenck's theory, these three factors are the most important dimensions of personality. If we locate an individual on them, then we can go a long way to understanding his personality. Thus the low E, high N subject who is normal on P becomes the obsessional neurotic, the high E, high N, normal P subject, becomes an hysteric. The high P, low E subject, the schizophrenic. Most people, of course, fall between the extremes on P, E, and N.

The theoretical structure

These factors have been woven by Eysenck into an elaborate theory which can account for a wide variety of experimental findings in psychology and various aspects of human behaviour in everyday life. Since a full description of this theory would be too lengthy we shall concentrate on two applied aspects which illustrate its scope and nature – crime and neurosis – as well as explicating its biological underpinning.

Physiological factors

Eysenck (1980) argues that the physiological basis of personality differences (subsumed by these three factors) can be located in the limbic system, the reticular formation and other paleocortical and brain-stem formations. Thus, extraversion is related to differences in cortical arousal (in reticular formation activity), and neuroticism (or emotionality as Eysenck sometimes calls it) to differential processes in the limbic system, reflected in lability of the autonomic nervous system. Differences in P appear to be related to levels of androgen and other hormonal secretions – that is, to maleness.

From this it is clear that the major dimensions of personality accounting for much of the variance in temperament are associated with identifiable, biological variables. From this two further points arise. First there should be some overlap with mammalian 'personality' in as much as there is any similarity of physiology between man and mammals. Eysenck claims this is so – emotionality (as defined by faecal counts) has been studied in rats by Broadhurst (1975) and all three factors have been identified in monkeys by Chamone et al. (1972). Secondly, there should be considerable genetic determination of these three factors, which is indeed the case (Eysenck, 1976).

Application to antisocial behaviour and crime

As recently expounded by Eysenck (1977), the theory states that there is a series of events underlying psychopathy. Inadequate functioning of the reticular formation leads to a low level of arousal (as experienced by extraverts). Low arousal leads to poor classical conditioning which is responsible for the acquisition of conditioned and socializing responses, that is the conscience – hence the link of extraversion and criminality. In addition low arousal leads to sensation seeking. Thus the extravert is biologically more open to temptation and has less resistance. Eysenck (1977) is able to cite some evidence for the lower level of arousal of psychopaths and for the involvement of extraversion in antisocial behaviour in a wide variety of cultures.

Although this implies that criminality is biologically determined, it does not ignore the obvious social determinants of crime since the conditioning by which the conscience is or is not acquired is clearly a social matter. It must be noted that this theory of crime is far from complete. As pointed out by Cattell and Kline (1977): not all criminals are extraverted; is there any evidence that conditionability is a unitary trait? Is the notion of crime a single homogeneous concept? Do not some criminals learn only too well – delinquent or criminal mores? All these questions render the theory less than entirely convincing. Nevertheless, the theoretical and practical power of the theory is impressive.

Application to neurosis

Eysenck (e.g. 1976a) has also applied the theory to neurosis. Here it is claimed that introverts, subjects with high arousal, who condition easily are more likely to develop neurotic disturbances which are considered to be conditioned emotional responses. However, such conditioned responses can be extinguished and behaviour therapy is based upon this principle, and is the only therapeutic procedure held by Eysenck to be of any value.

Summary

We have described the three main dimensions of personality, orthogonal higher-order factors, their measurement and their physiological substrates according to Eysenck. We have shown how his theorizing allows application to two important areas of applied psychology, in one case even suggesting treatment.

The work of Cattell

Cattell and Kline (1977) contains a detailed account of the work of Cattell on personality and readers are referred there for an amplification of the essence of Cattell's theorizing which spreads over 40 books and more than 300 papers.

The empirical basis

Cattell (1946) makes clear the basis of the original work. He hoped to map out, using factor analysis, the most important dimensions of personality. Since to do this it is essential to put all variables into the analysis, a method had to be found of defining the population of variables. This was done by utilizing the concept of *semantic personality sphere*. To define this a dictionary search of all words describing behaviour (for undefined behaviour cannot be said to exist) was carried out. All synonyms (as judged by scholars) were removed and subjects were rated on the remaining traits. When all highly correlated traits were removed, the remaining traits were subjected to a simple form of factor analysis (cluster analysis) and 12 L or life factors were found. These can be said to embrace the semantic personality sphere, which by virtue of its construction covers the most important personality variance.

Points of note and terminology

Before setting out the most recent list of factors, a few special terms must be mentioned and other points should be noted: (1) Cattell's factors are oblique, that is, correlated. He presents primary factors and their higher-orders. (2) The factors are regarded as source-traits, fundamental dimensions of personality. Surface traits are syndromes of trait-elements (e.g. the anal character – a syndrome of neatness, orderliness and pedantry). (3) Much of a person's behaviour is held to depend on his position on these personality dimensions. Because of their importance, these are the personality variables deserving of intensive study. (4) Cattell distinguishes L factors based on ratings, Q factors based on questionnaires and T factors based on objective tests. As yet the T factors are not clearly identified, although it is assumed there will be an overlap with L and Q factors. Our discussion of Cattell's factors will be restricted to L and Q factors. It is to be noted that the factors prefaced by Q are found only in questionnaires. The other factors are found in L data also. (5) In addition to these normal factors which, incidentally, discriminate neurotics clearly, there are some abnormal factors which discriminate psychotics. These factors are: D_1 hypochondriasis, D_2 suicidal disgust, D_3 brooding discontent, D_4 high anxious depression, D_5 fatigued depression, D_6 high guilt and resentment, D_7 bored depression, P_a paranoia, P_p psychopathic deviation, S_c schizophrenia, A_s psychosthenia (compulsive ideas), P_s high general psychosis. On these abnormal factors, normal subjects usually score low.

Since these factors are oblique, it is possible to factor the correlations between them to give higher-order factors. These factors, it will be remembered, load on the first order primary factors. They are, therefore, broader dimensions than the primary factors and, being fewer in number, describe the personality sphere with greater economy.

The factors

Temperamental factors.   Q and L factors amongst normal adults are shown opposite:

Source trait index	Low-score description	High-score description
A	*Sizia* Reserved, detached, critical, aloof, stiff	*Affectia* Outgoing, warmhearted, easygoing, participating
B	*Low intelligence* Dull	*High intelligence* Bright
C	*Low ego strength* At mercy of feelings, emotionally less stable, easily upset, changeable	*High ego strength* Emotionally stable, mature, faces reality, calm
E	*Submissiveness* Humble, mild, easily led, docile, accommodating	*Dominance* Assertive, aggressive, competitive, stubborn
F	*Desurgency* Sober, taciturn, serious	*Surgency* Happy-go-lucky, gay, enthusiastic
G	*Weaker superego strength* Expedient, disregards rules	*Stronger superego strength* Conscientious, persistent, moralistic, staid
H	*Threctia* Shy, timid, threat-sensitive	*Parmia* Venturesome, uninhibited, socially bold
I	*Harria* Tough-minded, self-reliant	*Premsia* Tender-minded, sensitive, clinging, overprotected
L	*Alaxia* Trusting, accepting conditions	*Protension* Suspicious, hard to fool
M	*Praxernia* Practical, 'down-to-earth', concerned	*Autia* Imaginative, bohemian, absent-minded
N	*Artlessness* Forthright, unpretentious, genuine, but socially clumsy	*Shrewdness* Astute, polished, socially aware
O	*Untroubled adequacy* Self-assured, placid, secure, complacent, serene	*Guilt proneness* Apprehensive, self-reproaching, insecure
Q1	*Conservatism of temperament* Conservative, respecting traditional ideas	*Radicalism* Experimenting, liberal, free-thinking

Source trait index	Low-score description	High-score description
Q2	*Group adherence* Group-dependent, a 'joiner' and sound follower	*Self sufficiency* Self-sufficient, resourceful, prefers own decisions
Q3	*Low self-sentiment integration* Undisciplined, self-conflict, follows own urges, careless of social rules	*Higher strength of self-sentiment* Controlled, exacting will-power, socially precise, compulsive, following self-image
Q4	*Low ergic tension* Relaxed, tranquil, torpid, unfrustrated, composed	*High ergic tension* Tense, frustrated, driven, overwrought

These are the sixteen most well established factors found amongst normal adults. Recently the following additional factors have been established: D, Insecure excitability; J, Gregarious sociability; K, Mature socialization; P, Sanguine casualness; Q6, Social panache; Q7, Explicit self-expression.

Second-order adult factors (based upon the sixteen main adult factors) are as follows:

Second order factors	Description in terms of primary factors
(1) Exvia	Sociable (A), surgent (F), adventurous (H), dependent (Q2) – i.e. extraversion
(2) Anxiety	Weak ego strength (C), timid (H), suspicious (L), guilt prone (O), low self-sentiment (Q3), tense (Q4)
(3) Cortertia	Unsociable (A –), insensitive (I –), shrewd (N)
(4) Independence	Surgent (F), dominant (E), adventurous (H), unconcerned (M), suspicious (L)
(5) Discreetness	Shrewd (N), sociable (A)
(6) Subjectivity	Unconcerned (M), radical (Q1)
(7) Intelligence	Intelligence (B)
(8) Good upbringing	Superego (G), submissive (E –), desurgent (F), self-sentiment (Q3)

In addition, four other second-orders can be found if the complete set of twenty-three primaries is subjected to higher-order analysis.

Their tentative labels are: (9) 'humanistic involvement'; (10) 'tough stolidity'; (11) a genetic component involving F and J; and (12) 'hypomanic security'. Not too much should be made of these last four factors, as little research into their nature has yet been carried out.

In addition to these eight factors, three others can be found among abnormal subjects. These are a psychosis factor (resembling Eysenck's P), a depression factor, and a factor cautiously labelled 'inhibition'.

Such are the factors held by Cattell to embrace the major part of the personality sphere. Twenty-three primaries and eight second-orders among normals: twelve primaries and three second-orders in addition among abnormals. A full description of these factors, together with their psychological implications can be found in Cattell and Kline (1977). These are temperamental factors, concerned with how we do what we do.

Mood factors.   In addition to his studies of temperament, Cattell has extracted the main mood and state factors, since it is obvious that behaviour is affected by short-term variables of this kind: a normally phlegmatic and calm subject can be made anxious by a severe and prolonged stomach pain of unknown origin.

The most important mood and state factors are: exvia, anxiety, depression, arousal, fatigue, guilt, regression and stress. A special test, the Eight State Questionnaire (ESQ), exists to measure these.

Motivation factors.   Cattell has also used factor analysis to investigate the dynamics of personality. Here the factors are the main drives and the components related to strength of interest. This work is fully dicussed by Cattell and Child (1975) and Cattell and Kline (1977).

Two types of dynamic factors are distinguished: *ergs*, which are biological drives and *sentiments*, culturally moulded drives – a distinction similar to that of McDougall (1932) who postulated propensities and sentiments.

The main ergs so far found are: food-seeking, mating, gregariousness, parental, exploration, security, self-assertion, narcissism, pugnacity and acquistiveness. The main sentiments are: religious, professional, self-sentiment, superego (duty), spouse or sweetheart and mechanical interest. Five sentiments and five ergs are measured by the *Motivational Analysis Test*, the MAT.

In Cattell's theory, interest in any activity is accounted for by the implication of sentiments and ergs. Thus, liking the cinema, for example, could be related to: mating, gregariousness (if a party goes), self-sentiment and sweetheart. These intimate relationships of behaviour to ergs and sentiments are described in the *Dynamic Lattice*, which is essentially a flow diagram portraying them.

Strength of interest factors.   Finally the study of motivation has revealed that strength of interest is determined by seven factors: (1) alpha, conscious desire; (2) beta, realized interest; (3) gamma, feeling of ought to be interested; (4) delta, a physiological, autonomic factor; (5) epsilon, a factor related to conflict and (6) and (7) zeta and eta, as yet unlabelled. Of these, the first three seem the most important.

The tests

Cattell has subjected these factors to intensive study. Thus the scores on them of various clinical and occupational groups are known as well as their correlations with a large variety of critical criteria. They have been identified in children from the age of about 5, as well as in adults and the following personality questionnaires have been devised to measure tham: The Pre-School Personality Quiz (PSPQ) for ages 4-6 years; the Early School Personality Quiz (ESPQ) for ages 6-8 years; the Child's Personality Questionnaire (CPQ) for ages 8-12 years; and the Sixteen Personality Factor Test (16PF) for adults. For the abnormal personality sphere, the Clinical Analysis Questionnaire (CAQ) has been constructed. It is from these tests, together with the original rating studies, that all the factors set out above have emerged. They form the main data for all Cattell's work. By refining and developing his methods of factor analysis with the aim of obtaining simple structure it can be argued (see Cattell and Kline, 1978) that the Cattell dimensions are the main variables of personality.

Over the years, Cattell has developed objective tests as well as personality questionnaires to measure these factors. Personality questionnaires have severe disadvantages (see Chapter 6), whereas objective tests, as defined by Cattell (1957), can be objectively scored (i.e. have perfect reliability by different markers) and their purport cannot be guessed by subjects. This eliminates deliberate distortion. Ideally all personality measurement will be carried out by such tests. However, as yet the factors emerging from them cannot be fully identified although many are similar to the second-order Q factors. Further, their psychological significance is not beyond dispute. For this reason they will not be listed here. For a full list and interpretative description see Cattell and Kline (1977).

Theoretical structure

As is obvious, this work of Cattell is far more comprehensive and grander in conception than that of Eysenck. The theoretical structure that has been built up from this work is huge and still largely speculative as is clear in the account of Cattell (1978). Furthermore, in his theoretical account Cattell also includes a further set of ability factors, such as intelligence or verbal ability. These factors fall beyond the scope of this chapter, but a full discussion of them can be found in Cattell (1971) or Kline (1979).

On the basis of what has been covered, a number of essential points about Cattell's theoretical approach can be made:

(1) It is assumed that for any behaviour, a specification equation can be set up in principle. This equation consists of the appropriate weighting on the source traits of ability, temperament, dynamics and moods (the factors discussed in this chapter), together with some numerical index to describe the situation in which the behaviour occurs. In fact, specification equations based on the temperamental factors alone have been computed for a variety of jobs and Cattell and Butcher used all variables to specify academic success at school (Cattell and Butcher, 1968). Similar work is going on in the clinical field.

Thus the whole set of results in the field of abilities, motivation, mood and personality becomes essentially a theory in that the factors are inserted into specification equations. The most severe problem is attempting to assess the stimulus value of situations, a matter as yet relatively unexplored.

(2) Studies have been (and are continuing to be) carried out into the variables influencing the development of all these factors. Nature–nurture ratios, which have been worked out by appropriate statistical analysis, exist for most of them and the major environmental influences have, in some cases, been identified (see Cattell

and Kline, 1977). Thus, a great insight into personality development can be obtained.

(3) Cattell (1978) has developed a learning theory – structured learning theory – which involves all these factors. This recognizes that learning involves multidimensional changes which can be re-corded in changes in (a) the trait vector (the profile of scores on all factors), (b) the bearing vector which shows the changing bearing of factors on performance and (c) the involvement vector indicating emotional involvement with the situation. All these can be quantified and the algebra is set out in Cattell (1978).

(4) As part of the structured learning theory, reinforcement can be defined in terms of maximizing tension reduction over all ergs simul-taneously. This maximizing over *all ergs* (as distinct from satisfying one at the expense of the other) is known as integration learning.

These four points indicate the large scope of Cattell's work and the way in which it can be used empirically to give insights into real life behaviours and more theoretically to account for the phenomena of human learning.

Comparison of Cattell and Eysenck

In our discussion of factor analysis we raised the issue of the non-uniqueness of solutions. Here, in the case of personality, we seem to find this criticism amply proven: two elaborate and highly researched theories, one positing three factors, the other thirty-five together with other sets in different modalities. There are, however, a number of points that must be made concerning these two apparently disparate results:

(1) Cattell works with oblique factors rotated to simple structure. At the second-order there is good agreement between Cattell and Eysenck.

(2) Thus exvia and extraversion are clearly the same factor. Similarly, anxiety and neuroticism show the same factor pattern. The difference in nomenclature is merely one of interpretation. P too has its equivalent among Cattell's abnormal factors.

(3) Eysenck fails to find Cattell's primary factors in his data. However, his items are more circumscribed and his analyses typically under-factor (i.e. not all the factors are rotated). Thus there are technical reasons for the differences – sampling of variables and under-factoring.

Thus despite appearances, there is good agreement between Cattell
and Eysenck that N and E or Anxiety and Exvia are the two largest
personality dimensions. Their point of difference lies in the importance attributed to primary factors. Cattell finds them stable and
useful, Eysenck does not. The differences in results are due in part to
technical factor-analytic methods. This, in fact, is an empirical
matter and recent research into this point is discussed in Chapter 7.

Suggested further reading

Factor analysis

Harman, H. H. (1976) *Modern Factor Analysis*. Chicago: University of
Chicago Press (a complete account).
Nunnally, J. (1978) *Psychometric Theory* (2nd edn). New York:
McGraw-Hill (a succinct and lucid introduction).

Cattell

Cattell, R. B. and Kline, P. (1977) *The Scientific Analysis of Personality
and Motivation*. London: Academic Press (an up-to-date, easily
comprehensible, statement of theory and research).

Eysenck

Cattell, R. B. and Kline, P. (1977) *The Scientific Analysis of Personality
and Motivation*. London: Academic Press (an evaluation of the
factorial work of Eysenck and his colleagues).
Eysenck, H. J. (1967) *The Biological Basis of Personality*. Springfield:
C. C. Thomas (most comprehensive account of the main corpus of
work).
Eysenck, H. J. and Eysenck, S. B. G. (1976) *Psychoticism as a
Dimension of Personality*. London: Hodder & Stoughton (detailed
discussion of the most important part of the more recent findings).

6 Personality questionnaires

Paul Kline

Since many of the findings discussed in the previous chapter and those to be examined in the next are based upon personality questionnaires, it is obvious that to evaluate the work properly, personality questionnaires must themselves be clearly understood. In this chapter we shall describe the two basic approaches to the construction of personality questionnaires, the criterion keyed method and the factor analytic method or its equivalents, pointing out their problems and advantages. We shall also describe some problems common to personality questionnaires, however constructed, and finally in the light of this discussion briefly evaluate some of the personality questionnaires most widely used.

In a brief chapter such as this no point can be discussed at any length. For greater detail on all these issues, readers are advised to consult the *Construction of Psychological Tests* (Kline, 1980) and Nunnally (1978) who is useful for a theoretical underpinning to the methods introduced in this chapter.

Cardinal points in psychological measurement

There are certain characteristics possessed by all good psychological tests which we shall now briefly discuss. Many of the methods of personality questionnaire construction are devised with these characteristics in view:

Reliability

There are two distinct meanings to the concept of reliability with reference to tests. They should be:

(1) Reliable over time. If a test is used on two occasions with the same subjects, it should yield the same scores (if we assume subject's status on the variable remains the same). This test – retest reliability is measured by correlating sets of scores on two occasions. Since the standard error of a score is related to the reliability of the test from which it was obtained, when used with individuals (as in practical vocational guidance or selection), a test should have a reliability of at least 0.7.

(2) Internally consistent. This refers to the homogeneity of the test items, the extent of which each item in the test measures the same variable. Although internal consistency reliability should be high (for if every item measures something different, the total test score cannot be meaningful), too high homogeneity can limit the validity of the test. An example can make this clear. If we had a personality questionnaire in which all the items were virtually paraphrases of each other: 'Do you like noisy parties?' 'Do you enjoy a good party?' 'Do you enjoy an evening on your own?', the test would be highly reliable, but so specific that it would be unlikely to be measuring a variable of any importance. The alpha coefficient is the best measure of internal consistency reliability. Others measured are the split-half or the odd – even and Hoyt's analysis of variance method (Hoyt, 1941).

Validity

Tests have to be reliable only inasmuch as low reliability naturally precludes high validity. A test is valid if it measures what it claims to measure. This may sound obvious and banal. However, as an examination of Buros (1978) shows, the majority of published tests are not, in fact, valid. A severe problem lies in demonstrating that a test is valid. Because of this difficulty there are several uses of the term valid, depending upon the kind the evidence cited. These are:

(1) Face validity. A test is said to be face-valid, if it looks as if it measures what is intended. Since, in personality questionnaires, face validity is a notoriously poor indicator of real validity, we shall say no more about it, other than to emphasize that it cannot be used as evidence for validity. Its only value lies in the fact that some adults may refuse to carry out tests of low face validity.

(2) Concurrent validity. This refers to the correlations of the test with other tests at the same time. Thus, the concurrent validity of the EPQ could be demonstrated by correlating it with the EPI taken at the same time. There is an obvious problem inherent in the notion of concurrent validity. If there is a test so good that high correlations with it establish the validity of other tests, it is reasonable to enquire into the value of the new tests. Unless they have some distinctive feature, for example, quick to give or suitable for a wide variety of subjects, they are adding nothing new for the test user. Even worse, in most areas of psychological testing, there are no tests for establishing concurrent validity, that is, upon which there is general agreement on their own validity.

(3) Predictive validity. This refers to the correlation of a test with future criteria. Thus the predictive validity of Eysenck's N scale would be its correlation with psychiatric treatment in the future. Clearly this is a powerful indicator of validity, although as with all studies of validity there is a severe difficulty in setting up adequate criteria.

(4) Construct validity. The idea of construct validity, first developed by Cronbach and Meehl (1955), is to set up as many hypotheses concerning the test variable as possible, bearing in mind its psychological nature. Thus if we had a test of neuroticism we could propose the following hypotheses, investigation of which would then establish its construct validity: neurotics would score higher than non-neurotic controls on the test; the test would correlate positively with other tests of neurosis; the test would not correlate significantly with tests of abilities or motivation; the test would be independent of E and P (see last chapter); the test would, if followed up, predict those needing psychiatric treatment.

If all these hypotheses were supported, we would have good evidence that our purported test of neuroticism was valid. Two points deserve note. First, construct validity embraces both concurrent and predictive validity. Second, it is also useful to show what the test does not measure, definition by exclusion in the Platonic style.

Tests should be discriminatory

An important advantage that tests have over rating scales or interview data, is that they can be made highly discriminatory. In terms of distribution of scores the most discriminating is the rectangular since any deviation from this would produce more subjects in some categories. Ferguson has compiled a discriminability index – delta (Ferguson, 1949). Delta is a coefficient, like the correlation, measuring the discriminating power of a test. A delta of 0.95 indicates a test which really spreads out subjects. Such a rectangular distribution contrasts well with personality ratings where inevitably there are few in extreme categories while the majority are rated in the middle.

These then are the characteristics of efficient psychological tests which sound test construction methods aim to build in. However, before we go on to discuss test constructional methods, there are certain other problems with questionnaires; problems which these methods aim to exclude.

Problems with personality questionnaires

Response sets

These are defined as tendencies to answer test items in certain ways, usually regardless of the item-meaning. Cronbach (1946, 1950) has singled out two as being especially important in disturbing the validity of personality questionnaires.

(1) Social desirability. This is the tendency to endorse items because to do so is socially acceptable. Edwards (1957) showed that this was an important influence on responses to the Minnesota Multiphasic Personality Inventory (MMPI) (Hathaway and McKinley, 1951) items. He found a high correlation between endorsement rate and judged social desirability.

(2) Acquiescence. This is the tendency to respond 'yes' or to agree with items regardless of content. Guilford (1959) has shown that this occurs most often when items are vaguely worded and refer to general rather than specific behaviours. Such item phrasing also tends to increase the social desirability response set.

Generally, by writing precise items of great clarity, using balanced scales where some items are keyed 'No', others 'Yes', and by avoiding item content that is likely to produce the socially desirable response set, for example, items about marriage or negroes or womens' lib, it is possible, if not to eliminate, at least to minimize the effects of these response sets.

Deliberate distortion

Most personality questionnaire items are so easy to distort deliberately that it makes their use in selection especially dubious. That is why Cattell and his colleagues would prefer to use objective tests where faking is so much harder because subjects cannot guess the purpose of the test.

Response-sets to item type

Some kinds of item, for example, items with a scale ranging from 'agree' to 'disagree' or 'always' to 'never', can either create an extreme response set in a subject or the response set of using the middle category.

All these four sources of error can lower the validity of personality tests. Thus it is always necessary to have clear evidence that a test is valid. It is not sufficient to demonstrate that a set of items with face validity is homogeneous.

Questionnaire items

Types of item

The most commonly used item types in personality questionnaires are as follows:

(1) Yes – No items as used in the EPI and the EPQ. *Example* 'Do you sleep well?' A variant of this item type is the Yes – Uncertain – No variety.

(2) True – False items as used in the MMPI. *Example* 'I am a good cook.' These can have a similar variant with a middle category, as the items above.

(3) Items with a rating scale. *Example* 'Wars are evil.' Strongly agree, agree, uncertain, disagree, strongly disagree. Cattell and Comrey use items of this type.

(4) Forced choice items. *Example:* I prefer to (a) visit a bank, (b) visit a large sports complex, (c) uncertain. Items of this kind, in which each choice was matched for social desirability, were used by

Edwards (1957) in the construction of his Personal Preference Schedule in an effort to eliminate social desirability as a source of bias.

Other types are possible, but the ones above would account for most items in the best-known personality tests. The only other variety of any interest is the *single word or phrase item*, to which subjects have to indicate like or dislike, for example, rowing boats, four-leaved clover. Grygier has used this item format with his Dynamic Personality Inventory (Grygier, 1961).

Item content

In constructing tests the behaviours which we wish to measure are translated into the item forms or form above. The content is usually taken from clinical observation or from descriptions of the trait in previous research. Thus when the present writer was constructing a test of obsessional traits, all descriptions of obsessional personality were searched for examples of obsessive behaviour and all traits mentioned were noted. These were all changed into Yes – No items. Two examples will clarify the procedure. (1) Behaviour: Obsessives enjoy working through timetables and directories; item 'Do you enjoy studying railway timetables?' (2) Trait: Obsessives are mean; item 'Are you considered to be careful with your money?' This phrasing was chosen because the item 'Are you mean?' would indubitably be answered 'No' by almost all subjects due to the response set of social desirability.

When an item pool has been developed it is tried out on a sample or samples of subjects (as large and as representative as possible) and subjected to item analysis – to produce a reliable, homogeneous, discriminatory test. There are two radically different approaches to item selection which produce very different kinds of tests and these will now be described and evaluated.

Item selection

The criterion-keyed method.   In this method items are selected if they can discriminate a criterion group from its control group. The most famous test constructed by this method is the Minnesota Multiphasic Personality Inventory (MMPI) (Hathaway and McKinley, 1951). In the construction of this test, the item pool was administered to various clinical groups and a normal control group. Any items that could discriminate one of these clinical groups was included in the final version of the test. Thus, for example, if item X discriminated homosexuals, it went in to the homosexual scale. To avoid capitalizing on the chance features of the particular samples, as with other methods, cross-validation on further samples is necessary. The original MMPI test construction produced nine clinical scales. However, over the years the item pool formed by the nine scales has been given to a huge variety of clinical groups and by 1960 more than 200 largely criterion-keyed scales had been thus constructed (Dahlstrom and Welsh, 1960).

There are certain problems with this method which make its use advisable only where nothing more than discrimination (as in screening) is required. This, however, is rarely the case. These problems are: (1) In many fields of personality measurement the establishment of clear criterion groups is difficult. Indeed the adequacy of the MMPI groups can be challenged in the light of the known unreliability of clinical diagnosis (e.g. Beck, 1962). (2) Criterion groups may differ from each other on a variety of variables. Thus a criterion-keyed scale may consist of a hotch-potch of variables. This means that it has, by the nature of its construction, no psychological meaning. We can, therefore, draw no psychological inferences nor arrive at any psychological insights by using such scales. All we know is that the scale discriminates certain groups from others. (3) Thus, only by chance can a criterion-keyed scale be unifactorial. If it is not, the identity of the same score is not assured. For example, if the scale measures two factors, a scale score of 10 can be comprised of 10,0; 9,1; 8,2; and so on. Even the quantification is dubious.

The factor analytic and similar methods.   In this method the item pool is administered to a large sample of subjects and submitted to a rotated factor analysis. Items which load on one common factor, but no others, are then selected for the test. As we saw in Chapter 5, factors can be regarded as fundamental dimensions underlying the observed correlations. Hence factored tests, provided that the item pool is well chosen, should yield psychologically meaningful factors, and this is the great advantage of the factor analytic method compared with criterion-keying. It should be noted that factored tests should always have their factors experimentally identified in further studies.

Identification by item loadings alone is little more than face validity.

However, there are also problems with this method. (1) The correlations between dichotomous items tend to fluctuate according to the proportion putting the keyed response to each item and this makes subsequent factor analysis difficult. (2) Factors often account for only a small proportion of the total variance, due to problems of item unreliability. (3) This has led some workers, for example Comrey (1970) and Cattell (1973) to advocate item parcelling or correlating clusters of items. How this clustering is to be done is, however, a matter of dispute, and some clustering techniques can lead to the emergence of second-order factors, that is, the clusters virtually represent primary scales. (4) Reliable factoring demands a large number of subjects relative to variables. Nunnally (1978) argues that it should be 10:1. This demands, with a large item pool, considerable computing facilities – in the case of the MMPI, nearly 6000 subjects and 600 variables would have to be factored! However, studies by Barrett and Kline (in press) show that 10 is conservative and that a ratio of 3:1 produces stable results. (5) Since rotation to a simple structure is necessary, factor analytic scales should be constructed together, so that there are hyperplanes (see p.80) for the rotation to find. If one scale is constructed at a time (thus loading on a general factor) accurate location of vectors is difficult.

In the light of all these difficulties, especially the low variance of factors and their unreliability, an analogous technique is often used whereby the biserial correlation of each item with the total score on all items is completed The highest correlating items are then selected. This method tends to produce a unifactorial scale or one loading on two highly correlated factors. This method is easier and almost as efficient as the factor method and provided that the test factor is located in factored space with other known factors afterwards it must be regarded as virtually as good. Kline (1971) used it in the construction of Ai3Q, a measure of obsessional traits. In all cases, the test factors should be identified experimentally and in factorial studies with other personality tests with marker factors such as extroversion or anxiety.

These are the methods by which personality questionnaires are constructed. In the final part of this chapter we shall briefly examine some of the best known personality questionnaires (other than the 16PF and EPQ and EPI, which have already been described in connection with the work of Eysenck and Cattell).

Some personality questionnaires

The Minnesota Multiphasic Personality Inventory

Originally the MMPI had nine clinical scales measuring subjects' resemblance to the main psychiatric Kraepelinian groups. Its use with non-psychiatric patients was limited because there was not enough variance, low scores being almost inevitable. Furthermore, factorizations of the scales (as fully discussed in Cattell and Kline, 1977) indicate that there is a general factor running through the test, concerned with the admission of neurotic symptoms. Certainly the original scales are not independent if only because some of them share items. Furthermore, as the work of Cattell (e.g. 1973) has shown, factorization of the items reveals a number of abnormal factors which do not correspond to the original scales. All this suggests that for abnormal subjects the MMPI item pool is highly satisfactory, but the clinical scales as well as the many others developed by criterion-keying need treating with caution. The MMPI items should be used in scales which have emerged in adequate factored studies for there is no doubt that the items were originally constructed with great skill. The Californian Personality Inventory (CPI) has been developed by Gough (1957) as 'the sane man's MMPI'.

The Comrey Scales

This test (Comrey, 1970) is remarkable for two features. First, to improve item reliability, the items are such that seven-point response scales are used, thus allowing product moment correlations between items. In addition, items are not correlated together to form the basis of the factor analysis. Rather the items are grouped into factored, homogeneous item dimensions (FHIDs). These, it is claimed by Comrey, form a better basis for factor analysis than items. Eight factors are measured by this test: trust, orderliness, social conformity, activity, stability, extraversion, masculinity and empathy.

Cattell (1973) claims that FHIDs tend to produce second-order factors (when factored) because they are in essence primary scales, an argument supported by the fact the E and N appear in this test, factors which are higher-order in the work of Eysenck and Cattell. Cattell and Kline (1977) have further argued that the Comrey factors are not in the simple structure position and that when properly rotated, they align with the Cattell second-orders, as set out in the previous chapter.

The Guilford Scales

Guilford has been producing factored personality scales since 1934 (Guilford and Guilford, 1934). His work is remarkable for the fact that he prefers orthogonal uncorrelated factors. In the most recent handbook on these tests (Guilford et al., 1976) some effort has been made to relate these factors to external criteria. However, as Cattell and Kline (1977) have argued, it is *a priori* unlikely that the major dimensions of personality would be uncorrelated, hence these factors really need rotating into the oblique positon. When this is done (e.g. Cattell and Gibbons, 1968) there is considerable overlap with the Cattell factors. Guilford's scales are: general activity, ascendance, masculinity, confidence, calmness, sociability, reflectiveness, depression, emotionality, restraint, objectivity, friendliness, and co-operativeness.

Questionnaires and theoretical rationale

As a glance at the latest edition of Buros (1978) would show, there are many other personality inventories, all constructed essentially by one of the methods discussed above. The MMPI, the CPI, the Comrey and the Guilford Inventories are all good examples of tests developed empirically: there was a rationale for the items, clinical and research reports, but no theoretical rationale. However, personality questionnaires can be constructed, by the methods we have discussed, with a clear theoretical background. For example: the Myers Briggs Indicator (Briggs and Myers, 1962) which tests Jungian theory; the Dynamic Personality Inventory (Grygier, 1961) is based on Freud's developmental theory; the Ai3Q, OPQ and OOQ (Kline, 1971 and Kline and Storey, 1977) relate to Freudian psychosexual theory; and the Edwards Personal Preference Schedule (Edwards, 1959) relates to Murray's Personology and work on social desirability.

7 Recent research into the factor analysis of personality

Paul Kline

As was made clear in Chapter 5, there are a number of outstanding problems in the factor analytic study of personality which need solution before a definitive picture can be drawn. The chief of these are: (1) What are the factors needed to describe fully, but elegantly, the domain of personality? How many of them are there? (2) What are the relationships between the apparently different sets of factors emerging? (3) To what extent are differences in results artefacts of particular factor analytic methods used? Although these three questions are separate, it is obvious that the answers to each are related. For example, if, in answer to (2) we find certain factors to be essentially identical, then our answer to (1) must be modified accordingly.

The research that we shall examine in this chapter bears upon these questions. However, we shall not simply summarize all the research findings. We shall submit the studies to a critical evaluation and much of our discussion must inevitably turn on factor analytic methods. All these essential points, however, have been discussed in the section on factor analysis in Chapter 5. Our reasons for adopting this approach are simple: as Vaughan (1973) has argued, the majority of factor analytic researches in personality are flawed by technical deficiencies, such that their results are misleading. Hence a catalogue of findings is itself misleading. Furthermore, the programmatic factorial research into personality (typified by the work of Cattell and Eysenck) has begun to yield a number of well-defined factors which should be the basis of a quantitative theory of personality. That is why, essentially, the fundamental question which this chapter must try to answer is (1) – what are the factors that can most efficiently embrace the field of personality? Thus we shall address ourselves to this question, but in so doing we shall find answers to the other problems.

The work of Cattell and Eysenck and its relation to other factors

The issue here is whether it is better to measure reliable and easily replicable second-order traits (favoured by Eysenck) or whether to abandon the primaries is to throw away much valuable information, as claimed by Cattell. Eysenck and Eysenck (1969) carried out a massive study of the items in the EPI, 16PF and Guilford scales on a total of 1200 subjects. The results indicated that the primary factors (both of Guilford and Cattell) did not emerge. The variance was better embraced by two large third-order factors, extraversion and neuroticism.

This study, therefore, appears to support Eysenck's contention. However, the research can be impugned on the grounds that only six or seven items per Cattell factor and ten items per Guilford factor were used, hardly enough to get clear factors. In contrast, forty-eight items per factor were used for the Eysenck scales, although it is true that if the primaries were truly robust they could have emerged. In addition there were technical problems with the factor analysis. Despite all this, this study does cast some doubt on the stability and thus utility of the Cattell primaries. Nor can it be argued that this result is a fluke since Vagg and Hammond (1976) in Australia found essentially the same factors in a replicative study.

Some light on the possible reason for the failure of the Cattell factors to emerge was thrown by the study of the Cattell scales among a large sample (2500) of British undergraduates, although it must be noted that this was a study of scales not items (Saville and Blinkhorn, 1976). They found that many of the factors were unreliable, thus supporting Eysenck's argument and that the reliabilities of the different forms of Cattell's test were low. Indeed, when the variance due to N was extracted it was found that Cattell primaries, supposedly contributing to N, had virtually no other variance. Thus there was no value in measuring personality with these primaries rather than the more reliable and stable, higher-order N factor (although it should be noted there are inconsistencies in their results, ranging from 90-23 per cent redundancy in the Cattell scales).

Krug (1978) has, however, criticized this work by Saville and Blinkhorn. First, the greater stability of N as measured by the EPI compared with the Cattell primaries is simply a function of test length – that is, the reliability is no higher if adjusted for the number of items. This makes it difficult to argue that the reliability of the second-order factor is in some way inherently higher than that of the primaries.

Even more important is Krug's reanalysis of the Saville and Blinkhorn data, using their statistical methods appropriately modified. He found that more than 50 per cent of the reliable Cattell variance is unshared by the EPI and that, conversely, only about one-tenth of the variation in the EPI cannot be predicted from the 16PF. Finally, using canonical correlation and factor analysis (a much superior method) Krug shows that *70 per cent of the information is contained in the 16PF and only 22 per cent of the information in the 16PF is contained in the EPI.* Furthermore if the reliabilities of the tests are taken into account 99 per cent of the reliable variance of the EPI is shared with the 16PF, whereas the EPI can account for only 32 per cent of the variance on the 16PF. Since the P factor of Eysenck, in the EPQ, is independent of normal personality traits (Krug and Laughlin, 1977) it cannot be argued that this would improve the situation, and add in more variance. This study by Krug is clear evidence that the primary normal factors of the 16PF test measure more widely than the higher orders of Eysenck and yet are able to measure those factors also. It is, therefore, firm support for the claims of Cattell, that it is more efficient to measure the primaries (and thus the higher orders) than the higher-orders alone.

Krug examined the factor scales of Cattell and Eysenck. However, as the first study by Eysenck and Eysenck (1969) indicated, the emergence of these scales from the items is not as clear cut as is desirable in test construction (as discussed in Chapter 6), and we must now consider further evidence concerning the factor structure of items.

Browne and Howarth (1977) searched through all personality

inventories for items that were not synonymous and finally selected 400 for an inter-item factor analysis, having administered them to 1000 subjects. Twenty factors, a number decided upon from a study of the previous research into personality factors, were rotated and nineteen were identified. What is clear from this study is that the Cattell primaries did not emerge. The mean correlation (of the oblique solution) between factors was only 0.16.

Browne and Howarth (1977) certainly use these findings as evidence against the Cattell system. However, this study has certain technical problems which render the results perhaps less than definitive. The decision to rotate twenty factors may well have affected the solution. As we have discussed in our chapter on Cattell and Eysenck's work, both under- and over-factoring can lead to poor solutions, and failure to reach simple structure. A further possible technical defect lies in the ratio of variables to subject. Nunnally (1978) argues that ten times the number of variables is necessary and few writers would venture as low as three in an exploratory study of this kind, despite the finding of Barrett and Kline that a ratio of three to one did give stable results. Perhaps even more serious is the fact that Browne and Howarth rewrote many of the items, understandably to obtain conformity of style. However, without evidence that the rewritten items are in fact highly correlated with their originals, it is not necessarily safe to assume so especially in the light of the problems of assessing the validity of personality test items from their face validity. Finally since there was no test to see whether simple structure was obtained, it is difficult to trust these factors, as being the best account of personality variance in the questionnaire realm. One further point needs to be made about this study. These factors have been identified only from the items loading on them. This contrasts ill with the factors of Eysenck and Cattell which have a multitude of external referrents supporting their identity.

Despite these problems of factor identification and rotation, Eysenck (1978) carried out an oblique second-order (Promax) analysis of the correlations and identified three factors, not surprisingly N, E and P, from their loadings on the Browne and Howarth primaries. He claims in this paper that psychologists familiar with the field identified these three factors from their loadings as he did. Nevertheless, some of the loadings are not as might be expected. Thus, social shyness loads on both the putative N and E factors, although these are supposed to be independent. Low superego loads on both N and P and social conversation on both E and P. Despite these unexpected loadings, generally the pattern is that of E, N and P, although the P loadings are unconvincing because the right primaries were not present. This finding is somewhat odd because in the Eysencks' own 1969 study (discussed above), these super-factors emerged at the third-order whereas here they are at the second-order.

In summary, this research by Browne and Howarth and the gloss on it by Eysenck leads to the firm conclusion that the three second-orders postulated by Eysenck do seem to emerge (clear in the case of E and N, probable rather than definite in the case of P), while the position concerning primaries remains unclear for the technical statistical reasons discussed above. Thus, to the questions at the beginning of this chapter, one answer is beginning to appear – second-order factors E and N are ubiquitous even where the primaries are somewhat dubious.

In the previous chapter on personality questionnaires, the scales developed by Guilford and Comrey were briefly described. A pertinent question here is, therefore, how do these relate to the factor systems of Cattell and Eysenck. We shall consider first the research with the Guilford scales. The Guilford scales are orthogonal, hence it is a simple geometrical point that they cannot align themselves with an oblique set such as those of Cattell. However, if rotated to oblique simple structure it could well be the case that they embrace much the same variance as Cattell's factors. On the other hand it might also emerge from the study of the items that these primaries were somewhat stable and elusive.

Eysenck and Eysenck (1969) in the study previously discussed in connection with the Cattell primary factors also included some Guilford items. Although these emerged with a little more clarity than the Cattell primaries, they did not load up on their items as they should and much the same conclusions concerning both the Cattell and Guilford primaries would have to be drawn from this research, thus strengthening Eysenck's arguments that primary factors are not stable enough to warrant measurement. Needless to say, all the arguments adduced against this study in respect of the Cattell factors apply here and it is not possible to disregard all these sources of possible error in evaluating the results.

Sells et al. (1970) factored 300 Cattell and 300 Guilford items in a large joint study of the two factor systems. Neither set of factors emerged clearly and they concluded that at least 400 of the 600 items did not load up as intended by their authors. However, this study is, if not vitiated, at least beset by a number of technical problems which again call the value of the results into question. In the first place the ratio of subjects to variables was about four to one which falls short of what is generally considered ideal (N = 2550) despite the finding of Barret and Kline. This could have affected the final structure. Secondly, the rotations used, Varimax and Promax, may well not have reached simple structure, for which there was no test. Furthermore the product moment correlation was the coefficient used, one which is affected by differences in the proportions putting the keyed responses to each item – an important source of error in factor analytic studies. Even more detailed technical problems concerned the communalities inserted into the diagonals where the authors used the highest correlation for each variable. Finally there was a problem over how many factors should be rotated. The Scree test (Cattell, 1966a) was not used and there is a distinct possibility that too few factors were rotated thus allowing second-orders to emerge as primaries (Cattell, 1973).

For all these reasons this study by Sells et al. must be regarded as less than definitive. Since, of course, no attempt has been made to verify the nature of these factors experimentally or by study of criterion groups, there is little point in listing them. The only conclusion that can be safely drawn from it is that the Guilford and Cattell primary factors failed to emerge, a result that could be due to the technical inadequacies of the study, inadequacies which we have discussed above. However, it would not be safe to conclude that the Guilford and Cattell primaries are not stable on the basis of this study.

Cattell and Gibbons (1968) also carried out a joint study of the Cattell and Guilford items. Here 424 items were administered to 302 undergraduates. However, by a clustering technique known as item-parcelling, these items were reduced to sixty-nine variables, but even here the ratio of subjects to variables was not ideal. In this study the fourteen Cattell factors included were all confirmed and three Guilford factors were aligned with Cattell factors (Guilford letters first) M and I, N and O, S and H. Four Guilford factors were confused together, E, G, R and T while 5 (C, D, F, O and P) aligned themselves with Cattell's O (guilt-proneness). Cattell and Gibbons concluded that seven Cattell factors were in common with three of

Guilford – Cattell's A, H, I, M, O, Q2 and Q4 – while six were not measured in the Guilford system – Cattell's C, E, F, G, L and Q3. Conversely Guilford's AA (artistic interest) was not measured on the Cattell system. This research, therefore, using item parcelling, supports the Cattell primaries and demonstrates that the Guilford scales, when rotated obliquely, align themselves with those of Cattell (other than AA). This study, therefore, is relevant to questions (1), (2) and (3) of our introduction. Guilford's factors appear different from those of Cattell because they are orthogonal.

This study by Cattell and Gibbons (1968) overcomes many of the technical problems of the researchers failing to find the Cattell primary factors. Thus, the Scree test was used to select significant factors for rotation. Furthermore, rotation was oblique and was tested for simple structure using the Bargman (1953) test. The rotation used was the Maxplane with adjustment by Rotoplot to maximize the hyperplane count (see Cattell 1966). Thus the only possible deficiency lay in the ratio of subjects to variables. However, such a deficiency is likely to add in error rather than produce the desired results and it seems to us that the results of this study can stand scrutiny. This means that essentially the Guilford and the Cattell factors are not different. Their apparent differences stem from the orthogonal factoring preferred by Guilford which prevents their immediate alignment with those of Cattell.

If Guilford's scales can be regarded as essentially similar to those of Cattell, it is arguable that Comrey's scales can be accounted for in the same way: factors that have not been properly rotated to simple structure.

Comrey and Duffy (1968) investigated the factor structure of the Comrey scales, the EPI and the 16PF factors, in a study of 272 undergraduates, using scales and FHID's (factored, homogeneous item dimensions), not items. The principal components analysis was subjected to an oblique rotation which was hand adjusted, a procedure which is not favoured by the leading factor analysts. In fact, two clear factors emerged – extraversion and neuroticism or anxiety, thus supporting the claim that by using FHIDs as the basis of correlation, rather than items, secondary rather than primary factors emerge at the first order. This process would be exaggerated if, as is likely, Comrey and Duffy failed to insert all the significant factors into the rotation, for we must remember that no test for significant factors was employed. The fact that the other factors emerging from this study were not close fits to the other Cattell second-orders could be attributed to the technical deficiencies of the study, particularly the subjective hand-rotation by which simple structure is unlikely to be attained.

Thus, the only conclusion from this early study of the Comrey scales is that extraversion and neuroticism clearly account for some of the variance in these scales and it is probable (but not certain) that the factors are essentially second-order but not rotated to the most elegant position. Barton (1973) replicated this early study, but utilized all the technical advances advocated by Cattell (1973) and Cattell and Kline (1977) – thus ensuring that simple structure was closely, if not perfectly, attained. In this investigation Barton (1973) found considerable overlap between the Comrey scales and the Cattell second-order factors and concluded that they were essentially similar. Cattell and Kline (1977) concluded their discussion of these Comrey scales by arguing that they were garbled versions of the Cattell second-orders, garbled on account of the failure to reach simple structure and second-order because of the preliminary grouping of items in homogeneous clusters.

Thus, we can conclude that two other well-known sets of personality factors, those of Guilford and Comrey are not essentially different from the factors claimed by Cattell and Eysenck. Eysenck's two second-orders are clearly the most pervasive personality factors among questionnaires and the Cattell primaries (as the work of Krug (1978) indicates) are still about the best located set of primary factors.

Although the factor-structure of the 16PF test seems quite firm when the scales are factored with other scales, it is noteworthy that the researches by Eysenck and Eysenck (1969), Vagg and Hammond (1976) and Browne and Howarth (1977), in which items are factored, have failed to reveal the Cattell factors. Our explanation of this, as we have seen, is error caused by the technical deficiencies of these studies. Nevertheless, this explanation is not fully convincing. If the factors were clear they should emerge despite the noise created by the deficient methods, for this certainly occurs with the examples (e.g. the twenty-four psychological variables where the results can be clearly predicted) cited by Harman (1976). Cattell and Vaughan (1974) have carried out a factor study of the 16PF items, using the methods advocated by Cattell (1973) and have found the factors stable, but this is the only research to have done so and it requires some replication. In summary we would argue that failure to find these factors from a study of the items is probably due to technical problems, as the successful study by Cattell and Vaughan indicates. Nevertheless it seems to us that more empirical studies are needed to demonstrate beyond doubt that the flaws are the causes of failure. Work is currently under way in Exeter (Barrett and Kline, in press) in which items are being refactored with all the technical variables, ratio of subjects to items, type of factor-solution, type of rotation, number of significant factors and different communalities inserted into the diagonals manipulated so that their effects can be observed.

Finally we want to examine some research with the Dynamic Personality Inventory (Grygier, 1961). This test is particularly interesting for a number of reasons. First, the item form is ingenious (see Chapter 6) and is claimed by the author to have some of the advantages of projective testing. Second, it is that rare phenomenon, the example of factor analysis applied to a theory – in this case Freudian developmental, psychosexual theory – rather than being used simply empirically. Finally, in various studies it has shown itself able to discriminate among art and architecture students (Stringer, 1967) and among arts and science students (Hamilton, 1970). In addition, in these studies there were correlations with academic success. All this strongly suggests that the DPI is, in fact, measuring variables of some power, and since the items in this test are quite different from those in the Cattell and Eysenck systems, it seems highly interesting to investigate the validity of these scales, that is, to find out just what these DPI factors are and where they are located in factor space.

Kline (1968) carried out a Varimax (orthogonal) analysis of the DPI scales on a small sample of seventy students. The results of this study have to be treated with great caution for there were many technical inadequacies. However, only one factor loaded up on the Grygier scales as hypothesized from what they claimed to be measuring: an obsessional factor emerged loading on the anal scales of the DPI and on Ai3Q (Kline, 1971) a measure of the anal character. The validity of the other scales was not, therefore, supported. Stringer (1970) replicated this study on a much larger sample. However, none of his factors supported the validity of the scales and they were difficult to identify.

These two investigations examined the internal structure of the DPI. Even if the factors emerging had loaded up as hypothesized for example, all the oral scales on one factor, and the anal scales on another, they would have been inadequate for answering the critical question of where these DPI factors lie in factor space. This question demands that the DPI be factored with the EPI and 16PF tests at least, and preferably with any other tests purporting to measure psychosexual variables. Such an investigation has, in fact, been carried out by Kline and Storey (1978). All these tests were administered to 128 undergraduates and the scale intercorrelations were subjected to a Promax oblique rotation.

The technical inadequacies of this study, the Promax rotation and the small number of subjects, can be disregarded, because the factors emerging from the well known tests were clear and as expected, thus demonstrating that in this case the factor analysis had worked well. In fact, the results were so clear-cut that we were able to draw a number of firm conclusions at the end of this study (an unusual event in psychology):

(1) The DPI factors are independent of the two large personality factors extraversion and anxiety or neuroticism. No DPI scales loaded on the N factor and only three, Sa sociability, Pe exhibitionism and Ei initiative, on the E scale. This means that the DPI is clearly in a different category from the Comrey and Guilford scales.

(2) The DPI scales are independent of general intelligence 'g'. This is important to establish since it indicates that the DPI has one of the basic features of any test of personality, i.e. is independent of ability.

(3) The 'a' (anal) scales of the DPI do load up as expected, together with the Ai3Q (Kline, 1971) a measure of the obsessional or anal character. This factor also loads on G (superego) and Q3 (self-sentiment) and is, in the terminology of Cattell, a surface rather than a source trait. It is to be identified as a factor of obsessional personality or possibly superego. It certainly resembles the anal character as described by Freud (1908) although, of course, there is no connection, in this study, with anal eroticism.

(4) A factor emerged concerned with feminine interests.

(5) A factor emerged concerned with masculine interests. Neither of these personality traits is measured in the 16PF and thus the DPI does seem to be adding in some useful new variance, although the variance accounted for by these factors was small – around 8 per cent.

These were the findings relevant to the problems of this chapter. In summary, this study of the DPI indicated that there are other factors beyond those of the 16PF test and indeed the full twenty-three normal factors. Thus, it cannot be argued that the Cattell factors embrace all the personality variance. However, these factors were small in terms of variance accounted for, although the masculine and feminine factors would seem likely to be useful.

Conclusion

We have now critically examined some of the recent research relevant to what we argued are the most important questions in the factor analysis of personality. From these researches the following answers seem reasonable summaries of the current position.

(1) What are the relationships between the different sets of factors? Generally it appears that the best test constructors are essentially measuring the same variables. The differences lie in the rotations, and the extent to which simple structure has been obtained. All the available evidence still points to the Cattell factors as being about the best account in terms of primary factors, despite the problems in identifying the factors from the study of items. The DPI does seem to be measuring new factors, but these are certainly of small variance.

(2) Are differences in results artifactual due to different factor-analytic methods? As implied above, the answer to this is in the affirmative. Many divergent results are due to the technical inadequacies of the factor analyses or (in Guilford's case) his preference for orthogonal rotation.

(3) What is the best and most elegant description of personality? This question is the hardest to answer. It would be a bold investigator who claimed, for example, that the twenty-three Cattell factors were the final solution. Nevertheless, it is clear that about 25-30 questionnaire factors, some of them aligned exactly with those of Cattell, will probably suffice to describe personality embracing most of the variance. Further studies are needed, with larger, more diverse samples, larger numbers of variables, preferably items and parcels of items, and various methods of rotation to compare simple structure. These factors will also need to be compared with L and T data, as indeed Cattell et al. (1976) have recently done.

As for the question of higher order factors, there can be no doubt that extraversion and anxiety are the most important, although the other factors are also useful. For quick measurement E and N are probably the best variables to concentrate upon, but as Krug (1978) showed, to use these is to lose, *vis-à-vis* the 16PF, a considerable amount of information. The P factor of Eysenck is probably best seen as an abnormal rather than a normal factor, although normals do score low on the dimension.

From this summary it can be seen that despite the apparent confusion of results in the factor analysis of personality, order can be maintained. Clear personality factors have emerged and it is argued that future theories of personality should be based upon studies of these variables and not the shadowy entities of clinical theorizing and speculation.

Part IV
Cognitive styles

8 Theoretical approaches to cognitive style

Kenneth M. Goldstein
and Sheldon Blackman

For centuries the study of personality was cognitively oriented; that is, the thinking processes of the individual were considered central in understanding personality. With the beginning of the behaviourist movement in psychology, attention shifted from the thinking to the behaviour of the individual.

In recent years, however, the pendulum has swung back so that thinking is once again being considered. With this renewed interest there has been a shift in the way thought processes are viewed. The individual's thinking is now considered important as it relates to his behaviour and is viewed as a mediator between impinging stimuli and the individual's responses to those stimuli.

People are constantly being bombarded by many and varied stimuli, so there must be methods for selecting those stimuli to which they will react. At the physiological level the reticular formation is considered to serve a selecting function; at the psychological level various processes have been postulated. In particular, one hypothesized mediator has been termed *cognitive style*. This refers to the consistent ways in which individuals organize their environments. Thus cognitive style is hypothesized to mediate between environmental stimuli and the responses that people make to those stimuli.

Considered in this way, cognitive style is a *hypothetical construct*. That is, it is an idea developed to aid conceptualization. As with intelligence and personality, cognitive style has no physical existence, but is a useful device to explain regularities in the behaviour of people. In the case of cognitive style, it is consistency in information processing, which in turn leads to consistency in behaviour, that is of interest.

Various investigators have taken different approaches toward defining the construct cognitive style. In this chapter the major approaches will be reviewed and material presented in an attempt to dimensionalize and organize them.

It should be understood that the common thread in all the approaches is a concern with the structure, rather than the content, of thought. That is, individuals are distinguished in terms of *how* they think, rather than *what* they think. For example, the political liberal and the political conservative are at different ends of a political continuum of thought content. Yet, knowing an individual's political beliefs tells us nothing about his style of thinking. A political conservative may hold his beliefs in a rigid manner, closed to new sources of information, or in a more flexible, open manner. 'Openness' relates to the underlying structure of the belief; 'conservatism' relates to what is believed.

The following approaches to cognitive style will be summarized: (1) authoritarianism and dogmatism, (2) cognitive complexity and integrative complexity, (3) field dependence, (4) cognitive controls and (5) reflection – impulsivity.

Authoritarianism and dogmatism

The study of authoritarianism began with a focus on the content of thought. During the Second World War a group of scientists, based in California, conducted a series of studies on anti-Semitism. From this rather narrow focus on content the investigators moved to a study of rightist conservatism in general. As the investigations progressed, it was noted that the style of thinking of rightist conservatives was characterized by two traits: *rigidity* and *intolerance of ambiguity*. Rigidity is the tendency to maintain a belief or practice in the face of evidence that it is untenable and inefficient. Intolerance of ambiguity is the tendency not to tolerate the existence of an ambiguous situation but rather to move quickly to one side or the other of a question. Rigidity and intolerance of ambiguity are stylistic characteristics. They describe how individuals hold ideas, not what the ideas are.

The major report of the research by this group was published as a book entitled *The Authoritarian Personality* (Adorno et al., 1950). The investigators' basic premise was that attitudes (that is content of thought) are a reflection of underlying personality. The underlying personality is also reflected in a number of other ways, including consistencies in perception, cognition and behaviour. The particular consistencies in cognition of interest here, rigidity and intolerance of ambiguity, are stylistic in that they deal with consistencies in how information is processed. Since information-processing is not directly observable, rigidity and intolerance of ambiguity are inferred from consistencies in behaviour.

In their summary of analyses of interview data, the researchers concluded that the rightists' tendency to be rigid and intolerant of ambiguity was due, in part, to the need of prejudiced individuals to keep out of conscious thought impulses that were unacceptable to them. In order to accomplish this, it was necessary to have rigid defences.

The transition from analyses of interview material to the laboratory study of the behaviour of political rightists was not long in coming. One frequently used technique for studying rigidity in the laboratory makes use of what is known as the Einstellung problems. The German word 'Einstellung' means a mental set, a predisposition to respond in a specific way. In the case of the Einstellung problems, subjects were presented with examples of how to solve a problem using an indirect method. Next they were presented with problems that had to be solved using that same indirect method. Following this, problems were presented that could be solved in the same indirect way, or by using a direct method. Subjects who persisted in using the indirect method when the more direct method was also applicable were termed rigid. It was found that authoritarian, or political rightist, subjects were more likely to show rigid behaviour, particularly when under stress, than were low authoritarian subjects (e.g. Rokeach, 1948).

With regard to the study of intolerance of ambiguity, an often used technique involves the autokinetic phenomenon. It has been noted that a stationary pinpoint of light in a dark room appears to move. Subjects who were tolerant of ambiguity were likely to demonstrate inconsistencies when reporting the amount of 'perceived' movement, whereas authoritarian subjects were likely quickly to stabilize their reports of perceived movement and so were judged to be intolerant of ambiguity (Block and Block, 1951).

The Einstellung problem as an approach to the study of rigidity, and the autokinetic phenomenon as a vehicle for the study of intolerance of ambiguity, represent classic approaches. Over the years there have been a number of other techniques employed by various investigators to study how rigidity and intolerance of ambiguity relate to authoritarianism. In general, the results of these later investigations have corroborated the earlier findings (see Goldstein and Blackman, 1978, for details).

It is reasonable to inquire why authoritarian individuals should be rigid and intolerant of ambiguity. It was originally believed (Frenkel-Brunswik, 1948) that the nature of the home environment of the prejudiced person requires the suppression of aggression toward authority figures. In order to ward off the anxiety that is generated, there is a tendency to keep conflicting ideas out of consciousness; this leads to a style of intolerance to ambiguity. Further, once an idea is adopted, it is rigidly maintained, again to avoid the anxiety of searching for new solutions. Consistent with this view is evidence that authoritarian individuals are often reared by cold, controlling parents who do not allow their children to express aggression toward them.

If rigidity and intolerance of ambiguity are stylistic attributes of political rightists, the question arose as to whether individuals who hold leftist political views exhibit similar stylistic tendencies. This question was central to the work of Milton Rokeach, who was concerned with an approach to cognitive style that would be independent of content. He believed that there are similarities in the way rightists and leftists process information. Rokeach (1960) posited a dimension of open-/closed-mindedness, which cuts across specific ideologies. In his early work he observed that individuals who were closed-minded tended to be so in a variety of areas, not just those involving political ideology.

Rokeach postulated several aspects of functioning that were characteristic of the dogmatic person. He believed that such people glorify authority figures who support their beliefs and are intolerant toward those who oppose them. Rokeach then developed the Dogmatic Scale, which will be presented in more detail in the following chapter. It is important to note here that research has indicated that individuals with rightist political orientation are likely to score as more dogmatic on the Scale than are individuals of leftist political orientation, indicating that Rokeach was not entirely successful in developing an instrument in which style is independent of content.

Researchers have generally found that dogmatic subjects, like authoritarian subjects, tend to be rigid and intolerant of ambiguity, and this is reflected in the fact that various studies show dogmatism and authoritarianism to be correlated from 0.5 to 0.7. But dogmatism has also been studied with regard to other variables that are likely to be influenced by information-processing strategies. A classic illustration comes from studies of the relationship between dogmatism and problem solving. Rokeach distinguished two phases of complex problem solving. The first, analysis, involves the replacement of old beliefs with new beliefs; the second, synthesis, involves an integration of the new beliefs into a system (cf., Goldstein and Blackman, 1978).

Rokeach et al. (1955) hypothesized that because dogmatic individuals tend to maintain isolation among beliefs, they would have difficulty synthesizing new beliefs into a belief system. However, with regard to the ability to analyse, that is, to replace old beliefs with new ones, high dogmatic subjects should perform no differently from low dogmatic subjects. The Denny Doodlebug Problem was used to provide data on this issue. The problem posed is how does an imaginary bug, Joe Doodlebug, reach a dish of food when his movements are limited by a set of rules. To solve this problem it is necessary for subjects to overcome a number of implicit sets. For example, nothing in the movement rules prevents Joe from jumping west when he is facing north. Analysing ability was measured by the time required by subjects to overcome the sets, and synthesizing by the time required to solve the problem once the sets were overcome. As hypothesized, nondogmatic subjects were superior to dogmatic subjects in synthesizing, but not in analysing, ability. However, in research in which tasks other than the Doodlebug problem were used, similar findings have not been generally obtained.

Cognitive complexity and integrative complexity

In a second approach to the study of cognitive style, the central concern is with the ability of individuals to perceive distinctions among stimuli and to organize those distinctions. The first element, that of making distinctions among stimuli, grew out of the work of George Kelly (1955). The second element, the organization of distinctions among stimuli, was developed by O. J. Harvey, David E. Hunt and Harold M. Schroder (1961).

One aspect of Kelly's personal construct theory (see Chapter 10) involves the complexity of the construct system. Of particular interest in the study of cognitive style is the number of independent constructs an individual uses in organizing his interpersonal perceptions. The greater the number of constructs, the greater the cognitive complexity of the individual. From Kelly's point of view, individuals with greater cognitive complexity are expected to be better predictors of events. The next chapter describes how James Bieri adapted Kelly's Rep Test to develop a standard procedure for assessing cognitive complexity (see also Chapters 11 and 12).

In a typical study, Adams-Webber (1969) had undergraduates complete Kelly's original form of repertory grid involving twenty-two constructs. After allowing subjects to interact in dyads, each subject was asked to guess from a total of forty-four constructs which twenty-two constructs his partner had used. Cognitively complex individuals were more accurate in judging which constructs had been used by their partners than were the cognitively simple subjects. In their review of the literature, Leitner et al. (1974) concluded that cognitively complex individuals were more accurate than cognitively simple individuals in assessing differences between themselves and others, but not in assessing similarities. Based on our reviews (Goldstein and Blackman, 1978), we would question the finding even with regard to the assessment of differences.

Work on cognitive complexity was an important step in the development of cognitive style measures directly concerned with information processing. However, in the research by Harvey et al. (1961) an instrument was specifically developed with a focus on information-processing without any reference to the content of thought. Their approach, which may be termed 'integrative complexity', emphasized the measurement of structure, without reliance on content.

Thus, not only was there an interest in how many independent concepts, or dimensions, individuals used in perceiving their environments, but also interest in how these dimensions were organized, or integrated. Individuals who are more integratively complex are those whose perceptions are ordered along many dimensions, and who organize these dimensions in a complex, integrated manner.

From Kelly's point of view, the superior performance of cognitively complex individuals was independent of the environment in which the performance was occurring. In integrative complexity theory, however, the environments in which individuals perform become an important consideration. It was posited that, for all individuals, behavioural output is best in environments of moderate informational complexity. Integratively complex individuals perform better at all levels of environmental complexity; in addition, they perform best in environments that are somewhat more complex than do integratively simple individuals.

To study behaviour in simple and complex environments, two research approaches have been used: sensory deprivation to study behaviour in informationally simple environments, and game-simulations to study behaviour in informationally complex environments. As an example of the latter, Streufert and Driver (1965) studied the performance of integratively simple and integratively complex undergraduates in a situation in which decisions about how to respond to an 'enemy's' invasion of an island were scored for integrative complexity. The complexity of the simulated environment was varied by manipulating the amount of information provided to the players – the more information, the more complex the environment. The data indicated that, for all subjects, perceptions of the complexity of the enemy were at a maximum at intermediate levels of environmental complexity. Further, integratively simple subjects tended to perceive the enemy in a less complex way than did integratively complex subjects.

Developmental considerations play an important role in integrative complexity theory. It is postulated that individuals progress through a series of stages during their development. The direction of progression is from integrative simplicity to integrative complexity. Here again, the interaction between environmental factors and the integrative complexity of the individual is emphasized. The progression to maximum integrative complexity requires a special type of parental training, termed interdependent informational, which essentially involves the parent's structuring the environment so that the child may explore and learn from the consequences of his explorations. At the other extreme training is termed reliable unilateral. In this case the parent is autocratic, rewarding and punishing the child for adherence to a set of rules that the parent has developed. This type of training is hypothesized to arrest development so that the child never progresses beyond an integratively simple, concrete cognitive style.

Field dependence–independence

Perhaps the most extensively researched of all approaches to cognitive style was developed by Herman A. Witkin and his associates (Witkin et al., 1962). While the other approaches to the study of cognitive style dealt with in this and the following chapter began from what is essentially a personality-orientation, Witkin's study of field dependence originated in his research on perception. Witkin noted that when subjects made judgements about whether a rod was in an upright position, there was a consistency in their performance. Some subjects were able to make relatively accurate judgements, uninfluenced by environmental cues designed adversely to affect performance. Other subjects made consistently greater errors in the face of these same cues. Witkin concluded that in order to study perception of the upright it was necessary to take into consideration factors about the individual, in addition to factors directly related to the task.

Individuals who made accurate judgements and were uninfluenced by the environmental context were termed 'field-independent'; those whose judgements were adversely affected by the environmental context were termed 'field-dependent'. As Witkin's study of field-dependent and field-independent individuals continued, it was found that there were consistent differences between the two types on nonperceptual tasks as well.

The concept of field dependence was eventually broadened to include an underlying dimension of differentiation. This refers to the stylistic component of personality, to the complexity of the personality system. Differentiation as used by Witkin is similar to the concept of differentiation found in the theory of integrative complexity and to complexity as it is used in the theory of cognitive complexity. As in integrative complexity, Witkin also uses the construct of integration to include the elaborateness of the relationship of the differentiated subsystems and the facility with which they interrelate.

One of the concerns in the study of cognitive styles has been the relationship between cognitive styles and intelligence. The independence of the two constructs has been especially studied in the area of field dependence, where a number of investigators have shown that various measures of field dependence are significantly and moderately related to various measures of intelligence. One such study was conducted by Karp (1963), who administered three measures of field dependence, along with six subtests from the Wechsler Adult Intelligence Scale and other measures, to 150 male undergraduates. Karp's data indicated that there are high positive correlations between the measures of field dependence and intelligence.

Reflection–impulsivity

Second only to field dependence–independence in current interest is the cognitive style dimension of reflection–impulsivity. The study of reflection–impulsivity began with an interest in information processing by children. Kagan et al. (1963) had been studying ways in which children categorize complex stimuli. One style that they were particularly interested in was termed an *analytic* style. Children who could be characterized as analytic tended to group objects together on the basis of shared similarities. For example, shown a picture of a zebra, a white shirt and a striped shirt, the analytic subject would group the zebra and striped shirt together because they both have stripes. In the course of their work, Kagan and his associates noted that analytic responders tended to delay making decisions. The researchers inferred an underlying process of reflection versus impulsivity as mediating the analytic performance. Reflection appeared to involve a process of considering alternate hypotheses before making a decision.

This line of research was soon extended by Kagan et al. (1964). In order to further study the relationship between the analytic style and reflection–impulsivity, it was necessary to develop an instrument to measure reflection–impulsivity. As discussed in the next chapter, the Matching Familiar Figures (MFF) Test was devised for this purpose. An impulsive child was defined as one who responds to the test items quickly and inaccurately.

There has been great interest in the modification of reflection–impulsivity, in the direction of reducing impulsivity. The research design usually involves a pre-test, some training procedures designed to reduce impulsivity, followed by a post-test. Most of the studies have indicated that it is possible to increase the time that an individual takes to make a response, but that the accuracy of the responses is not affected by the training procedure. In the first reported attempt to modify reflection–impulsivity, Kagan et al. (1966) worked with children in the first grade at school. The children were given a variety of training tasks and required to wait a specified interval of time before giving their responses. When re-tested on the MFF Test, it was found that latency of response had increased from pre-test performance levels, but that accuracy had not improved.

Cognitive controls

The final approach to the study of cognitive style to be considered here is based on a number of different dimensions, or 'cognitive controls'. As defined by George Klein (1954), these cognitive controls have in common the function of acting as delaying mechanisms, that is, mechanisms to delay the expression of needs. In this regard cognitive controls are similar to Freud's concept of the ego, which exerts a controlling function on the primitive id urges (see Chapter 2).

As the work advanced at the Menninger Foundation in Topeka, Kansas, different cognitive controls were delineated. An individual's cognitive style was conceived of as the pattern of interrelationships among the various cognitive controls. Most of the research, however, has been on the cognitive controls taken one at a time, rather than on their relatedness.

The major cognitive controls are as follows:

(1) Tolerance for unrealistic experience, which is defined as the degree of readiness of subjects to report experiences that appear contrary to reality.

(2) Conceptual differentiation, originally termed 'equivalence range', refers to the extent to which an individual is likely to break a dimension up into many categories.

(3) Constricted–flexible control deals with the degree to which individuals are susceptible to distraction.

(4) Levelling–sharpening refers to the degree to which new experiences are integrated with existing ones.

(5) Scanning refers to the extent to which the individual monitors his environment in order to verify his judgement.

(6) Field-articulation, which is essentially field-dependence.

Most of these cognitive control dimensions have not been extensively studied. Currently, however, major work is being carried out by Santostefano (1978). Over the past twenty years Santostefano has been investigating cognitive control dimensions in his studies of children. He developed a battery of cognitive control tests for use with children, based on earlier work with adults. In addition to adapting four of the controls that had been studied with adults, Santostefano found it necessary to develop a new cognitive control that he termed 'body movement/ego-motility'. This dimension relates to the way children think about their bodies and how their bodies move.

Santostefano's work on cognitive controls in children is closely tied to the treatment of children with academic and behaviour problems. He makes the point that such problems are often the result of inadequate matching between the level of cognitive control development in the children and the environment demands placed on them. This concern with the match between cognitive style and environment was previously noted in the work on integrative complexity. The treatment is to provide training aimed at increasing the maturity of the various cognitive controls, to bring them into balance with environmental demands.

The organization of cognitive style

We began this chapter by defining cognitive style as a concern with the structure, rather than the content, of thought. Each of the cognitive-style approaches considered has this concern in common. It has also been noted that different investigators have taken quite different approaches to the conceptualization of cognitive style. And, as will be seen in the next chapter, the approaches to measurement are equally diverse.

Given the apparent diversity among approaches, a number of researchers have attempted to organize and conceptualize the approaches into a simpler model. This has been done in two ways. One way is empirical and involves the use of statistical techniques to study the interrelationships among the various approaches; a second way is to relate the approaches on a theoretical basis.

The major statistical technique in the empirical approach has been that of correlation; occasionally, factor analyses have been conducted (see Chapter 5). The data indicate a fairly high relationship between authoritarianism and dogmatism, a relationship that is likely to be due, in part, to the similar format of the measuring instruments and to the rightist content of the two measures. Authoritarianism relates moderately to cognitive complexity, integrative complexity, and field-dependence, relationships that cannot be attributed to content or instrument similarly. The latter three measures do not relate well to each other or to dogmatism. Based on our review of a number of studies (Goldstein and Blackman, 1978), we conclude that the data show field-dependence and the error-dimension of reflection–impulsivity to be related.

At the theoretical level there have been several attempts to organize the diverse approaches to cognitive style. Messick (1970) originally developed a system that involved nine categories, but in a later presentation (Messick, 1976) found it necessary to delineate nineteen categories. In an attempt to consolidate the area, Kogan (1973, 1976) suggested that cognitive styles could be grouped into three types. Type I involves performance against a standard of correctness (for example, field-dependence), Type II implies a value judgement by the investigator (for example, it is better to be cognitively complex than to be cognitively simple), and Type III involves neither performance against a standard nor value judgements regarding superiority at one pole of the dimensions of style (for example, category width, a cognitive style discussed by Pettigrew (1958) that relates to individuals' judgements about the range within which events are likely to occur).

In summary, cognitive style is a hypothetical construct designed to describe the manner in which individuals process the stimuli that impinge on them. It may be understood as occupying the ground between intelligence and personality. Like intelligence it relates to thinking and the ability to manage information. Like personality it relates to characteristic modes of responding over time and across situations.

We have presented a number of different approaches to cognitive style that have been developed over the past forty years. The approaches are notable in the diversity of their theoretical orientation. They share in common a concern with style rather than the content of thinking. In the next chapter the equally diverse approaches to measurement are considered.

Suggested further reading

The reference list for this chapter cites a number of the original reports that might be of interest to students requiring additional information. Students needing more extensive and recent information might consult:

Goldstein, K. M. and Blackman, S. (1978) *Cognitive Style: Five Approaches and Relevant Research.* New York: Wiley.

9 Cognitive style: research and measurement

Sheldon Blackman
and Kenneth M. Goldstein

As was noted in the preceding chapter, techniques for assessing cognitive styles are many and varied. Not only do the measurement techniques differ from one theoretical orientation to another, but there are often a variety of measurement techniques within a given theoretical orientation. In this chapter we examine the measurement techniques associated with each orientation and consider their similarities and differences. This chapter is organized to parallel the preceding chapter, and it is assumed that the reader is familiar with the material contained in that chapter.

In what follows the emphasis is on the rationales of the assessment procedures and on descriptions of the techniques. All measures of cognitive style discussed here have acceptable levels of reliability. The question of their validity relates primarily to the effectiveness with which measures can be used to predict theoretically derived effects. A number of studies provide evidence for the predictive validity of these instruments (see Goldstein and Blackman, 1978, for details).

As in the preceding chapter, the material is organized in the following five sections: (1) authoritarianism and dogmatism, (2) cognitive complexity and integrative complexity, (3) field dependence, (4) cognitive controls and (5) reflection–impulsivity.

Authoritarianism and dogmatism

After several instruments were developed to measure anti-Semitism, ethnocentrism, and political and economic conservatism, another instrument, the F Scale (Adorno et al., 1950) was developed to assess the underlying personality of the authoritarian individual. In its final form the F Scale consisted of thirty items to which a subject had to indicate degree of agreement. The items made no reference to minority groups or prejudice, but sought to provide an indirect measure of level of prejudice.

For example, one of the items requires the respondent to agree or disagree with a statement to the effect that our lives are controlled by people plotting in secret places. The investigations maintained that the prejudiced person views interpersonal relations in such terms as strength and weakness, dominance and submission. Since agreement with this item reflects the belief that our lives are subject to the power manipulations of others, such agreement is more likely to be made by a prejudiced individual.

In assembling the F Scale, items were selected to represent nine areas of functioning of the authoritarian individual. The areas were as follows:

Conventionalism: adherence to middle-class values.

Authoritarian submission: submission to middle-class moral authority.

Authoritarian aggression: hostility toward individuals who violate middle-class norms.

Anti-intraception: toughminded orientation.

Superstition and stereotype: relating to belief in external control.

Power and 'toughness': tendency to behave in a powerful, dominant manner.

Destructiveness and cynicism: hostility.

Projectivity: projection of unconscious impulses.

Sex: exaggerated concern with sexual misbehaviour.

As discussed below, attempts to validate these nine dimensions empirically have shown that the F Scale is multidimensional, but research provides evidence for only some of the dimensions (cf., Kerlinger and Rokeach, 1966).

The F Scale was not developed as, nor claimed to be, a measure of cognitive style. As noted in the previous chapter, it was found that individuals who scored in an authoritarian direction were found to be rigid and intolerant of ambiguity. Rigidity and intolerance of ambiguity are information-processing characteristics that were fore-runners of the study of cognitive style.

Shortly after the development of the F Scale a question of bias in the instrument was raised. Since each item in the Scale is worded so that agreement with the statement contributes to a high authoritarianism score, some investigators were concerned that what was being measured was the tendency to agree, or acquiescence-response tendency, rather than the subjects' responses to the content of the items. However, subsequent research indicated that the validity of the instrument was not adversely affected, since it was found that acquiescence is characteristic of authoritarian individuals (e.g. Messick and Frederiksen, 1958).

In the area of dogmatism, instrument development was much more closely tied to a concern with cognitive style, in that both rightists and leftists could be dogmatic. The final version of the Dogmatism Scale, Form E, contains forty items, items that were written to reflect different aspects of Rokeach's theory (Rokeach, 1960).

The Dogmatism Scale contains three major dimensions, each of which is further subdivided into different levels. The major dimensions are as follows:

Belief–disbelief dimension: beliefs are all ideas that a person accepts as true; disbeliefs are all that he rejects as false.

Central–peripheral dimension: central beliefs are primitive and unverbalized, dealing with the nature of the world and one's self; central beliefs are differentiated from beliefs at an intermediate level, which deal with the nature of authority, and from peripheral beliefs, which emanate from authority.

Time–perspective dimension: the organization of the belief–disbelief system in terms of past, present and future.

Test items were written for each dimension to reflect the functioning of dogmatic individuals on each dimension. Regarding the belief–disbelief dimension, for example, the dogmatic individual tends to hold beliefs and disbeliefs that are isolated from one another. Such an individual might agree to an item that states that the United States and Russia share virtually nothing in common.

An example of an item that relates to the central–peripheral dimension is one that deals with the idea that man is helpless and miserable. The tendency to agree with such an item is taken as an indication of dogmatism (or closed-mindedness) since Rokeach posits that the closed-minded individual views the world as threatening and hostile.

Rokeach also posits that closed-minded individuals are past- and future-oriented, rather than present-oriented, and so would tend to agree with an item that states that the present is full of unhappiness and only the future counts. Such items reflect the time-perspective dimension.

The F Scale and Dogmatism Scale are presented in a Likert scaling format (that is, a five-point scale ranging from 'strongly agree' to 'strongly disagree'). As we have noted, agreement with the items contributes to a high score. Such a procedure raises the objection that what is being measured is the tendency to agree or acquiesce, regardless of the content. With regard to these two scales in particular this was not a major problem because the tendency to agree is found to be a characteristic of the authoritarian/high-dogmatic individual.

The Likert technique also raises an important question regarding unidimensionality. The items are weighted equally and are summed to arrive at a total score. This implies a unidimensionality that may not be inherent in the Scale. This question can be studied empirically by factor analysis (see Chapter 5). In a factor analysis, items that are responded to in a similar manner are grouped together to form factors. If all of the items on a test are responded to similarly, there will be one general factor. If the Scale is made up of clusters of items that are responded to similarly (but differently from other items), the scale will contain several factors. In the latter case, a total score may not be meaningful. In such an instance, each cluster, or factor, should be scored separately. Research has indicated that the F Scale and the Dogmatism Scale are indeed made up of a number of factors (e.g. Krug, 1961; Pedhazur, 1971), raising a serious question about the appropriateness of using a single, total score. Despite this problem, research with the two instruments has yielded interesting and fruitful results (Kirscht and Dillehay, 1967; Vacchiano et al., 1969).

Both the F Scale and the Dogmatism Scale are similar in that they are, as indicated in the previous chapter, measures of presumed underlying characteristics. They differ in that the F Scale was designed to measure characteristics of the fascistic individual, while the Dogmatism Scale was designed to measure characteristics of the dogmatic, or closed, individual, without regard to rightist or leftist ideology.

Cognitive complexity and integrative complexity

The two approaches to be considered in this section were developed with a specific interest in the measurement of information-processing styles. In his development of personal construct theory, George Kelly (1955) devised the Role Construct Repertory Test (Rep Test) to aid in the analysis of constructs used by individuals to view their environments. As developed by Kelly in its grid form, the Rep Test can be used in many ways. For example, one's perceptions of oneself might be compared with one's perceptions of one's parents.

Of interest in the study of cognitive style was the modification of the Rep Test introduced by James Bieri (Bieri et al., 1966). Bieri focused on the number of different constructs that are used by a subject in completing a Rep Test. The number of independent constructs was considered a measure of differentiation, the greater the number of such constructs the greater the differentiation, and the greater the cognitive complexity. In the Bieri modification of the Rep Test the subject is asked to make ratings along ten scales (for example *outgoing–shy, adjusted–maladjusted*) for each of ten role-types (for example, yourself, person you dislike). The ratings assigned to each of the role-types are analysed. Cognitive structure is simple to the degree that the ratings of each role-type are identical. The cognitively complex individual makes different ratings of the role-types, implying greater differentiation among constructs (see also Chapter 12).

The second system that we are considering here, integrative complexity, was an extension of the work on cognitive complexity to include the dimension of integration. The major approach to measurement taken by Harvey et al. (1961) made use of a stem-completion format, originally termed the Sentence Completion Test, and later modified to the Paragraph Completion Test (PCT) (Schroder et al., 1967). The latter presents the subject with a series of stems (e.g. When I am in doubt ..., Rules ...) and requires the subject to complete the stem and write several additional sentences. The responses to each stem are then scored in terms of the differentiation and integration inherent in each response, presumably without regard to the content of the paragraph. In order to receive a high score indicative of abstractness, the response must show that the writer views his environment along a number of dimensions and that he has the capacity to weigh, order and hierarchically integrate the dimensions in a complex way. Schroder and colleagues (1967) give details of scoring criteria and examples of responses that differ in abstractness.

A number of other approaches to the measurement of integrative complexity have been developed. One of the more important ones is the 'This I Believe' Test (TIB Test) developed by O. J. Harvey (1964). As with the PCT, the TIB Test uses a stem-completion approach. However, unlike the PCT, it is scored on the basis of content. For example, reliance on external authority is posited to be a characteristic of the integratively simple. concrete individual. If the subject's responses indicate reliance on external authority, then the TIB Test protocol would be scored for concreteness. In this regard, the TIB Test is similar to the Dogmatism Scale.

As distinct from all other measures of cognitive style considered in this chapter, these measures of integrative complexity require extensive training to attain scoring proficiency and the necessary inter-scorer reliability. Since the questions are open-ended, scoring requires intimate knowledge of the theory and scoring criteria. It is probably this difficulty with scoring that is primarily responsible for the relatively little research involving integrative complexity that has taken place outside the laboratories of the original investigators. At least one attempt to develop an objectively scored measure of integrative complexity, Tuckman's (1966) Interpersonal Topical Inventory, has not related well to the original instruments.

In considering the approaches to the study of integrative complexity, one distinction that we have already alluded to is the content approach represented by Harvey's TIB Test as compared with Schroder's structurally based approach represented by the PCT. While there are some data that indicate that complexity on the PCT is associated with length of response and sophistication of vocabulary (Schroder et al., 1967), it is unclear whether this is a bias in the scoring or a reflection of characteristics of the more complex subject. The reason that open-ended approaches have been emphasized in this area is that it has been argued that a cognitively simple person might be able to agree with a complex statement but could not generate one. This leads to an approach that requires subjects to generate their own responses, with the attendant scoring problems.

Field dependence–independence

There have been two major approaches to the measurement of field dependence. One involves measurement of the subject's perception of the upright, the other involves the subject's ability to locate a simple figure that is hidden in a complex, embedding surround.

The initial approaches to measurement in the area of field dependence were cumbersome. The Tilting-Room–Tilting-Chair tests had two major components, the Room-Adjustment Test (RAT) and the Body-Adjustment Test (BAT). In both tests a chair was suspended in a special room. Both the chair and the room itself could be tilted to the right or left by the experimenter. In the RAT both room and chair tilted, and the subject's task was to instruct the experimenter to reorient the room until the subject believed the room was in an upright position. In the BAT both room and chair were again tilted, but this time the subject was required to instruct the experimenter to manipulate the chair on which the subject was seated so that it was brought to what the subject perceived as the upright.

After initial work with the BAT and RAT, Witkin and his associates (Witkin et al., 1962) developed the Rod-and-Frame Test (RFT). In administering the RFT the subject is seated in a dark room in which a luminous rod is suspended in a luminous frame. Both rod and frame can be tilted independently. The subject's task is to instruct the experimenter to manipulate the rod until the subject believes the rod is in an upright position. Performance is measured in terms of deviation of the rod from a true vertical position. Subjects whose performance manifests greater inaccuracies, presumably because of the distracting cues provided by the tilted frame, are considered to be more field-dependent.

The second approach is illustrated by the Embedded Figures Test (EFT), in which the subject is presented with a design and required to locate it within a distracting, embedding context (Witkin et al., 1962). In total, twenty-four designs are available for presentation. The measure of field dependence is the speed with which the figures are located, the slower the performance the greater the field dependence. In practice, only the first twelve figures are used, with a 3-minute time limit for each figure. The logic of the EFT is that the individual who is more field-dependent is more distracted by the embedding context and is less likely to be able to locate the figures quickly.

A number of versions of both the RFT and the EFT have been developed. Most notable of the RFT modifications is Oltman's (1968) portable version, performance on which relates well to performance on the standard version. Among the important variations of the EFT are a short form developed by Jackson (1956), and the Group EFT, the Children's EFT (Witkin et al., 1971) and the Preschool EFT (Coates, 1972). Data indicate that scores derived from different versions of the EFT intercorrelate well. When performance on various versions of the RFT is related to performance on various versions of the EFT, the correlations are in a moderate range, indicating the two types of instruments for the assessment of field dependence are measuring somewhat different things.

In the study of field dependence, the two major assessment instruments are both perceptual measures. This reflects the initial interest in perceptual work, rather than in personality (authoritarianism and dogmatism) or cognitive style (cognitive complexity and integrative complexity) as such.

Cognitive controls

As noted in the previous chapter, there has been limited research on most of the cognitive control dimensions. Constricted–flexible control, measured by the Thurstone (1944) modification of the Stroop Color–Word Test (1935), is an exception. The first part of the Stroop Test presents the subject with a list of the names of four colours (red, yellow, green, blue) repeated many times. The names of the colours are printed in black ink. The subject is required to read aloud the names of the colours. On the second part of the test the names of the colours are printed with coloured inks that correspond to the name of the colours, for example, the word *red* is printed with red ink. The subject is again required to read the names aloud. On the third part of the test the names of the colours are printed with coloured inks that do not correspond to the names; for example, the word *red* may be printed with green ink. On this part of the test the subject is required to name the colour of the ink and disregard the printed name. Individuals who are not distracted by the printed name are considered to be flexible.

Santostefano's (1978) development of instruments that are appropriate for use with children represents a major research effort in the area of cognitive controls. For example, to measure constricted–flexible control, Santostefano uses the Fruit–Distraction Test, which was patterned after the Stroop Test. In this test, line-drawings of vegetables (for example, lettuce) are appropriately and inappropriately coloured (for example, green and red). The logic of the test is largely unchanged from that of the Stroop Test.

Santostefano's interest in the assessment of the patterning of cognitive controls in children led him to develop a Cognitive Control Battery, which measures the child's level of maturity on each of the five cognitive control dimensions with which Santostefano worked. As such, Santostefano's work represents the only attempt to remain faithful to that aspect of cognitive control theory that holds that an individual's cognitive style is represented by a pattern of specific cognitive controls. For example, Santostefano (1978) reported that different cognitive controls correlate 'meaningfully and predictably' with different dependent variables in various environments for different populations. He therefore urges an approach in which a number of cognitive controls are considered simultaneously.

Reflection–impulsivity

The Matching Familiar Figures (MFF) Test is used to measure reflection–impulsivity (Kagan et al., 1964). The test consists of twelve items. For each item the subject is presented with a standard figure and six comparison figures, only one of which is an exact match to the standard. For example, one of the items presents a sketch of a tree with one branch jutting out to the right. Five of the comparison figures differ in some degree. In two of the figures the isolated branch is at the wrong angle. In a third picture the branch points to the left. In a fourth picture the trunk is curved rather than straight. In the fifth non-matching picture the outline of the top of the tree is incorrectly drawn. The subject's task is to indicate which of the six comparison figures exactly matches the standard. Subjects who respond rapidly and inaccurately are termed impulsive; those who respond slowly and accurately are termed reflective. In most research, subjects are categorized as impulsive if they are above the median of the group of subjects in the study on speed of responding and below the median with regard to accuracy (cf., Messer, 1976).

This procedure for identifying reflective and impulsive subjects has been criticized by a number of investigators (e.g. Block et al., 1974). One problem is that speed and accuracy are confounded in the definition of reflection–impulsivity. Since response speed is moderately correlated with response inaccuracy, the two dimensions are not independent. The basic model does not consider the subject who responds rapidly and accurately, nor the subject who responds slowly and inaccurately. In an attempt to deal with this problem, some investigators use all four types (slow-accurate, slow-inaccurate, fast-accurate, fast-inaccurate), and some use the two dimensions separately, sometimes with interesting results (cf., Messer, 1976). As noted in the previous chapter, in attempts to train individuals to be less impulsive, there is generally more success in reducing the response speed than in improving response accuracy.

The Matching Familiar Figures Test is appropriate for use with children above six years of age. There have been several attempts to develop versions that are suitable for younger children, as well as for adults. The Kansas Reflection–Impulsivity Scale for Preschoolers (Wright, 1973) is designed for 3-6 year olds. Another version for young children involves the use of only three variants (Banta, 1970).

Summary

As one might expect, approaches to the measurement of cognitive style are as diverse as the underlying theories. It may well be that each approach to measurement is capturing a different aspect of the complex construct of cognitive style. Possibly combining different cognitive style measures in studies attempting to predict behaviour would yield better predictive accuracy than when only one measure is used.

Part V
Personal constructs

10 Personal construct psychology

Fay Fransella

In 1955, George Kelly launched an alternative psychology on the world. For him neither Freudian theory on the one hand nor behaviourist theories on the other provided an adequate framework within which to attempt to come to an understanding of that most complex of living organisms – the human being.

His is not so much a theory of personality as a total psychology. Kelly sought to incorporate within the same theoretical framework those areas in psychology usually coming under separate chapter headings. In the theory of personal constructs the person is not segmented into 'learning', 'cognition', 'motivation', 'emotion' or 'psychophysiology'. It is in this sense that the theory provides a total psychology about the total person.

The model of the scientist

Kelly suggests we might profitably use the 'as if' philosophy of Vaihinger (1924). 'Suppose we regard the floor as if it were hard', he says.

> If I make such a statement I immediately find myself in an interesting position. The statement leaves both the speaker and

the listener, not with a conclusion on their hands, but in a posture
of expectancy – suppose we do regard the floor as if it were hard,
what then? A verb employed in the invitational mood, assuming
our language had such a mood, would have the effect of orient-
ating one to the future, not merely to the present or to the past. It
would set the stage for prediction of what is to ensue. It suggests
that the floor is open to a variety of interpretations or constructions. It invites the listener to cope with his circumstances – in this
case, the floor – in new ways. But more than this, it suggests that
the view of the floor as something hard is one that is not imposed
upon us from without, nor is it isolated from external evidence, as
a phenomenological proposition would be, but is one that can be
pursued, tested, abandoned, or reconsidered at a later time.
(Kelly, 1969, p.149)

So, instead of looking at the person 'as if' he or she were a
'psychodynamic' product or a 'Skinnerian' product, Kelly suggests
we might look at ourselves 'as if' we were all scientists and products of
our own creation. Scientists in the sense that we can be seen as
placing our own interpretations (theories) upon the world of events
confronting us and, from these personal theories, deriving hypotheses
and making predictions about future events. From this point of view,
behaviour becomes the independent variable – *it is the experiment*.
The resulting perceived validation or invalidation of our predictions
determines the nature of our subsequent behavioural experiments.

For Kelly human behaviour, like science, is an evolutionary
process and he places it in historical perspective thus:

Psychology, emerging in the late Nineteenth and Twentieth
Centuries, sought to identify itself with a science it had no part in
creating. It seemed enough that the science of the day was
wonderful and good. In the world that scientists envisioned nature
was a relatively stable entity. Evolution had run its course. At last
the outcome of the long slow process could be studied to see what
nature's assembled menagerie had turned out to be.

But it is increasingly clear that human behaviour has not settled
into orbit. It is, indeed, the one part of nature that now is most in
transition – perhaps transforming itself at a pace no other aspect
of nature has ever matched. Man, inquisitive chap, is irrepressibly
engaging in new enterprises, just as psychologists themselves seek
to do, and the formulas we derive from binding events to his

subsequent actions keep losing touch with the novel human engagements of our day. Man is not content to cope with his circumstances forever in the same way. At an ever-increasing tempo he casts his anticipation in fresh varieties of searching questions and, to pose them, the behaviour that psychologists want so much to explain is redeployed in an ever-varying encounter with circumstances. (Kelly, 1969a, p.23)

Claxton's (1979) comparison between psychology and twentieth century physics is argued along similar lines. Physics has found that it is impossible to study 'an event' or 'matter' since all is intimately bound up with the environment in which it exists. The implications of such an altered view of science are taken up again in Kelly's philosophy.

The philosophy of constructive alternativism

Both the model of the person as a scientist and the Fundamental Postulate (elaborated by eleven corollaries) of the theory stem from a stated philosophical position. This argues that although there is a real world of events, no one organism has the privilege of 'knowing' it; all we are able to do is place our personal constructions upon it. The better able we are to 'fit' our constructions to the events swirling around about and within us, the more control we have over our personal world.

> *We assume that all of our present interpretations of the universe are subject to revision or replacement* ... we take the stand that there are always alternative constructions available to choose among in dealing with the world. No one needs to paint himself into a corner; no one needs to be completely hemmed in by circumstances; no one needs to be the victim of his biography. (Kelly, 1955, p.15)

A constructive alternative approach to scientific inquiry means that a research finding in line with the hypothesis merely indicates that one's ideas are working well at the moment; but the researcher knows that one day there will be a hypothesis that will account for the data in some way that will be an improvement on the existing one. The classic view of science, which Kelly called *accumulative fragmentalism*, saw the world as knowable and each research finding as a fragment of knowledge or truth in the jigsaw puzzle of nature that would one day be completed. The researchers within this framework only question that fragment of truth if future evidence suggests they are wrong; and to avoid this they are careful to replicate their experiments.

It is the implications that construct theory has for the nature of the science of psychology that Tyler (1978) sees as:

> an insight the importance of which can hardly be over-emphasized. If the subject matter of psychology is not a finite collection of behaving objects but rather the limitless domain of human possibilities from which generation after generation of individuals draws without depleting the resources, then our science cannot be content with models borrowed from physics and chemistry. We must create new models, new rules for playing the game of scientific inquiry, new guidelines for our research. George Kelly realized this. (Tyler, 1978, p.130)

In Chapter 1 Rychlak pointed out that philosophy is basically the study of assumptions made by human beings. In this general sense Kelly's philosophy is concerned with some general assumptions about our psychological nature, and his theory focuses on the nature of the philosophical outlooks of individual persons.

> We have taken the basic view that whatever is characteristic of thought is descriptive of the thinker; that the essentials of scientific curiosity must underlie human curiosity in general. If we examine a person's philosophy closely, we find ourselves staring at the person himself. If we reach an understanding of how a person behaves, we discover it in the manner in which he represents his circumstances to himself. (Kelly, 1955, p.16)

This exemplifies the reflexive nature of personal construct theory. It as much accounts for the ways in which Kelly, as a person, construes people as it suggests how we attempt to understand our own personal worlds. Kelly, the theorist, started his academic life by studying physics and mathematics and trained as an engineer before coming into any meaningful contact with psychology. It is therefore small surprise that he takes 'the scientist' as his psychological model of the person.

The basic theory

Anticipation and motivation

The Fundamental Postulate states that *a person's processes are psycho-*

logically channelized by the ways in which he anticipates events.

The theory is thus primarily focused on individuals (although another corollary states how it can be applied to more than one person); it is about psychological, nor neurological or physiological, processes; and it is forward-looking – it is about a person's anticipations.

If people have heard only one thing about Kelly it is most often that 'he has done away with motivation'. Indeed he did. He argued that there was no need to copy the old notion from physics and see all matter (including the living organism) as inert and so feel the need to develop a concept of some energy system to account for why we move. He argued that all living matter can be seen as constantly on the move, in which case concepts of drives or needs or psychic energies are not needed (Kelly, 1962).

He finds two other reasons for rejecting the concept of motivation. The first is that our understanding of someone is not increased when we use our own interpretations of their behaviour and attribute a 'motive' to him or her. We may describe someone as 'lazy' and yet, when we observe what they are actually doing, we find they are being 'active'; what is happening is that they are not doing what *we* think they *ought* to be doing.

> Life itself could be defined as a form of process or movement. Thus, in designating man as our object of psychological inquiry, we would be taking it for granted that movement was an essential property of his being, not something that had to be accounted for separately. We would be talking about a form of movement – man – not something that had to be motivated ...
>
> How else can we characterize this stand with respect to motivation? Perhaps this will help: motivational theories can be divided into two types, push theories and pull theories. Under push theories we find such terms as drive, motive, or even stimulus. Pull theories use such constructs as purpose, value, or need. In terms of a well-known metaphor, these are the pitch fork theories on the one hand and the carrot theories on the other. But our theory is neither of these. Since we prefer to look at the nature of the animal himself, ours is probably best called a jackass theory.
> (Kelly, 1969b, pp.80-1)

Yet the personal scientist is not devoid of direction. To understand it we simply have to find out what the jackass thinks he is up to rather than impose our own interpretations upon him. As scientists we seek to predict and hence gain control over as much of our environment as we can, for our psychological processes are indeed channelized by the ways in which we anticipate events. As he defines 'anticipates' he says:

> Here is where we build into our theory its predictive and motivational features. Like the prototype of the scientist that he is, man seeks prediction. His structured network of pathways leads towards the future so that he may anticipate it. This is the function it serves. Anticipation is both the push and the pull of the psychology of personal constructs. (Kelly, 1955, p.49)

The nature of the construct

We anticipate events *by construing their replications*. The Construction Corollary is the first of eleven that elaborate the Fundamental Postulate. By noting that some events are similar to each other in certain ways and thereby different from others, we are able to anticipate future events. By noting that people who call themselves psychologists are similar in some respects and yet different from those who call themselves physiologists or geneticists, we are able to make certain predictions about the two groups of people. Prediction is the essential feature of a construct. We do not predict that all psychologists are totally alike, but merely that they are alike in certain abstracted ways, and it is in these ways that they differ from physiologists and geneticists. Of course, these construed similarities are not an objective part of each psychologist, but merely each person's subjective personal abstractions. Others may have abstracted other similarities that are equally meaningful to them. But the more we as psychologists share these abstractions, the better able we will be to communicate with each other, as a group.

Two corollaries deal with the range of applicability (*a construct is convenient for the anticipation of a finite range of events only*) and the dichotomous nature of constructs (*a person's construction system is composed of a finite number of dichotomous constructs*).

The Range Corollary means that few, if any, constructs refer to all events confronting us. The construct *good–bad* has a very wide range of convenience, yet most people will be able to think of some events, objects, people, that are neither good nor bad. Range of convenience problems were particularly important in the disenchantment with the semantic differential (Osgood et al., 1957). Not all concepts could be rated on all the bi-polar scales, as so nicely summed up in Brown's (1958) review of Osgood's work entitled 'Is a boulder sweet or sour?'

Without two poles, as stated in the Dichotomy Corollary, the construct would have no meaning. If all events were similar, there would only be a world of chaotic undifferentiated homogeneity leaving 'the person engulfed in a sea with no landmarks to relieve the monotony'; whereas if all were different the world would be chaotic heterogeneity, confronting the person 'with an interminable series of kaleidoscopic changes in which no other would ever appear familiar'.

It is often the opposite pole of the construct that gives one insight into what another is talking about. For instance, three people may be talking about *friends*; for one this means people who are not *enemies*, for another not *strangers* and for the third not *acquaintances*. If this were the case, one might expect considerable conversational confusion to arise at some point in time. Similarity of verbal label does not necessarily imply similarity of construct.

Levels of cognitive awareness

But not all construct discriminations have any verbal labels attached to them at all. It is here that construct theory links with Freud's notion of the unconscious. But instead of using a *conscious* versus *unconscious* dichotomy, Kelly prefers to talk of differing levels of cognitive awareness.

> A person is not necessarily articulate about the constructions he places upon his world. Some of his constructions are not symbolized by words; he can express them only in pantomime. Even the elements which are construed may have no verbal handles by which they can be manipulated and the person finds himself responding to them with speechless impulse. Thus, in studying the psychology of man-the-philosopher, we must take into account his subverbal patterns of representation and construction. (Kelly, 1955, p.16)

There is a very fundamental difference between Freud's 'unconscious' and Kelly's 'pre-verbal construing'. For Freud, there is psychic *energy* attached to the ideas, memories and so forth, that have been repressed and 'reside' in the unconscious (see Chapter 2). Not so for Kelly. The pre-verbal construct is only a discrimination that is taken out of the person's repertoire of constructs when it seems useful for ordering events in the present. For example, a child has construed that all *mothers* are *soft and cuddly* whereas *non-mothers* are not. This non-verbal way of discriminating between the women with whom he comes in contact, is related to how he behaves; he runs up to and cuddles the *mothers* and holds back from the others. In the years that follow he never needs to elaborate and verbalize this construct, it remains with him in his original form. In adult life he 'pulls it out' of his repertoire whenever *cuddly* women confront him. Some people might attribute to him the motive of seeking 'mother figures'. But in his terms he is seeking all the childhood security, feelings of warmth and satiation that accompanied the original discrimination.

But pre-verbal construing is not the only way of translating the term 'unconscious'. One pole of a construct may be *submerged*. As examples of this Kelly cites such statements as 'Everyone has always been good to me.' There is no stated opposite pole, but it is possible to look for one. Perhaps the person is emphasizing *me* – 'Other people are mistreated but not me'; 'Everyone has always been good to me BUT I have not always been good to others'; or he may be saying 'See what a good person I am, I am the kind of person who goes around saying that others are always good to him,' with its implied contrast 'There are some people not a million miles from here who go around saying that people are mean to them'; or there could be an emphasis on the *has* – 'Everyone *has* always been good to me' contrasted with 'but I expect them to treat me badly at any time now'. A therapist suspecting this construction had better take care.

The other aspect of low level cognitive awareness is *suspension*. In order for an experience to be remembered or perceived clearly it must be supported within a system of constructs. When psychological movement occurs, some of the structure may be rejected because at that time it is incompatible with the overall system – it has been *suspended*.

The construct system

The Organization and Fragmentation Corollaries elaborate the nature of the construct system. The Organization Corollary states that: *each person characteristically evolves, for his convenience in anticipating events, a construction system embracing ordinal relationships between constructs.* It is this Corollary that has been most elaborated by research and has proved useful in generating hypotheses about psychological disorders (see Chapter 12).

In 1965 Hinkle described his theory of implications, so producing the first major elaboration of construct theory. He argued that a construct has meaning only in terms of that which it implies and that by which it is implied. To say someone is *kind* is meaningless, unless one has an idea about the nature of that kindness – other attributes are implied by, and certain others imply, being *kind*.

Since the Organization Corollary suggests that constructs are related in a hierarchical fashion, then *kind* may be a superordinate construct in relation to *patting the dog* versus *kicking the dog*, and subordinate to *good* versus *bad*. In order to elicit superordinate constructs, Hinkle developed the procedure of 'laddering'. For this, the person is asked to indicate the preferred pole of each construct previously elicited from him (see Chapter 11 for details). They are then asked to give a reason for their choice. So the questioning might run: 'Why would you prefer to be the sort of person who *pats dogs* rather than *kicks them?* What are the advantages, for you, in being a patter rather than a kicker?' The person may say that they believe one should be *kind to dumb animals* as opposed to being *cruel to them*. This belief is then treated as another construct and the same questioning repeated. This time the person may say that being kind to dumb animals as opposed to being cruel to them is important since one should be *kind to all living creatures*. 'Why is it important to be kind to all living creatures?' *Because all are made in God's image.*

This procedure of laddering theoretically leads the person successively to higher levels of abstraction. In practice, as in theory, most subordinate constructs ladder into a very few superordinate ones. From the Organization Corollary Hinkle argued that the more superordinate the construct the greater would be the number of its implicative linkages and so the more it would resist change. To test this first hypothesis he developed the implications grid and to test the latter the resistance-to-change grid (see Chapter 11 for details). The hypotheses were supported ($p < .001$). This relationship between construct superordinacy and number of implications has been cross-validated by several other studies (e.g. Fransella, 1972; Button and Fransella, 1980). A more detailed description of Hinkle's work can be found in Bannister and Mair (1968).

The other Corollary relating to the construct system is to do with fragmentation: *a person may successively employ a variety of construction subsystems which are inferentially incompatible with each other.* We do not have to give up an old idea before considering a new one. It is possible for someone who is a stutterer, an arsonist or an alcoholic to acknowledge that they fall into that category, but to deny that they are 'like' those other people in the group. It has been suggested (Fransella, 1977) that we are capable of having a subsystem of constructs (a stereotype) to do with a group of people, and also to acknowledge that we are, for instance, toe-nail nibblers, armpit sniffers or 'crotch-eyeballers', and yet not see ourselves as having all those other features characteristic of those groups – we, each one of us, see ourselves as unique. We are able to do this by having a superordinate construction that subsumes the undesirable behaviour – perhaps something along the lines that 'I do that thing, but that is just a personal hang-up, otherwise I am all right.'

Personal and interpersonal construing

As the theory's name suggests, this is a theory pre-eminently about the individual person and *persons differ from each other in their construction of* events. This Individuality Corollary thus forms the basis for the study of individual differences; it is the different ways in which we place our constructions upon reality that makes each one of us psychologically a unique human being. Even though the events which confront us are similar, no two people can play exactly the same role in relation to that event. Each will be experiencing the other as part of the external environment; each will have a different central figure – the individual themselves. And finally, as Kelly says, 'the chances are that, in the course of events, each will get caught up in a different stream and hence be confronted with different navigational problems.'

However, this does not mean that commonality of construing cannot, and does not, take place; for the Commonality Corollary states that: *to the extent that one person employs a construction of experience which is similar to that employed by another, his psychological processes are similar to those of the other person.* Thus, two people can have what seems to the outsider to be almost identical experiences, and yet behave very differently, because they construe the events differently. Or two people can have had very different experiences of life and yet behave similarly in a specific situation, because they are employing similar constructions concerning those events.

Just as Individuality provides a basis for the study of individual differences, so Commonality enables the researcher to study differences within and between cultures. Lemon (1975), for instance, studied the relationship between language development and conceptualization in bilingual Tanzanian children. Karst and Groutt (1977) studied a mystical religious community taking up the theme discussed by Kelly in 1930, that our personal construing is negotiated with those with whom we now live and is influenced by those who 'have bequeathed us our language, our customs and the consequences of their lives' (Bannister and Fransella, 1980).

Commonality alone is not enough for interpersonal understanding, and for the process of social interaction. For this we have to attempt to subsume another's construct system. The Sociality Corollary states that: *to the extent that one person construes the construction processes of another, he may play a role in a social process involving the other person.* This does not mean that we have to agree with another's views, we may disagree or misunderstand, but the act of trying to understand how another sees things defines a role relationship and is linked with one's behaviour. Your understanding of a listener's reactions to a story you are telling will, to a large extent, make you embellish it, curtail it, or simply play it as it comes. Kelly regarded this social aspect of his theory as of considerable importance.

> Here we have a take-off point for a social psychology. By attempting to place at the forefront of psychology the understanding of personal constructs, and by recognizing, as a corollary of our Fundamental Postulate, the subsuming of other people's construing efforts as the basis for social interaction, we have said that social psychology must be a psychology of interpersonal understanding, not merely a psychology of common understandings. (Kelly, 1955, p.95)

Relating socially to psychological research, Kelly says 'the psychologist can better understand his subjects if he inquires into the way in which they construe their stimuli than if he always takes his own construction of the stimuli for granted.' If the psychologist were always to focus on the subjects' constructions of events (play a role in relation to them), they would have to take into account the social nature of the enterprise for, as Mair (1970 comments 'psychologists are human too.' Salmon (1978) likewise points out the implications of sociality for the research student and supervisor. She argues that research should involve a personal commitment to the research topic, and this should be explored with the student (as subject).

> If the subject is truly a subject, then the research is about *his* questions, and he needs to be decisively involved in defining what situations, what outcomes, what criteria are critical, for him, to those questions. (Salmon, 1978, p.42)

An increasing amount of research has stemmed from the Commonality and Sociality Corollaries, particularly the latter. The most up-to-date account to be found is Stringer and Bannister (1979) in which they focus on Sociality and Individuality. And, of course, without Sociality there could be no psychotherapy.

Psychological change

There are three corollaries specifically to do with change. The *Experience Corollary* states that: a person's construction system varies as he successively construes the replications of events. The hypotheses we have about present events are put to the test and their outcomes construed. Simply being in a situation is not the same as having experience. Kelly uses the example of a teacher who gives the same lecture each year, ignoring the change in student needs, new research data and changing teaching methods, as contrasted with the teacher who modifies the lecture each year. The first teacher can be said to have had one year's experience repeated ten times and the other ten years' teaching experience.

The assumption built into the Experience Corollary makes it synonymous with learning.

> The burden of our assumption is that learning is not a special class of psychological processes; it is synonymous with any and all psychological processes. It is not something that happens to a person on occasion; it is what makes him a person in the first place.
>
> The net effect of incorporating learning into the assumptive structure of a psychological theory is to remove the whole topic from the realm of subsequent discourse. Some readers may be dismayed at this turn of events. Psychology now has a considerable investment of research effort in the topic ... If it is any comfort to do so, one may say that learning has been given a preeminent position in the psychology of personal constructs, even though it

has been taken out of circulation as a special topic. (Kelly, 1955, p.75-6)

So, just as with behaviour and motivation, Kelly built learning into his psychology of personal constructs. For his expressed aim was to describe a psychological approach to the understanding of the person that was sufficiently comprehensive not to require the use of constructs from other theoretical systems.

The *Modulation Corollary* discusses how the variation that occurs with experience takes place within the construct system. *It is limited by the permeability of the constructs within whose range of convenience the variants lie.* Permeability is a construct used to describe the relative ease with which a construct can incorporate new elements (events). Concrete constructs, such as *cricket ball*, are relatively impermeable, whereas *kind* may more easily allow new elements to be included within its range of convenience. The more impermeable the construct, the less likelihood there is to be learning or change. McGaughran and Moran (1956) suggested that permeability might be a more useful dimension to use in relation to conceptualization that the classic abstract – concrete, and discuss its application to the understanding of conceptualization in the schizophrenic person.

The *Choice Corollary* states that: *a person chooses for himself that alternative in a dichotomized construct through which he anticipates the greater possibility for extension and definition of his system.* Here motivation is built in. We each aim to make our world more predictable and thus more personally meaningful. Our choice does not always seem logical to the outsider. Why should a stutterer go on stuttering even though he desperately wants to be fluent? It is argued (Fransella, 1972) that this way of behaving is more meaningful to him – it is his personal way of life and always has been. He 'chooses' it because it offers greater possibilities for extension and definition of his construct system than does being fluent. To change to fluency would plunge him into a relatively meaningless world – and few are able to take that plunge. He therefore has to learn about being a fluent person and then, and only then, can he start to make the change. In this same way one can argue that obesity has meaning for the obese, smoking for the smoker and depression for the depressed.

McWilliams (1980) has pointed out a possible connection between the Choice Corollary and type of scientific approach (see p.150); the accumulative fragmentalist is one who focuses on definition of the construct system and the constructive alternativist on extension. The person-as-scientist can also be viewed as adopting one or other approach to life (Fransella, 1980) and, following McWilliams' line of thought, some can be seen as primarily 'self-definers' and other as 'self-extenders'. A stutterer, for example, may usefully be viewed as increasingly defining a construct subsystem to do with being a stutterer. If so, then a treatment aim becomes one of helping a person to stop being an accumulative fragmentalist and to become a constructive alternativist.

Constructs and their elements

The Modulation Corollary describes a mechanism whereby new elements are incorporated into the construct system, while other constructs deal with how constructs control their elements. A *preemptive* construct is one which says 'anything which is a ball can be nothing but a ball'. A person who uses a number of constructs preemptively may find decision-making easy but social relationships a problem; he relates to people on the basis that 'you are a negro and nothing but a negro,' 'he is a psychologist and nothing but that,' 'she is a singer and nothing but a singer' whilst seeing himself as a person who knows his own mind, plays football well, loves his mother and wonders why other people cannot be as easy to get on with as he is.

A *constellatory* construct allows its elements to belong to other categories or constructs, but fixes their membership. 'A thing that is called a ball must be something that is round, and will bounce.' Stereotyped or prejudiced thinking fits into this category. 'If a person is an X, they must be deceitful, unclean, work-shy and musical.'

A *propositional* construct leaves its elements free to be construed in other ways. 'Any roundish mass may be considered, amongst other things, as a ball.' This is the other end of a continuum from the preemptive and the constellatory construct. While propositional thinking may be desirable in many circumstances, as opposed to the preemptive, category type of thinking or the dogmatic thinking of constellatoriness, a person would have difficulty in making their way in the world on a diet of propositionality alone.

> Preemptive thinking, in a moment of decision, is essential if one is to take an active part in his universe. But preemptive thinking which never resolves itself into propositional thinking condemns

the person to a state of intellectual rigor mortis. He may be called a 'man of action', but his actions will always follow well-worn ruts. (Kelly, 1955, p.156)

Constructs in transition

Cycles of construction

Kelly describes two specific sequences of construction that deal with originality and decision-making – the cycles of Creativity and C–P–C (circumspection–preemption–control) respectively. *The Creativity Cycle is one which starts with loosened construction and terminates with tightened and validated construction.* Loose constructions lead to varying predictions but retain their identity. Extremes of loose construing (where constructs may even have lost their identity and only the verbal label is retained) may be found in the person diagnosed as a thought-disordered schizophrenic and in normal dreaming. In loose construing a person mumbles, ideas shift around, are left half said, communication confusion is caused. It is this type of thinking that is the start of the Creativity Cycle. In the course of this loose speculation, the person may suddenly glimpse the possibility of a new construction, or the juxtaposition of two constructs never contemplated before. The art is to 'capture' this gem, tighten the construing so that it can be looked at critically and, ultimately, to give it a suitable verbal symbol – for 'an idea is likely to take shape before a suitable symbol is chosen to represent it – it is born before it is named' (Kelly, 1955, p.1051).

Such creative activity is an essential part of the scientific enterprise, whether one is a professional scientist or merely a human being acting 'as if' they were one.

The C–P–C Cycle is to do with making decisions; it involves *in succession circumspection, preemption and control, and leads to a choice precipitating the person into a particular situation.* The person first looks at the possibilities available to them and then preempts or selects the one to be acted upon and hence bring the events under control. The decision is made. If a person only takes a very short amount of time during the circumspection phase of the cycle, they are said to be behaving *impulsively.*

Emotion

More controversy has surrounded Kelly's dealings with the concept of emotion than almost anything else. For many, personal construct theory is a 'cognitive' theory. Yet Kelly was very explicit about the place of emotion within his framework and about the limitations of dualistic thinking.

> The classic distinction that separates these two constructs (emotion, cognition) has, in the manner of most classic distinctions that once were useful, become a barrier to sensitive psychological inquiry. When one so divides the experience of man it becomes difficult to make the most of the holistic aspirations that may infuse the science of psychology with new life. (Kelly, 1969c, p.140)

As with motivation, behaviour and learning, Kelly sought to bring the experience we call emotion within the single theoretical framework of the psychology of personal constructs. He did this by relating certain emotions to the awareness of the construct system in transition.

Fear is the awareness of an imminent incidental change in one's core structures. The emphasis here is on the 'core structures'; these are to do with our central notions of the self, 'they govern our maintenance processes.' We are confronted with specific events – the car coming out of a side road, the speed of our own car, the apparent inevitability of a crash. The change is 'incidental' in that it only subsumes a small and immediate range of events.

Threat, on the other hand, *is the awareness of imminent comprehensive change in one's core structures.* Here the possible change is substantial; it looks as if it will have repercussions throughout the system. Psychologists may be threatened if they have spent a considerable part of their life working within one theoretical framework, and they then come across another that, if accepted, would make all their past work seem worthless. The client in psychotherapy may likewise be threatened if the therapy is proving too successful – he perceives that, if he continues the way he is at present he will soon have changed radically and he has not worked out exactly what that would mean – so he relapses or resists further change for the time being.

Landfield's exemplification hypothesis (1954) suggests that we may find a person threatening if they exhibit some behaviour that we have discarded, but to which we could still all too easily revert. Landfield's expectancy hypothesis states that a person may also be perceived as threatening if they seem to expect us to behave in ways that we have left behind.

Anxiety provides a basis for change and is *the recognition that the events with which one is confronted lie mostly outside the range of convenience of one's construct system.* Anxiety is normal and commonly present, since any attempt to extend the range of convenience of a part of a construct system must open it up to unconstruable events. Kelly points out that

> from the standpoint of the psychology of personal constructs, anxiety, *per se*, is not to be classified as either good or bad. It represents the awareness that one's construction system does not apply to the events at hand. It is, therefore, a precondition for making revisions. (Kelly, 1955, p.498)

Guilt is the awareness of dislodgement of the self from one's core role structure. The teacher who gives a sarcastic reply to a student's question may experience guilt if he construes himself as the kind of teacher who is sensitive to students' needs. A mother who slaps her child in a moment of anger experiences guilt since this is not how a good mother should behave.

The constructs of aggression and hostility relate to actions. *Aggression is the active elaboration of one's perceptual field.* This may, but need not, be synonymous with the type of behaviour we normally call aggression. The youthful vandal may be seen as actively testing out some hypothesis to do with the stupidity of society or the impotence of the police. On the other hand, the business executive can also be seen as being aggressive if he is actively elaborating notions concerning the limits of his own competence.

Hostility is defined as behaviour designed to retain the status quo. It is the *continued effort to extort validational evidence in favour of a type of social prediction which has already been recognized as a failure.* The parent of a university student may continue to point to childish misdemeanours such as muddy shoes, lateness at meals, hair out of place, until such time as the student rebels and answers back. The parent now turns round and says it was to have been hoped that he had grown out of his childish temper tantrums. The parent has 'cooked the books', has extorted evidence to validate a way of construing her son that is comfortable for her. Perhaps to acknowledge to herself that she has a grown-up son threatens her construing of herself as an attractive woman.

McCoy (1977) has considerably elaborated Kelly's coverage of types of emotion to include such things as happiness, love and shame (see also Bannister, 1977).

The process of reconstruction

Psychotherapy involves the application of the theoretical constructs of the psychology of personal constructs by one individual in an attempt to bring about reconstruction in another. Kelly described one particular procedure for aiding reconstruction which he called *fixed role therapy*. In this the client is asked to enact a person described in a sketch which has been written for him or her by the therapist. The sketch is not totally different from the one he or she has already written, but differs sufficiently to give the person glimpses of what the effects may be when events are approached from a different stance. However, the personal construct therapist is by no means limited to this. Where personal construct therapy differs from most other forms is in the level of abstraction at which its theoretical framework is pitched. With constructs described at such a high level of abstraction, methods characteristic of other frameworks become techniques to be used for specific purposes. For instance, if it is thought desirable to help a client loosen his construing, free association (borrowed from psychoanalysis) can be used or 'dream-work' or guided phantasy; if tightening is the aim, the Ellis' (1962) rational emotive approach may be used. Gestalt methods (Perls et al., 1965) aid those who need to work within a clear structure; and behaviour modification is useful with the less articulate and so on. But all, without exception, are used because professional diagnostic constructs derived from the psychology of personal constructs lead one to think a particular method is best for a particular client at a particular stage in therapy. There is no eclecticism here.

The framework also leads one to have different aims in research. It leads one to look for parameters of psychological change and to relate these to therapeutic procedures that will, or are likely to, bring about the desired results. The researcher seeks to relate therapeutic procedures to aspects of construing at different stages in therapy, and not to try and discover whether therapy A is better than therapy B.

A theory's life expectancy

Apart from having an appropriate focus and range of convenience, for Kelly, a good psychological theory should be stated 'in terms of abstractions which can be traced through most of the phenomena with which psychology must deal'. But, perhaps most important of all, and stemming from the philosophy of constructive alternativism, he believed that a theory should ultimately be expendable.

> Since a theory is an ad interim construction system which is designed to give an optimal anticipation of events, its life is limited by its period of usefulness. If this theory proves to be fertile in providing us with testable hypotheses and in suggesting new approaches to the problems psychologists face, it will have cleared its first hurdle. If, subsequently, it occurs that a considerable proportion of the hypotheses prove to be true, and many of the new approaches provide desired control over psychological events, the theory will have reached maturity. When its place is eventually taken by a more comprehensive, a more explicit, a more fertile and more useful theory, it will be time to relegate it to history. (Kelly, 1955, pp.102-3)

Suggested further reading

Bannister, D. (ed.) (1977) *New Perspectives in Personal Construct Theory*. London: Academic Press.

Bannister, D. and Fransella, F. (1980) *Inquiring Man* (2nd ed). London: Penguin Books.

Fransella, F. (1980) Man-as-Scientist. A. J. Chapman and D. Jones (eds) in *Models of Man*. London: The British Psychological Society.

Maher, B. (ed.) (1979) *Clinical Psychology and Personality: the Selected Papers of George Kelly*. New York: Krieger.

11 Repertory grid technique

Fay Fransella

Kelly offered two suggestions for eliciting constructs from someone with a view to understanding that person. The better known of these is called *repertory grid technique*, and the lesser known as *self-characterization*. Because of the increasing interest shown in grid technique, it is this that will be discussed in this chapter, but a word on the self-characterization is in order.

The self-characterization

Kelly said that his first principle in clinical work was 'if you do not know what is wrong with a person, ask him, he may tell you.' The self-characterization is an invitation to a person to 'tell' one what is personally meaningful. The instructions were worked out with great care so as to give the person maximum room for manoeuvre and yet to minimize threat. The person is asked to write a character sketch of themselves along the following lines:

> I want you to write a character sketch of (for example) Harry Brown, just as if he were the principal character in a play. Write it as it might be written by a friend who knew him very *intimately* and very *sympathetically*, perhaps better than anyone ever really could

know him. Be sure to write it in the third person. For example, start out by saying, 'Harry Brown is ...'.

In the analysis one is not interested in the truth or falsehood of the statements, nor in deriving scores of their relative negative and positive values; rather one hopes to gain some insight into how one person construes a personal world. Some details of self-characterizations can be found in Kelly (1955, vol.I), Bannister and Fransella (1980) and Fransella (1980a).

Repertory grid technique

Forms of grid

The original grid.   Kelly's second method for inviting a person to divulge some of their personal constructs was the Rep Test. This was aimed at helping the client give the interviewer some of the role constructs they apply to the people with whom they interact. For this purpose Kelly suggested that twenty-four such role titles might provide a representative sample of people with whom the subject relates. These include members of the immediately family, such as father and mother; and non-family members such as boy or girl friends, an employer who is hard to get along with, someone hard to understand, the most successful person the subject knows and so forth. In the Rep Test the person is presented with three of the role titles and asked to say in what important way two are alike but different from the third. Kelly gives eight different ways in which these triads of role titles can be compiled (see Kelly, 1955, pp.224-9 or Bannister and Fransella, 1980), but all focus on helping the person provide some of the personal constructs used in dealings with others.

From the constructs elicited, Kelly hoped the clinician might be able to derive hypotheses to aid in psychotherapy. However, being trained as a mathematician, he was not content to let matters rest there. In the chapter following that on the Rep Test he proposed a method for 'dealing with the way constructs and figures are interwoven to give substance to the fabric of society'. This, the Grid Form of the Role Construct Repertory Test was for 'looking beyond words'. That original repertory grid and all its subsequent variations consists of a matrix which, in most cases, has role titles, or other types of *element*, describing each column and bi-polar constructs describing each end of the rows. The data in the grid indicates whether, for instance, the person who nominated a column element as being *successful* also nominates the same element as *not believing in God*.

From such a matrix of ticks and blanks, Kelly devised his own method of non-parametric factor analysis which he describes in detail in the 1955 volume and later as follows:

> Factor analysis can be regarded as a way of displaying information in an economical way. As we have suggested before, this is the answer to a minimax problem – how to reduce a maximum of information to a minimum of terms. It is the baffling complexity of psychological processes that makes psychologists seek to encompass a maximum of information, and it is the limited ability of the human mind to orient itself in hyperspace that makes them try to keep the number of factors at a minimum.
>
> But there is another problem to. Man has difficulty construing along unfamiliar lines, even when they are drawn with mathematical simplicity. His notions are held fast in a network of personal constructs and any ideas or feelings that have not yet found their place in that network are likely to remain exasperatingly elusive. Science, therefore, not only has the task of coming to simple terms with events, but it also has the psychological task of achieving some accommodation between what man believes and what, indeed, confronts him. (Kelly, 1969d, pp.325-6)

One of the problems with such tick/blank data is that it is possible to get a lopsided distribution. If, out of twenty elements, two are described as *undesirable aliens* and two others as *Church of England*, the resulting correlation between the two rows will be high because of the preponderance of blank cells. It is perhaps unlikely that the person was actually saying that Church of England adherents were undesirable aliens – at least one might like further evidence before accepting that as a valid statement of the person's beliefs.

The rank order grid.   In an attempt to deal with this problem of lopsidedness, Bannister (1959) suggested that all elements should be divided equally between the two construct poles (split-half method). However, this proved to be a rather restrictive procedure and he introduced the rank order method. Here the person is asked to rank a set of elements in terms of each construct – from, say, the person who is most to the person who is least *successful*. The rank order grid has been widely used, particularly in Europe, but also has its limitations. Many find it difficult to discriminate between elements at the middle ranks. In all probability this does not distort the results, but will certainly contribute to error. One reason for its popularity is the relative ease with which it can be administered and scored. Spearman's rho rank order correlations can be run quite quickly between the sets of rankings using a pocket calculator, and two constructs extracted to act as axes along which the other constructs can be plotted (see Fransella and Bannister, 1977, for details).

The rated grid.   Another form of grid in common use is one in which the elements are rated in terms of the constructs. This is very similar to the semantic differential (Osgood et al., 1957). However, there the similarity ends. The grid, when used with an individual, is made up of that individual's personal elements and personal constructs and the findings are confined to a description of that individual alone. Semantic differential data are, however, nomothetic in that each individual's responses are analysed in terms of a specific set of predetermined factors – usually evaluative, activity and potency. Kelly is basically concerned with an understanding of an individual's meaning or construct space and Osgood with an individual's position in a universal semantic space.

The implications grid.   Kelly did suggest other ways in which a grid might be compiled, such that one may look at how a person dispersed his dependency on others, for instance, but these have rarely been used to date.

A form of grid that has been in use for some time resulted from Hinkle's (1965) theory of implications. This led him to devise a grid in which constructs were compared with constructs – there are no elements except, of course, those concerned with the elicitation of the constructs. In the Impgrid, the person is asked to think about each pair of constructs in turn and to say, for example, whether a change from their indicated preferred pole *relaxed* to the unpreferred *tense*, would also bring about a swing from being *soft-hearted* to being *hard-hearted*. An affirmative answer is indicated by a tick in the appropriate cell in the grid matrix and taken to mean that the one construct implies the other.

In clinical work it is often important to find out what is the meaning of the implicit as well as the emergent pole of a construct. For this reason, the bi-polar implications grid was developed (Fransella, 1972). In this form each pole of a construct is taken in turn and compared with all other poles, the person being told that 'all you know about a person is that they are *soft-hearted*' and they are asked to state which other characteristics, in terms of the constructs in the grid, they would expect to find in a *soft-hearted* person.

Hinkle also described the resistance-to-change grid to test, amongst other things, the hypothesis that the more superordinate construct would not only have more implications but be more resistant to change. Again each construct is here paired with every other. The subject is told that they have to change from the preferred side to the non-preferred side on one of a pair of constructs, and asked which they would find it easier to change on; so the grid matrix indicates the relative resistance to change of each construct. Unfortunately, in spite of its seeming potential usefulness problems may arise in the clinical setting, since many people already see themselves as described by the non-preferred sides of their constructs. They want to be *relaxed* but see themselves as *tense*, they want to be *confident* but *lack confidence*. However, the resistance-to-change grid may still be of use by giving an indication of the relative ease with which such individuals may be able to change to the desired pole of each construct; it can indicate where the person might most profitably focus their efforts toward change.

Types of element

Although most grids are matrices of responses indicating how particular constructs are applied to particular elements this does not mean that a construct is only a construct and an element is only an element. They are two sides of the same proverbial coin. 'Mother' can be an element in a grid to be construed in certain ways. She can also be a construct and used to construe elements – which elements are like *mother* and which are not.

Ryle and Lunghi (1970) were particularly interested in inter-personal relationships and used these as elements to be construed; for instance, self in relation to mother, mother in relation to self, self in relation to brother, brother in relation to self. Construct elicitation, usually with two such elements, takes the form of asking the person in what way the relation of self-to-mother is similar to or different from the relation of brother-to-self, and so on.

It is important to remember that all elements should be within the range of convenience of the constructs. All this means is that if one wishes to study people's views on bread, then the elements in a grid may well be loaves of bread; if the area of interest is how an individual construes him or herself, then the elements can be different aspects of the self – 'like me now', 'as I was before "X" happened to me', 'as I would like to be', 'as I was when a child' and so forth.

Types of construct

In Chapter 10 several terms were discussed which refer to constructs – they can be permeable, constellatory, preemptive and so forth. But it is not these dimensions that cause the grid designer concern, since there is little in the literature to indicate how they can be identified. What one can take into consideration is whether one wishes to supply or elicit the constructs (or both) and whether one wants a mixture of identifiable subordinate and superordinate constructs.

Supplied and elicited constructs. A considerable controversy has surrounded the issue of whether it is legitimate to supply or provide constructs. Part of the problem stems from the fact that some people appeared to think that to supply constructs is contrary to the spirit of Kelly's theory. Instead of using *elicited* as the polar opposite *supplied*, they used *personal*. Thus there arose the idea that supplied constructs are not personal constructs. This, of course, denies the existence of the Commonality Corollary which accepts that people in similar cultures will construe some events similarly and so share certain constructs. Of course, this is not to say that these constructs will necessarily be used in identical ways, since the *total* network of implications of a particular construct may differ from person to person; but there is enough implicative overlap for clear communication to take place. If one decides to supply constructs to subjects, perhaps because one wishes to compare grid responses across a number of people or to test out specific hypotheses, one makes the assumption that the constructs supplied mean what one thinks they mean to all the people and that all the people can make sense of them. One common practice is to elicit constructs from a sample of people and then to use those occurring most frequently.

One type of construct often supplied concerns the self. This usually takes the form of *like I am in character, like I'd like to be* and so forth. But it is clear that using the self (or father, mother and the like) as a whole-figure construct may not present the subject with the same task as asking him to construe these people as elements. Mair and Boyd (1967) found that the rating of 'self' as an element correlated 0.47 with rankings of *self* as construct, whereas the range of element/construct correlations for 'self', 'mother' and 'father' was from −0.58 to +0.89. Attempts have since been made to relate these person element/construct discrepancies to conflict concerning that person (Fransella and Crisp, 1979), but it is still far from clear how to interpret the discrepancy when it does occur. However, whole-figure constructs are widely used and it must be left to the investigator to assess the validity of their results. Salmon (1976) has, however, suggested that whole-figure constructs should not be used with children under 7 years of age.

Superordinate and subordinate constructs.   There is no way of knowing at what level in a construct hierarchy any particular elicited construct lies, although one might hazard a guess that, for example, *good* is pretty superordinate. For this reason it is often useful to use both elicited and laddered constructs (Hinkle, 1965) in a grid, since the latter ensures that the dimensions of construing that emerge from an analysis are 'anchored' to known personally important constructs.

Classification of constructs.   Landfield (1971) has taken a first step in outlining a procedure for the categorization of elicited constructs. Subsequent attempts to use these categories for constructs elicited from British as opposed to American subjects have met with only partial success. Too many constructs are found to be unclassifiable for the system to be adopted without modification.

Methods of analysis

It sometimes looks as if the interest in grids is due to the fatal fascination of the statistical games, including factor analysis, that can be played with the resulting matrices. It is impossible to discuss these here in any comprehensive way, so relevant references are given at the end of the chapter.

The concept of reliability

Kelly's comment that reliability is a measure of a test's insensitivity to change was not facetious, but a logical deduction from personal construct theory. This sees each person as a form of motion and so a static mind is a contradiction in terms. Instead of expecting a measure to yield similar scores for the same subjects on different occasions, we might do better to predict where stability and where change in a particular grid with a particular person is likely to occur.

Bannister (1962), for instance, used the correlation between two identical grids, one repeated immediately after the other, as a score to discriminate between those identified as showing schizophrenic thought disorder and both psychiatric and non-psychiatric groups (see pp.180-4 for a detailed description of Bannister's work). Later developments of this approach yielded test – retest correlations for non-psychiatric and thought-disordered schizophrenic groups of 0.8 and 0.18 respectively (Bannister and Fransella, 1967).

The grid literature is spattered with other example of average reliabilities with different grid methods and different populations. For instance, Watson et al., (1976) used a test–retest interval of from seven to ten days with a group of thirty-two prisoners, and report an average correlation of 0.74 with a range of 0.3 to 1.0. Fjeld and Landfield (1961) found stability of elicited constructs over a two-week period to be 0.8 (for other examples see Fransella and Bannister 1977).

In general, average reliabilities tend to be quite high, but the range for the individuals making up the sample is often very wide. But it really makes as little sense to talk about *the* reliability of *the* grid as it would to ask what the reliability was of *the* questionnaire. One would have to ask *what* grid/questionnaire? *What* is it aiming to measure? *What* kind of subjects and *what* method of analysis are being used? And so on.

In view of the extreme flexibility of grid technique, in that it can be designed to investigate aspects of the construing of individuals or groups, and of thought content or thought process, it seems reasonable to regard reliability as itself an aspect of construing rather than solely as an entity which is either 'acceptable' or not for a particular person.

The concept of validity

As grid technique is not a single test and has no specific content, its validity can only be discussed in terms of whether it effectively reveals patterns and relationships in certain kinds of data. The grid is therefore very different from a questionnaire designed, for example, to measure aggression. It is reasonable to ask about the validity of that questionnaire (see Chapter 6) but not so a grid, since it does not usually measure traits or characteristics in that sense.

Occasionally a grid is designed as a nomothetic test as was the Grid Test of Thought Disorder (Bannister and Fransella, 1967). When this is done its validity can be assessed in the traditional manner (e.g. Bannister et al., 1971; Heather, 1976). But grids are not usually made into standardized tests in this way. Nearly always they are designed for specific purposes – to yield measures of the construing process or to assess differences in thought content between groups or within an individual on different occasions and so on. Again, these can be assessed for their validity in the standard manner if the person wishes to do so. For instance, Fransella and Bannister (1967) validated a rank order form of grid against votes cast by the subjects in a British General Election. Based on how subjects ranked people they knew in terms of *like I'd like to be* and *like me in character* compared with the rankings of the same people (elements) on the constructs *likely to vote Conservative (Labour, Liberal)*, fairly accurate predictions could be made of how each subject would vote.

Kelly, however, equated validity with usefulness and saw understanding others as the most useful of activities. Thus, most grid studies have sought to increase our understanding of a problem, be it clinical, in the area of social relationships, linguistic meaning, children's construing, politics or sex differences. He deliberately chose the word 'anticipate' rather than 'predict' in the Fundamental Postulate (see Chapter 10, p.150) to suggest that we seek our own personal understanding of the world by being involved in it and acting upon it. If our anticipations are validated we have increased our understanding of the world. Kelly makes the distinction between prediction and action as follows:

> however useful prediction may be in testing the transient utility of one's construction system, the superior test of what he has devised is his capacity to implement imaginative action. It is by his actions that man learns what his capabilities are, and what he achieves is

the most tangible psychological measure of his behaviour. It is a mistake to always assume that behaviour must be the psychologist's dependent variable. For man, it is the independent variable. (Kelly, 1969a, p.33)

Applications of grid technique

The most systematic development of a line of argument stemming from construct theory, and tested out by a series of experiments, is Bannister's theory of schizophrenic thought disorder. This is mentioned in Chapters 10 and 12, so here the focus is on issues resulting from the form of grids used.

It was Bannister's work with this group of patients which resulted in the development of the split-half and rank-order forms of grid, and the latter has been used in most of his subsequent research and the Grid Test of Thought Disorder (Bannister and Fransella, 1966, 1967). Whatever the rights and wrongs of such diagnostic testing (and views have changed markedly over the last ten years), the test provides an example of how a grid can be used in a nomothetic fashion – it has standard elements, constructs and normative data.

Conceptual structure of the tightness – looseness type has also been looked at in the context of group psychotherapy (Fransella, 1970). As with the thought-disorder test, both constructs and elements were supplied to the group members in order to make inter-individual comparisons possible. In this study, the group members themselves were used as the elements. Thus, each person ranked all other group members, including themselves, on a number of supplied constructs. The tightness of construing (as measured by the strength of the interconstruct rank order correlations) did indeed fluctuate over the one-year therapy period, but of particular interest was the finding that the psychiatrist leading the group and the one there as observer, also fluctuated along with the patients. Loosening and tightening appeared to be a truly group process.

Again in a clinical context, Fransella (1972) used scores from bi-polar implications grids to define operationally 'meaningfulness'. She demonstrated that change in severity of stuttering as the result of personal construct psychotherapy correlated with changes in the meaningfulness to the stutterer of both being a fluent speaker and of being a stutterer – as disfluencies decreased, there was an increase in the implications of being a fluent speaker and a concomitant decrease in implications to do with being a stutterer.

In the field of social psychology, Duck (e.g. 1979) conducted a series of studies, based on the Commonality Corollary, focusing on interpersonal attraction. It seems that we do indeed choose our friends on the basis of construed similarity. Duck argues that the validation the friend gives us is experienced as evidence of the accuracy of our own construing. There do, however, appear to be some sex differences here. Construed similarity is found in same-sexed pairs but only in the women in cross-sex friendship pairs. Duck suggests that 'although both sexes use the same apparent cognitive strategy for choosing their friends of the same sex, when it comes to choosing friends of the opposite sex, males and females use different 'filter' strategies.'

Thomas and colleagues (e.g. 1978) have seen the grid, not as a static object, but as a tool for increasing one's awareness of the process of learning. Similarly, Boxer (1980) has found the feedback of grid data useful in the context of exploring the construing of managers in business settings and in providing a basis for learning.

These are a very few specific examples of the uses to which grid technique has been put. Sources for others are cited at the end of the chapter.

The grid and the theory

The grid was initially developed within the context of personal construct theory. No one would deny that. Argument arises when one asks whether it should always be used within that context or whether it should take on a life of its own. In some ways it actually does have a separate existence since some current forms bear only marginal resemblance to the original proposed by Kelly. It must be left to personal preference. What needs to be borne in mind is that, with more and more complicated statistical packages becoming available, the grid user is being taken a long way from the subject's original responses. My personal preference is to argue that some theoretical framework is needed within which to interpret the data obtained and to prevent too much wild speculation. If one is going to have a theory, why not use the one from which the technique originally emerged?

Suggested further reading

The technique and its uses

Fransella, F. and Bannister, D. (1977) *A Manual for Repertory Grid Technique*. London: Academic Press.

Ryle, A. (1975) *Frames and Cages*. Sussex University Press.

Slater, P. (ed.) (1976) *The Measurement of Intrapersonal Space by Grid Technique*. Vol.1. London: Wiley.

Analysis

Fransella, F. (1972) *Personal Change and Reconstruction*. London and New York: Academic Press (for description of the analysis of the bi-polar implications grid).

Goodge, P. (1979) Problems of repertory grid analysis and a cluster analysis solution. *British Journal of Psychiatry 134*: 516-21.

Slater, P. (ed.) (1977) *The Measurement of Intrapersonal Space by Grid Technique*. Vol.2. London: Wiley (for details of his principal components analysis package).

Thomas, L. (1978) A personal construct approach to learning in education, training and therapy. In F. Fransella (ed.) *Personal Construct Psychology*. London: Academic Press (for descriptions of the grids and methods of analysis proposed by Thomas and his co-workers).

12 Personal construct theory: research into basic concepts

J. Adams-Webber

It will not be possible in this brief chapter to provide a general survey of research in personal construct theory. More comprehensive reviews can be found in the following sources: Adams-Webber (1979), Bannister and Fransella (1980) and Bannister and Mair (1968). The present discussion will deal specifically with several representative lines of investigation which have played an important role in the development of this system during the past twenty-five years. Consideration will be limited to research which has clearly formulated theoretical implications. Many interesting findings will not be discussed either because there is not yet sufficient evidence to evaluate their significance in terms of the basic principles of personal construct psychology, or they involve applications of Kelly's ideas that are of more practical than theoretical importance. Finally, we shall not be concerned with developments in repertory grid methods as such or with specific clinical techniques derived from personal construct theory, as these have been discussed extensively elsewhere (Fransella and Bannister, 1977; Landfield, 1971; Slater, 1977).

The central focus of research in personal construct psychology since its inception has been the formal analysis of individual conceptual structures. Kelly (1955, 1969) assumes that psychological development is essentially an evolutionary process involving the progressive differentiation of systems into independently organized subsystems ('fragmentation'), and the integration of the functions of these subsystems at increasingly higher levels of hierarchic organization ('modulation'). He argues that the specialization of subsystems serves to enhance the applicability, or 'range of convenience', of a construct system in terms of the *variety* of different events which can be discriminated meaningfully within its framework. The integration of the functions of separate subsystems allows the individual to maintain the overall *unity* of her or his construct system as an operational whole. Thus, from the standpoint of personal construct theory, *differentiation and integration are logically distinct, but equally necessary aspects of all psychological development*.

As previously outlined in Chapter 8, it was Bieri (1955) who first attempted to assess the relative level of development of personal construct systems in terms of their degree of differentiation, which he labelled 'cognitive complexity'. His specific index of differentiation was based on the extent to which an individual used different constructs independently of one another in categorizing persons. The main problem with this particular approach to evaluating the organizational complexity of construct systems is reflected by the fact that thought-disordered schizophrenics typically exhibit a high degree of independence between constructs in characterizing people; however, their social judgements are better described as *random* than as complexly organized since they are also very inconsistent from one occasion to the next (Bannister et al., 1971). This suggests that 'their ideas about people are poorly related to one another' (Bannister and Fransella, 1966). Thus, as Langley (1971) points out, 'it is unknowable whether this measure reflects high differentiation, as Bieri suggests, and/or low integration.' Radley (1974) concludes that 'it seems unlikely that the degree of functional independence of constructs is a sufficiently comprehensive measure to encompass such disparate modes of thinking.' (Cf., Space and Cromwell, 1978.)

An alternative method of assessing the level of differentiation of a personal construct system, which enables us to surmount this particular problem, has been devised by Crockett (1965). His index of 'cognitive complexity' is based on the relative number of different constructs used by a person in writing brief character sketches of several acquaintances. Although this index does not correlate with Bieri's measure, described above, there is considerable evidence which supports Crockett's claim that his own method taps some important aspects of the complexity and flexibility of an individual's social construing. For example, the scores of children on this measure increase systematically with age (Scarlett et al., 1971); it relates to frequency of interaction with the persons being described (Zalot and Adams-Webber, 1977); ease in learning sets of social relationships differing in degree of symmetry (Delia and Crockett, 1973) and the ability to resolve inconsistencies in information about people (Nidorff and Crockett, 1965).

Crockett (1965) contends that the development of a personal construct system involves not only differentiation among constructs, but also increasing integration of constructs both *within* and *between* separate subsystems. There is now ample evidence that different subsystems within the same construct system can vary independently of one another in terms of their relative levels of internal organization. For example, Bannister (1965) demonstrated that:

> If two separate constellations (subsystems) of constructs are available to normal subjects and one is serially validated and the second is serially invalidated then intercorrelations in the former will rise while in the latter the pattern of construct relationships will repeatedly change and the strength of correlations will ultimately fall. (Bannister, 1965, pp.381-2)

Further observations from outside the laboratory are consistent with Bannister's findings. For instance, student teachers during their first six weeks of classroom experience show gradual increases in the degree of interrelationship between those specific constructs used to define their professional roles with no corresponding changes in other sectors of their systems (Adams-Webber and Mirc, 1976). Similarly, Tanzanian school children, who study geography in English and interact with their peers outside of school mostly in Swahili, manifest higher levels of construct relatedness when they judge their peers on 'Swahili constructs' and foreign nations on 'English constructs' than vice versa (Lemon, 1975).

Kelly (1955) assumes that changes in the form and content of our construing occur mainly in response to disconfirmation of our anticipations. He posits that those constructs that are closely related to the construct(s) upon which our original expectations were based will be the most affected by predictive failure. It follows that *the more highly interrelated all the constructs within a given system or subsystem, the greater will be the impact of any invalidating experience in terms of its range of 'implications' throughout that system or subsystem.* For example, when Bannister (1963, p.685) provided normal adults with feedback concerning their judgements of strangers on a set of 'psychological constructs' (e.g. mean, honest, etc.), the effect of this information depended on the initial level of interrelationship among these constructs for each individual. Specifically, it was observed that subjects who exhibited relatively high degrees of construct relatedness at the outset showed 'catastrophic reactions to validational experience by zig-zagging from very high to very low strengths of structure while the low intensity (of relationship) group were markedly less affected'; In a similar vein, Crockett and Meisel (1974) have shown that subjects who manifest relatively high levels of relatedness among psychological constructs revise their impressions of people more in response to 'strong disconfirmation' than to 'weak disconfirmation'. In their experiment, strong disconfirmation consisted of having inferences based on the subject's most central construct invalidated; whereas weak disconfirmation involved more peripheral constructs. Crockett and Meisel (1974) conclude that:

> for a subject whose personal constructs are massively connected, a change in inference along one construct dimension demands a change in many others ... unless his impressions of other people are to vacillate continuously as he obtains new information about them such a subject must show little or no response to weak disconfirmation of his impressions. (Crockett and Meisel, 1974, p.298)

Bannister (1963, 1965) proposes that in the face of repeated disconfirmation ('serial invalidation') of her/his anticipations, a person may loosen relationships between constructs in order to minimize the 'reverberatory' effects of further invalidation through-out her/his system as a whole. One effect of this loosening will be to isolate those constructs which are the primary focus of invalidation from the rest of the system, thereby limiting the 'implications' of any further predictive failures. Although this loosening is undertaken to conserve the system, the *progressive loosening of construct relationships must, by definition, lead ultimately to the collapse of all conceptual structure.* It has been shown repeatedly that thought-disordered schizophrenics manifest less construct relatedness than either normals or other clinical populations (e.g. Bannister et al.,

1971). There is also considerable evidence that schizophrenic thought disorder does not involve a general cognitive deficit, but rather is specific to psychological construing (Bannister and Salmon, 1966; McPherson et al., 1978).

In a recent experiment, Higgins and Schwarz (1976) validated normal adults for applying typically related psychological constructs, such as *kind* and *sincere*, to people in 'an atypical, inversely related manner'. That is, they were validated whenever they construed someone as either 'kind and insincere' or 'sincere and unkind'. This produced a gradual loosening of the initially high degree of relationship between these constructs, which was most pronounced for subjects classified as 'schizotypic' (on the Sc scale of the MMPI; cf., Hathaway and Meehl, 1951).

In a subsequent study, Cochran (1977) presented normal adults with descriptions of hypothetical people containing 'inconsistent' combinations of psychological traits such as those used by Higgins and Schwarz. This produced differential effects depending upon each subjects' initial, 'baseline' level of construct relatedness. Those subjects who originally manifested a high degree of construct relatedness reacted to inconsistent information by loosening construct relationships; whereas subjects with low levels of construct relatedness at the beginning tended to strengthen them under the same conditions. This suggests that the 'schizotypic' subjects in Higgins and Schwarz's experiment may have exhibited relatively high levels of construct relatedness at the outset, and thus 'inconsistent' information led to their loosening relationships between their constructs. We shall return to this point later.

Another relevant finding is that when the interpersonal judgements of normal adults are repeatedly invalidated in the laboratory, relationships between their constructs frequently reverse in direction, producing 'atypical' patterns of implication, for example, *insincere* being positively related to *honest* (Bannister, 1963). Moreover, the psychological judgements of thought-disordered schizophrenics tend to deviate from the general pattern of construct relationships for normal populations (Bannister et al., 1971). This is probably not merely a 'side-effect' of the loosened structure of their psychological construing since their 'social deviation' scores do not correlate with the overall degree of relatedness among their constructs (Bannister et al., 1971). The 'social deviation' scores of schizophrenics also relate ($r = 0.58$; $N = 19$) to psychiatrists' ratings of the severity of thought disorder (McPherson et al., 1973). Bannister et al. (1971) suggest, in the light of this evidence, that the psychological construing of thought-disordered schizophrenics may have become deviant before it became disorganized.

Radley (1974) indicates that schizophrenics who are free of thought disorder tend to have construct systems in which all psychological constructs are closely interrelated. Thus, their social construing is 'homogeneously tight'. In this type of system, constructs are concretely pyramided in such a way that all lines of implication will eventually converge upon a single superordinate construct. Therefore, regardless of the number of constructs constituting the subsystem (which is Crockett's operational definition of *differentiation*), all of an individual's expectations about people must 'fit' the constraints of one fixed pattern of logical possibilities. This type of monolithic conceptual structure is prototypical of Bieri's (1955) notion of 'cognitive simplicity'.

As the experiment by Crockett and Meisel (1974), discussed above, illustrates, it is difficult to make changes in a monolithic subsystem in response to invalidating feedback, because even minor revisions can have sweeping implications and may present a prospect of impending chaos. Cochran's (1977) findings, cited above, suggest further that, the more monolithic the organization of one's psychological constructs, the more likely it is that one will be forced to loosen relationships between these constructs in order to deal with people whose behaviour is not consistent with the current 'logical' structure of one's system. This implies that a lack of functional differentiation between psychological constructs (Bieri's operational definition of 'cognitive simplicity') could be a predisposing factor in the genesis of clinical thought disorder (Adams-Webber, 1970).

In contrast, thought-disordered schizophrenics are 'homogeneously loose' in construing people (Radley, 1974). That is, their psychological subsystems are so fragmented in structure that, although they may still have a fairly large repertory of constructs and these may be functionally differentiated from one another, there is not enough linkage between constructs to relate one aspect of experience to another. Thus, it is clearly not differentiation alone which determines the efficiency of an individual's interpersonal construing. We must, as Crockett (1965) argues, also take into consideration the relative levels of integration both within and between subsystems.

When we directly compare thought-disordered and non-thought-disordered schizophrenics, it seems possible that the former are now floundering in the wreckages of what were at one time highly monolithic conceptual structures in which the 'rules' for interpreting behaviour were inflexible. In such subsystems it is very difficult to resolve inconsistencies in one's experience and to accommodate one's thinking to events which do not fit into the existing patterns of interrelationship between one's constructs (cf., Crockett and Meisel, 1974; Cochran, 1977). Such 'ambiguous' events will tend to remain on the periphery of one's construct system where they can become important foci of confusion and anxiety.

In the normal course of development of a personal construct system, according to Kelly (1955), it is the ambiguity of new experience within the framework of current conceptual structures which routinely leads to progressive changes in their organization and content. A given event can be said to be ambiguous when it becomes the focus of expectations which are inconsistent with the specific relationships between constructs which articulate the structure of an individual's system. It follows that *new structure evolves within a personal construct system to accommodate events which are ambiguous within the context of its existing structure* (Adams-Webber, 1970). That is, when people are confronted with events which lie outside the ranges of convenience of their construct systems as they are currently organized, which is Kelly's (1955) definition of *anxiety*, they normally attempt to make specific changes in order to accommodate their construing to those events. This usually involves the further differentiation and reintegration of their construct systems (cf., Adams-Webber, 1979).

Kelly (1955) points out that:

> From the standpoint of the psychology of personal constructs, anxiety, per se, is not to be classified as either good or bad. It represents the awareness that one's construction system does not apply to the events at hand. It is, therefore, a precondition for making revisions. (p.498)

He does note, however, that persons whose construct systems are relatively undifferentiated in structure, because of their heavy dependence on a single pattern of construct relationships, are reluctant to risk adjustments at any level within their systems for fear that this will place them in an even more ambiguous position with respect to the anticipation of events. In short, people with monolithic conceptual structures will tend to resist change in the face of increasing ambiguity in order to avoid further confusion and anxiety. Again, this point is well illustrated by Crockett and Meisel's (1974) finding that the more closely interrelated all an individual's psychological constructs, the greater will be her/his resistance to changing impressions of people in response to invalidating feedback.

Radley (1974) also indicates that normal adults exhibit relatively more *variability in construct relatedness than either thought-disordered or non-thought-disordered schizophrenics*. That is, in Radley's own words, 'normal subjects have, overall, a system of closely related constructs, but within the system there is high variability in the extent to which particular constructs relate to one another'. This is consistent with the finding of Makhlouf-Norris et al. (1970) that the construct systems of normal adults are typically composed of a number of separate subsystems of closely interrelated constructs, which are, in turn, interconnected by means of several 'linkage' constructs. Given this kind of differentiated and abstractly 'cross-referenced' conceptual structures, independent lines of implication can be developed simultaneously within separate subsystems and then re-integrated within the context of superordinate constructs (Adams-Webber, 1979). Thus, at the highest level of hierarchic organization, superordinate constructions can provide a thread of consistency throughout a construct system as a whole by co-ordinating the functioning of different subsystems, which can operate more or less independently at lower levels.

On the other hand, when superordinate constructs are too impermeable to admit new substructures to their ranges of convenience and still maintain overall coherence, fragmentation under the pressure of events in a continually changing environment can be haphazard rather than systematic, and may lead ultimately to the collapse of all conceptual structure (Adams-Webber, 1970). In Kelly's own words:

> The variety of construction subsystems which are inferentially incompatible with each other may, in the train of rapidly moving events, become so vast that he is hard put to it to find ready-made superordinate constructs which are sufficiently permeable and open-ended to maintain over-all consistency. (Kelly, 1955, p.89)

In short, thought disorder, which Bannister operationally defines as 'loosened construing', may result eventually from the failure to find permeable superordinate constructions to subsume changes in a construct system that are made in response to invalidating feedback from the environment. Thus, within the framework of personal construct theory, *research concerned with individual cognitive development and that concerned with the aetiology of clinical thought disorder have begun to converge on the same basic principles of conceptual organization.*

Recent research has uncovered another principle governing the structure of construct systems. It has been demonstrated repeatedly that we have a general tendency to allot other persons to the same poles of constructs as we use to characterize ourselves approximately 62 per cent of the time (Adams-Webber, 1979; Adams-Webber and Davidson, 1979; Benjafield and Adams-Webber, 1975). About the same proportion of 'like-self' judgements is observed when we describe strangers whom we have just met for the first time as when we describe our own parents and siblings (Adams-Webber, 1979). Moreover, the distribution of 'like-self'/'unlike-self' judgements seems to have stabilized at approximately 62/38 by mid-adolescence (Adams-Webber and Davidson, 1979). An explanation of this finding in terms of the psychology of personal constructs requires that we import some concepts from both early Greek philosophy and modern information theory.

Pythagoras, the presocratic philosopher, developed an elaborate system of numbers and geometrical forms to which he and his followers attributed great moral significance. A central concept in this system was the 'golden section', which can be constructed by dividing a line into two segments so that the shorter is to the longer as the longer is to the whole. This requires that the longer segment be approximately 62 per cent of the entire line. The golden section has had an ubiquitous influence on western culture. For example, the Greeks based much of their art and architecture upon it; and many painters, including Piero della Francesca, Bellini, Vermeer, and Seurat divided their canvases on the basis of this ratio. At least since Fechner, psychologists have studied its aesthetic properties. For instance, Fechner measured many common rectangles, including windows, playing cards, book covers, and writing pads; and found that their proportions were often quite close to the golden section (cf., Berlyne, 1971). However, the advantages of assigning others to the same poles of constructs as the *self* 62 per cent of the time may not be purely aesthetic.

It can be shown in terms of the basic axioms of information theory that the contribution of a given category of event to average information is maximized when its relative frequency of occurrence is approximately $1/e$, which works out to about 0.37 (Berlyne, 1971). This value is, as Berlyne notes, very close to the minor element of the golden section, that is, 0.38. He suggests, in the light of this relationship, that the golden section has such great aesthetic appeal because it allows the minor element to occupy that proportion of the whole which makes it stand out as maximally striking. Following Berlyne, Adams-Webber (1979) hypothesizes that people tend to organize their interpersonal judgements in such a way that perceived differences between *self* and others will stand out maximally as 'figure' against a diffuse background of perceived similarities.

Kelly submits that:

> the *self* is, when considered in the appropriate context, a proper concept or construct. It refers to a group of events which are alike in a certain way and, in that same way, necessarily different from other events. The way in which the events are alike is the self. That also makes the self an individual, differentiated from other individuals. (Kelly, 1955, p.131)

It follows that each person has a clear and distinct notion of his/her own identity only to the extent that he or she is able to discern a specific pattern of similarities and differences between the *self* and others (Adams-Webber and Davidson, 1979). As Bannister and Agnew (1977) point out, 'the ways in which we elaborate the construing of self must be essentially those ways in which we elaborate our construing of others for we have not a concept of self but a bipolar construct of *self–not self*'. Lemon and Warren (1974) hypothesize that an individual's judgements of others 'automatically involve a kind of self comparison process ... (in which) the self-construct will act as an anchoring point to produce the effects of assimilation and contrast familiar in psychophysics'. The fact that people tend to allot themselves and others to the opposite poles of constructs approximately 38 per cent of the time suggests that it may be perceived contrasts between oneself and others which define the contours of *self* as an unique figure against a general background of similarities (Adams-Webber, 1979).

Previous research has shown that individual differences in the extent to which other people are construed as similar to the *self* on specific sets of constructs are highly stable (Benjafield and Adams-

Webber, 1975). It has been demonstrated as well that this variable relates closely to several other basic indices of conceptual structure, including the overall degree of interrelationship between constructs and the average level of differentiation among elements (Adams-Webber, 1979). This suggests that the golden section proportion may play a central role as a formal principle of organization in the development of personal construct systems (cf., Adams-Webber, 1978; Benjafield and Adams-Webber, 1976). This would not be surprising in the light of the fact that this proportion is manifested frequently in natural patterns of growth (Mitchison, 1977).

This discussion has dealt exclusively with research concerned with the formal analysis of individual conceptual structures, which seems to be the current focus of convenience in personal construct psychology. In drawing to a conclusion, however, I should like to point out that there has been a great deal of important work carried out within the framework of this theory which is concerned with the 'content' of our construing. Although there is not space to review this research in the present chapter, I have discussed it extensively elsewhere (Adams-Webber, 1979).

Suggested further reading

Adams-Webber, J. (1979) *Personal Construct Theory: Concepts and Applications*. New York: Wiley.
Bannister, D. and Fransella, F. (1980) *Inquiring Man* (2nd edn). London: Penguin Books.

Part VI
The humanists

13 The self with others: the person and the interpersonal context in the approaches of C.R. Rogers and R.D. Laing

Keith Oatley

We each of us have the sense of ourselves and others persisting through time. Despite ageing, despite doing different things in different places, I am the same person (in some respects) as I was a dozen years ago. Despite discontinuities in my waking consciousness I have some sense of a continuity in my experience, as my friends do of my patterns of behaviour.

It is presumably to this sense of what is constant in people's own experience and the behaviour of others that the idea of personality pays tribute: the idea that there is some predictability in the way I go about this, or react to that. Tests or inventories of personality set out to capture these characteristic modes of behaviour, and pin them down, butterfly-like, so that character can be exhibited.

A quite different view of people arises if we ask someone 'What is your experience of being here?' or if we ask 'How does this person continuously create the reality in which she lives?' (with assumptions of 'growth' and agency mentioned by Rychlak in Chapter 1). Yet further differences arise if one considers that one might be quite different with different people, and that much of one's sense of being, and of one's behaviour arises interactively from relationships with others. These aspects are not captured in attempts to make context-free diagnoses of other people's personalities.

These themes are recognizable preoccupations of existential and phenomenological psychology. I shall here explore them in the work of Carl Rogers and Ronald Laing.

In some ways the approaches of Rogers and Laing seem worlds apart. They are in fact the width of the Atlantic Ocean apart. Rogers, so far as I can gather, has only since his work has become well-known been told that he is 'existentialist', or 'phenomenological' in his thinking. The influences on him to which he admits (e.g. Rogers, 1974) are primarily his clients and his younger colleagues. 'Reading,' he says, 'has most of its value for me in buttressing my views. I realize I am not a scholar.' He is none the less recognizably within a tradition – it is the distinguished American tradition exemplified by John Dewey: the tradition of no nonsense, of vigorous self-reliance, of exposing oneself thoughtfully to experience, of practical innovation, and of careful concern for others.

In his writing, Rogers is straightforward and homely. He exudes the sense of a gentle, caring, older friend. From his pages I get the impression of someone honest and (this is the unusual part) sufficiently concerned about his clients to let them be and to trust them to find themselves without manipulation on his part.

In contrast to Rogers' lack of scholarship, Laing is steeped in the literature of European existentialist thought and feeling. If anyone writing in English today carries the torch of existentialist mood, and the phenomenological method, it is he. His writing is dense, allusive, engaging; sometimes obscure, sometimes mysterious, often clarifying into limpid insight. Laing is an accomplished iconoclast and a mordant commentator on society.

Though his experience of the world has evidently been radically different from that of Rogers and though he has indeed courted experiences which many would regard as unusual, he has allowed himself to be touched by that experience, and in so doing emerges in his writing as a man of passion and humanity. It is not a humanity that is bland or comfortable – but it is real.

Despite their differences there are shared themes, and of these I shall choose three: the nurturing of experience, the issue of defensiveness versus creative growth and the emergent properties of human relationship. For the sake of expressing a continuity of each man's work I shall write first about Rogers on all three themes, and then about Laing.

Carl Rogers

Rogers writes:

> I was brought up in a home marked by close family ties, a very strict and uncompromising religious and ethical atmosphere.... I came along, the fourth of six children. My parents cared a great deal for us, and had our welfare constantly in mind. They were also, in many subtle and affectionate ways, very controlling of our behaviour. (This quotation and the following biographical material is from *On Becoming a Person,* 1961.)

When he was twelve, the family moved to a farm and Rogers took up natural history, 'becoming an authority ...on the moths which inhabited our woods'. He also read learned works on scientific agriculture, acquiring 'a knowledge of and a respect for the methods of science in a field of practical endeavour'.

The experience of the client

The most fundamental notion in Rogers's work is that a person becomes herself, and gets in touch with her own experience in a certain kind of nurturant atmosphere provided by another person. In the relationship between therapist and client the Rogerian therapist makes no attempt to diagnose, to tell the client how to live or how not to live. Instead the therapist simply (though it is of course by no means simple) makes sure that she is herself there with the client as a real person (not being phoney or defensive), accepts and values the personhood of the client unconditionally (neither approving nor disapproving of what the client says), and endeavours to understand and empathize with the client's own experience as she is expressing it.

This set of three characteristics: genuineness, warmth, and accurate empathy, have been known as the Rogerian triad. It is Rogers' contention (e.g. Rogers, 1959) that when, in a therapeutic relationship, these three conditions are created by the therapist and are perceived by a troubled client, then therapy occurs.

The metaphor that comes to mind is that of the person as a growing plant which, given appropriate conditions of soil, of light, of humidity, will grow strong and healthy, unique and yet characteristic of its species. The resources for this growth, for this actualization of itself, are already within the organism. The plant does not need to be pulled or pushed by gardeners. All the outside environment needs to provide is a benign climate.

One can see in Rogers' agricultural interests, glimpsed in his autobiographical sketches, the seeds of this optimistic and positive philosophy – or at least in those interests combined with his evident rebelliousness against the religious constraints of his upbringing, and the subtle (if affectionate) control of his parents. To allow people to become themselves one needs not to control them in 'their own best interests' but to let them be.

This preparedness to let the client be, for her own account of her experience to be taken seriously, valued, affirmed – as opposed to having her attitudes and behaviour questioned, diagnosed, judged, approved, disapproved, or in many more or less subtle ways arranging for the person to be given the impression that she should be something other than she is, is a decisive step. It is a step first taken unequivocally by Rogers, at least within the ranks of psychologists, and it is important both for therapy and for theories of personality.

There is, in these conditions for therapy, a large degree of paradox. Only if the therapist is real, that is not practising the method as some kind of technique, will the conditions be met. Only if the therapist is prepared to be open about her feelings, to say she is bored or angry if that is how she feels, will progress be made. But is the expression of anger compatible with unconditional positive regard? As Smith (1980) has argued it might be precisely this kind of paradox, that is that this person values her and can be angry sometimes, that might allow the client to learn that (for instance) anger and rejection are not necessarily synonymous.

The implication of Rogers' work is that those theories of personality which try to capture some essential feature of the person in a psychiatric or psychoanalytic diagnosis, or on a scale or an inventory, using the result as a springboard for an intervention of some sort, do not simply miss the point of what it is to be human – they actually militate against the possibility of the person to whom they are applied becoming a whole person, that is being her own self, acting and thinking on her own behalf.

Rogers has said that he has 'little sympathy with the rather prevalent concept that man is basically irrational and that his impulses, if not controlled, will lead to destruction of self and others' (Rogers, 1961, p.194). Rogers argues that if one believes that man is fundamentally destructive (and bad) then one can see why some members of society try and direct and control other members, who they believe to be suffering from this destructiveness, and why some theories of personality reflect this view by trying to identify these unfortunate traits. At the same time it becomes difficult to see by what manoeuvre those attempting the control exempt themselves from the general condition they assume to exist.

Rogers challenges such views making it clear (e.g. particularly in Rogers, 1977) that whatever else is going on when one person is (with however good intentions) attempting to control or direct the behaviour of another, that other is being treated not as a person (capable of autonomy and responsibility) but as a thing, and that this is no basis for any science of persons.

Of defences and growth

The key notions in what Rogers (1959) calls 'A theory of personality' are those of congruency and incongruency. At the beginning of life an infant simply assimilates her experience, valuing it in so far as it helps to actualize the whole organism. But social processes intervene – the baby learns to need her mother's 'love', or at least the experience of maternal acceptance. The baby then comes to regulate her behaviour not on the basis of what might be actualizing for her own organism; instead she courts maternal approval, and avoids disapproval. She creates a sense of who she is as seen through the eyes of her mother, and it is this social sense that Rogers identifies with the self. In interaction with her mother or with significant others she comes to like or dislike herself in some total way as she has felt liked or disliked by her significant others. So some behaviour might be intrinsically satisfying for her, but be regarded negatively. Equally some behaviour might be intrinsically unsatisfying, but be performed because it is seen positively according to the introjected values.

This sets up congruences and incongruences between what one thinks, feels, or experiences for oneself, and an introjected sense of what one ought to think, feel, or experience. If what one experiences is consonant with what one ought to experience, all is well; and the world is (on the whole) perceived accurately. If they do not match then what happens is selective perception, distortion, denial and the rest of the processes of defence.

This as we see it is the basic estrangement in man. He has not been true to himself, to his own natural organismic valuing of experience, but for the sake of preserving the positive regard of others has now come to falsify some of the values he experiences and to perceive them only in terms based on their value to others. (Rogers, 1959, p.226)

Therapy, as Rogers sees it, is an undoing of this incongruent, disunited view of oneself, by providing a significant other who will, instead of giving one selective positive regard, give one positive regard unconditionally, allowing one to regain the sense of who one truly is.

Rogers is not simply putting forward some bland view of contented people in a world where everything is comfortable so long as everyone is nice to each other, but proposing the possibility that people can live more closely in touch with their feelings, experiencing the world more intensely and relating to others more directly.

Perhaps rather surprisingly, Rogers, who is one of the pioneers of humanistic psychology, has also pioneered empirical research on psychotherapy. His theory of therapy can be stated as saying that if certain conditions are fulfilled then personality change occurs. As Peter Smith points out in the next chapter, this idea casts his propositions into an easily recognizable behavioural research framework with independent and dependent variables. Smith also reviews the results of this research, and it seems appropriate that it should be on the basis of its results that Rogers' theories of personality change should be judged.

A theory of interpersonal relationship

More speculatively, Rogers' theory lays out the conditions for deteriorating and improving relationships in the ordinary world. In a deteriorating relationship, two people in contact (Rogers calls them X and Y, but I will call them Alice and Ben) are in contact and communicating on some subject. If Alice's experience of the subject of communication, her awareness of this subject, and her consciously communicated expression to Ben are incongruent then her communications will become contradictory. If the incongruence is principally between what Alice is aware of and what she consciously communicates, then we call this deceit. If the incongruence is between what she is aware of and what she is experiencing at some other level (though Rogers by certain contortions here avoids using the term 'unconscious') then Alice is deceiving herself. Rogers uses the idea of 'experience' to mean 'to receive in the organism the impact of the sensory or physiological events which are happening at the moment'. This experience may or may not be perceived accurately, and brought to awareness by the person. To the extent that it is, then the person is congruent, and to the extent that it is not then the person is incongruent.

Ben receives this contradictory communication, and experiences the contradictions and ambiguities, but tends to be aware only of the part of the communication that Alice has consciously intended, not allowing into awareness the contradictory elements of the communication. Hence, his awareness and experience tend also to be incongruent, and his response to Alice, reflecting this incongruity, will also be contradictory. The relationship deteriorates in reciprocally escalating defensiveness.

Rogers gives the example here of a relationship between mother and child.

> The mother feels 'You annoy me because you interfere with my career,' but she cannot be aware of this because this experience is incongruent with her concept of herself as a good mother. Her perception of this experience in herself is distorted, becoming 'I am annoyed at this instance of your behaviour. I love you but I must punish you.' This is an acceptable symbolization of her experience, and it is this which she consciously communicates to the child. But (the child) receives not only this conscious communication. He also experiences (but tends to be unaware of) the expressive behaviours indicating a general dislike of himself....One possibility is that he will experience himself as bad and unloved, even when his awareness of his behaviour is that he is 'good'. Hence, he will act and feel guilty and bad....This type of response is threatening to the mother, because his behaviours expressing badness and unlovedness threaten to bring into awareness her own rejecting feelings. (Rogers, 1959, p.238)

It comes as no surprise to find that Rogers' theory of an improving relationship requires that Alice and Ben are communicating with each other congruently, that is, their experience, their awareness, and their consciously intended communications are in harmony with one another, these communications being perceived as clear. As they feel understood by the other, their needs for positive regard are satisfied, and they can each convey unconditional positive regard in response, thus decreasing the threat to the other, decreasing the consequent need for defensiveness, and drawing back from further twists of the spiral of incongruence.

From the point of view of theories of personality, it is here that we begin to depart from the realm of purely intrapsychic, intrapersonal analyses. Even in Rogers' account of the therapeutic relationship, not very much about the relationship as such emerges. The client simply grows more true to herself in the benign climate provided by the therapist. But in this interpersonal theory are the seeds of an account of how people affect one another in reciprocal fashion. Here are beginnings of an interpersonal account of personality where there emerge those other facts of personality, that (as well as being the same person constant in oneself) one is different with different people, experiencing oneself and behaving as a naughty child here, as an employee there, as a valued friend with someone else.

Ronald Laing

Ronald Laing in an autobiographical preface to *The Facts of Life* (Laing, 1976) writes:

> I was born at 17.15 hours on 17 October 1927 into a family that consisted of my mother and father, living in a small three-room flat on the south side of Glasgow....My mother went into 'a decline'....My father was the only one in his family to marry and, with one possible exception, the only one to commit sexual intercourse....From as far back as I can remember, I tried to figure out what was going on between these people.

Laing studied medicine at Glasgow University and was drafted into the army after qualifying. He worked for a time at a mental hospital in Glasgow and then moved to the Tavistock Clinic in London. Howarth-Williams (1977) – whose study of Laing's work is the best and most comprehensive that I know – quotes Laing as saying that he 'never felt completely comfortable as a doctor'. His work has, of course, become known for its uncompromising stand against the medical establishment. In this chapter, I shall pick out three themes, corresponding to those that I discussed in the work of Rogers.

The affirmation of experience

It seems to me that there are two kinds of writing on the subject of psychiatry, psychotherapy, and the like. There are those which talk in terms of 'they'; their inadequacies, neuroses, illnesses, and so on. Then there are those which talk in terms of 'we' and the vicissitudes of the human condition. With rather few exceptions I have found it a worthwhile heuristic to avoid the former category.

The writings of Laing do not just fall into the latter group, they go further than those of most other writers in making aspects of our own and others' experience real and intelligible even when this experience is of the kind which we are most apt to deny in ourselves or to invalidate in others.

Laing enjoins us to look at what actually goes on in psychiatric interviews. Here, from *The Politics of Experience* (Laing, 1967), is an account of Kraepelin (the first to describe what is now called schizophrenia as a distinct syndrome) exhibiting a patient to an audience.

> Gentlemen, the cases that I have to place before you today are peculiar. First of all you see a servant girl, aged twenty-four... the patient is in continual movement, going a few steps forward, then a few steps back again....*On attempting to stop her movement,* we meet with unexpectedly strong resistance....*If one takes firm hold of her,* she distorts her usually rigid and expressionless features with deplorable weeping....*If you prick her in the forehead with a needle,* she scarcely winces.

And so forth. Laing sums up:

> Here are a man and a young girl. If we see the situation purely in terms of Kraepelin's point of view, it all immediately falls into place. He is sane, she is insane....But if we take Kraepelin's actions (in italics) – he tries to stop her movements... sticks a needle in her forehead, and so on – out of context as defined by him, how extraordinary are they. (Laing, 1967, pp.88-9)

Yet, this is a standard method of clinical examination used today. It is the method, as Kraepelin makes clear, by which we can indeed discover 'syndromes' like schizophrenia. What is going on, of course, is that:

> in a sequence of an interaction between (a person) p and (another) o, $p_1 \longrightarrow o_1 \longrightarrow p_2 \longrightarrow o_2 \longrightarrow p_3 \longrightarrow o_3$ etc., p's contrib-

bution p_1, p_2, p_3 is taken out of context....This artificially derived sequence is then studied as an isolated entity or process and attempts may be made to 'explain' it. (Laing, 1967, p.43)

This of course is the kind of method on which many notions of 'personality' are also founded.

The observer or diagnostician somehow forgets that he, too, is part of the interaction. Kraepelin has overlooked the fact that he is doing strange, or demeaning things to this other person; in short, treating her like a thing.

In a diagnostic interview of this kind the clinician may not be paying much real attention to the person as a person. He is, no doubt, paying close attention to the process of her disease, as if to some rather fascinatingly intricate piece of clockwork that has gone wrong. Wondering what makes her tick. Acting as if with a twist of the pliers here, or a prod of the screwdriver there, he might be able to put it right.

But as Laing points out, though our bodies and brains are no doubt composed of physiological mechanism, we as people are not that mechanism, that thing. Nor is experience a 'thing'. Indeed, if a patient were to complain of feeling like a piece of mechanism she would be regarded as mad.

An alternative is simply that one person meets another and this in turn means that each takes the other's experience seriously. It is to this end that *The Divided Self* (Laing, 1960) and *Sanity, Madness and the Family* (Laing and Esterson, 1964) are directed. What is made real and comprehensible here is respectively the experience of being schizoid, and the experience of being 'schizophrenic' in certain families.

Here, for instance, is a fragment of a portrait of a schizoid person – David.

The boy was a most fantastic looking character – an adolescent Kirkegaard played by Danny Kaye. The hair was too long, the collar too large, the trousers too short, the shoes too big, and withall, his secondhand theatre cape and cane! He was not simply eccentric. I could not escape the impression that this young man was playing at being eccentric.... He was indeed quite a practised actor, for he has been playing one part or another since his mother's death... his idea was *never to give himself away to others*. Consequently, he practised the most tortuous equivocation towards others in the parts he played. (Laing, 1960, p.71)

As we read through these portraits of experience, of the experience of Laing with various people (as in the above) and the experience of the people themselves, we are struck by resonances with our own experience: in our own perceptions of others, and in our own playing this part for one person and that part for another. Instead of conceptually banishing patients to states called 'neurosis' or 'psychosis', thus reducing them to a level of being that is less than fully human and so justifying our treating them as less than human, we acknowledge our own personal involvement in these kinds of curious manoeuvre.

For Laing, the playing of parts, the acting, is a response to others' demands that we be this or that: a response to injunctions made without anybody necessarily realizing what was going on. These injunctions (like the manoeuvres of Kraepelin with the servant girl) are a violence to the person.

> Love and violence, properly speaking, are polar opposites. Love lets the other be, but with affection and concern. Violence attempts to constrain the other's freedom, to force him to act in the way we desire, but with ultimate lack of concern. (Laing, 1967, p.50)

Nothing could be more ridiculous, of course, than to announce that the cure to our ills is to love each other more, as if loving is something we can just decide to do, like waving a handkerchief. But none the less, perhaps... maybe... psychotherapy as 'an obstinate attempt of two people to recover the wholeness of being human through the relationship between them' (Laing, 1967, p.45) is possible.

Alienation and liberation

Laing is notable for his formulation both of intrapersonal and interpersonal theories of defences. I shall briefly mention the former here.

As with Rogers, the central idea in Laing's conception of human suffering is that of not being true to oneself. For Laing, the concept is alienation; more trenchant than Rogers' idea of incongruence, and rising from a century of radical and dialectical thought.

Alienation is the result of pretending to ourselves and then, to make it more convincing, pretending that we are not pretending. We act on our own experience to distort it or deny it in various ways, perhaps for our own purposes, perhaps under pressure from others – especially when that pressure is exerted under the name of love.

There are various mechanisms of pretence or defence described in psychoanalysis: repression, splitting, denial, projection and the like.

> These 'mechanisms' are often described in psychoanalytic terms as themselves 'unconscious', that is the person appears to be unaware that he is doing this to himself. Even when a person develops sufficient insight to see that 'splitting' for example is going on, he usually experiences this splitting as indeed a mechanism, so to say an impersonal process which has taken over. (Laing, 1967, p.30)

But these defences appear as mechanism precisely because the person is alienated – dissociated from his own experience – the battle is not just to realize that these defences are happening, but that we do them to ourselves. In such a realization we may begin to convert process back to praxis, and become again agent rather than patient.

> Ultimately it is possible to regain the ground that has been lost. These defence mechanisms are actions taken by the person on his own experience. On top of this he has dissociated himself from his own action. The end product of this twofold violence is a person who no longer experiences himself fully as a person. (Laing, 1967, p.30)

Interpersonal perceptions

Classical psychoanalysis has no real way of conceptualizing people's relationships. Though the analytic transference is a decisive step in the study of relationship, in the psychoanalytic tradition the psychological takes place inside the person not between people. Laing, mentioning Sullivan (1947), Berne (1961) and drawing from the existentialist and phenomenological movement, attacks some of the problems of relationship in a way which is (in the psychological literature at least) both striking and fresh.

Laing states that:

> I may not actually be able to see myself as others see me, but I am constantly supposing them to be seeing me in particular ways, and I am constantly acting in the light of the actual or supposed attitudes, opinions, needs, and so on the other has in respect of me. (Laing et al., 1966, p.4)

A personal relationship is made up not just of me acting towards another, and the other acting towards me, each of us out of our own intrapsychic 'personality'. We contrive our behaviour in the light of what we think the other thinks. Even what we think the other thinks we are thinking becomes important for what we allow ourselves to think and do in that relationship.

It is, for Laing, axiomatic that behaviour is a function of experience, and that both experience and behaviour are always in relation to some one or some thing other than the self. So in an interpersonal relationship, let us say between Alfie and Betty, each has his or her own experience, and each must interpret the behaviour of the other. There is no direct access to the experience of the other. It is a matter of inference. Moreover, each person's experience of the other strongly influences that person's behaviour, which in turn influences the other's experience.

If Alfie and Betty are lovers; then for Alfie to feel loved is to interpret, that is to say, to experience, Betty's actions as loving. But since interpretations of the other's actions are only made from the view point of his own beliefs there is room for misunderstanding. Betty might see her behaviour towards another man as friendly: Alfie experiences it as flirtatious and provocative. She might see her behaviour towards Alfie as feminine: he sees it as helpless and dependent.

Laing et al. (1966) give an example of a couple who after eight years of marriage described one of their first rows, on the second night of their honeymoon. They were sitting in a bar at a hotel when the wife struck up a conversation with another couple sitting next to them. The husband became gloomy and refused to join in. She became angry at his leaving her in an awkward social situation. They had a bitter row.

Eight years later they discovered that for her the status of 'wife' had meant that she would be able to relate as part of a couple to other couples and what better time than the honeymoon was there to try out this new role as wife? For the husband it was equally clear that a honeymoon was exactly that time when he could be together with his new wife, and ignore the whole of the rest of the world. For her to need to talk to anyone else could only mean she found him inadequate. Eight years after the incident they could laught at it. He said, 'If only I'd known how you felt it would have made a great difference.' At the time each experienced the other as inconsiderate and even deliberately insulting.

One might take the view that rows are precisely the occasions for finding out that one's interpretations of the other's intentions have been mistaken. Maybe they are; but the anger generated by this row demonstrates nothing if not that the woman could not be a wife if she did not experience the man as her idea of a husband. He could not be a man if he did not experience her as his woman. Moreover, mismatches in our systems of expectancy tend only to be seen by us as the upsetting behaviour of the other.

The couple on their honeymoon had a row arising from their mismatched expectations. Others give up more easily, settling instead for trying to be what they think the other wants them to be. As Laing points out, this leaves a sorry spectacle of relationships consisting of a kind of double absence, as each strives to be the other that he or she imagines the other wants him or her to be.

Laing et al. (1966) set out as cartographers of this fundamental region of existence. They argue that if one takes some particular event (say, the honeymooning wife's conversation at the bar) then he has a view of that – this is a direct perspective. He also has a view of his wife's view: a metaperspective. From the story, his view of her view was that he thought she was 'telling me in effect that I was not man enough for her, that I was insufficient to fill her demands'. Also relevant, no doubt, is his view of her view of his view: since he was making it clear that he viewed her conversation unhappily, she must have perceived this and therefore felt satisfied that her intention to drive her point home had indeed been effective in upsetting him. (Peter Smith discusses research on this in the next chapter.)

For the couple to have wanted different things on their honeymoon was in light of their different upbringing and expectations about marriage very probable. It is a measure of the difficulty of relationships that we do not just have to deal with conflicts – as if that were not difficult enough. We have to deal with them through a haze of only dimly recognized misapprehensions. From this haze arise many of the manifestations known as 'psychopathology', and because the life of people is interpersonal it is this domain in which our personality, or rather, our different personalities (as we act differently for different others) are evoked, developed and displayed.

Goffman (1961) has a sentence, which Laing (1967) also quotes: 'There seems to be no agent more effective than another person in bringing a world for oneself alive, or, by a glance, a gesture, or a remark, shrivelling up the reality in which one is lodged.' And thus it is that one can descend in spirals, not of wanting:

> Someone to love or someone to love me, but I need someone to
> need me, and the other is someone who needs me to need her....
> My need has then ceased to be a matter of direct loving and being
> loved. My need is for the other's need of me... my solicitude is not
> for the other, but for another to want me. (Laing et al., 1966,
> p.34)

These are dimensions of 'personality' not to be conceived of as
residing in the mind, but emerging in the relationships we have. If we
are to make portraits of people, we must not just make measurements
in some contrived isolation, but portraits of a person and of his or her
experience, making this experience and action intelligible by
explicating the social context (as Laing and Esterson, 1964, and
Esterson, 1970, have done). Or, if we wish to develop psychometric
instruments, ask not just what a person habitually does in this or that
situation, but (as Laing et al., 1966, do in their interpersonal
perception method) ask questions about how he sees her, how he
thinks she sees herself, how he thinks she sees him and so on.
Thereby, we can uncover some of what emerges in and between
people in their relationships.

The person in the social context

Both Rogers and Laing have attracted dismissive criticism: Rogers
for being simplistic, for being groundlessly optimistic, for ignoring
the problem of evil, and so on; Laing for being incomprehensible,
mystical, irresponsible, for glorifying schizophrenia. I do not intend
here to give a critical appraisal of these issues (see Holland, 1977, for
such a discussion). Rather I have intended to give a brief glimpse of
their work, in a way which is expository and reflects some of its mood.

Fundamental here is the way in which both have sought to explore
a science of persons that takes people's experience seriously, and
views people in relationship with each other.

Methodologically, Rogers stands astride two different positions.
He has been in the forefront of developing the encounter group as an
activity in which people, rather than studying others for the purpose
of writing scientific papers, find out about themselves and others
through interaction. He has also (1973) written portraits of people's
experience in marriage and other relationships. However, much of

the research on his theory of personality change has been squarely in the tradition of a behavioural paradigm, as Peter Smith describes in the next chapter.

Laing's methodology has been more consciously formulated. The issue is well discussed by Howarth-Williams (1977). It consists of an explicit rejection of the monopoly of natural scientific methodology which is addressed to things, and in which the things are expected, more or less, to remain as they are while the observer, whose characteristics are irrelevant, is studying them. Without denying the validity of natural scientific methodology for processes where it is appropriate, Laing argues that for a science of persons something different is necessary. From 1962 onwards, following his study of Sartre's *Critique of Dialectical Reason* (of which Laing and Cooper (1964) contains an exposition), he adopts an explicitly Sartrian dialectical methodology. If man creates himself in the choices he makes, and affects the world which then affects him, it is not much good simply studying people as if they were static, as if they were things (though of course one might also want to study physiology, etc.). Dialectical (as opposed to natural) science involves the reciprocal effects that people have on each other, including the effects of an observer. It seeks to make intelligible the way in which people create their world intentionally, by praxis, rather than seeing the social world as process with mechanical causes.

With such methodologies, theories of personality might be transformed into theories of persons, where 'theory' might be understood in something closer to its original Orphic meaning interpreted by Cornford (1912) as 'passionate sympathetic contemplation'.

Out of this contemplation perhaps may arise the sense that others are not simply objects to be manoeuvred in our fantasies. By becoming aware of our own experience, we can allow others their experience, and that in such a world not just a science of persons, but the possibility of our being human might be created.

Note

I am grateful to Anthony Ryle and Peter Smith for reading and commenting on a draft of this manuscript.

Suggested further reading

Rogers

(1961) *On Becoming a Person: A Psychotherapist's View of Psychotherapy.* London: Constable.

Laing

(1967) *The Politics of Experience.* London: Penguin.

14 Research into humanistic personality theories

Peter B. Smith

The theories advanced by humanistic personality theorists do two things. They assert a particular view of human nature and of how it comes to be as it is. They also assert, sometimes in a no more than implicit manner, how research relating to these theories shall be undertaken. The preceding chapter has clearly shown the manner in which two such theorists have developed their ideas and formulated them in a manner in which they are amenable to some form of empirical investigation. A substantial part of this chapter will be taken up with the studies which have been triggered by the work of Rogers and Laing. However, the phrase 'humanistic personality theory' encompasses a somewhat wider range of work and it may be worthwhile initially to examine some other attempts to contribute to this field.

Humanistic personality theories are those which accord some kind of primacy to the immediate experience of the person. An element in many humanistic theories is the concept of 'growth' or progression toward a more ideal state, often referred to as self-actualization. In Rogers' model the state where the person is congruent is one in which the person's self is at that moment actualized. Maslow (1954) has constructed a total personality theory around the concept of self-actualization. In Maslow's view we are subject to two quite different motivational states, deficiency-motivation and being-motivation. Under deficiency-motivation we seek to behave in a manner which reduces various aversive states such as physiological needs, insecurity, lack of love or status. Under being-motivation we engage in behaviours which are intrinsically satisfying. We 'do our thing', not in the expectation of any particular reaction from others, but just because it expresses some particular aspect of ourself which we value.

Self-actualization

In theory one might expect that if Maslow and those who have been influenced by him wished to encompass the range of human experience, they would pay equal attention to deficiency-motivation and to being-motivation. In practice, since deficiency-motivation has been the focus of many non-humanistic personality theorists, attempts to describe and measure the state of self-actualization provide both the novelty and the enthusiasm of these workers. Maslow (1962) himself made a study of 'peak-experiences', that is moments of ecstatic happiness, which most of us experience on occasion, but some more frequently than others. Maslow undertook interviews with a range of people, many of whom were particularly successful in their chosen field, and sought to establish the frequency and quality of these peak experiences. The descriptions he received sustained his view that at such moments the person is given over to 'being' and is not in any way aware of deficiency needs or the possible reactions of others. Czikszentmihalyi (1975) interviewed a wide range of prominent sportsmen and reported a similar experience of ecstatically losing oneself, or as he called it 'flow', in the highly skilled performance of one's ability.

Moments such as those reported by Maslow and by Czikszentmihalyi are seen by them as rare and precious and on the whole not something which one could consciously *plan* to experience. Many writers in the field of humanistic psychology see personal growth as a planned or at least plannable process within which one learns to choose how one will act, to take responsibility for what one does rather than to depend on the reactions of others as the sole arbiter of what is right. It is perhaps therefore not surprising that, for some, the development of humanistic psychology as a field has become almost synonymous with the development of an ever growing diversity of methods which seek to enhance self-actualization through the provision of some particular kind of short but intensive experience. The range of such experiences includes not only psychotherapy, but also encounter groups, bioenergetics, meditation, guided fantasy, massage and many others.

Rogers and Maslow would both agree that self-actualization is not a state which one either has or does not have. They would see it as a state which one might experience either rarely or more frequently. Thus in researching the various forms of personal growth experiences one might most usefully ask not 'do they make people more self-actualized?', but 'do people achieve greater self-actualization during the experience?' and also 'does this make it any more likely that they will experience self-actualization subsequently?' Rogers (1970) quotes from interviews with participants in encounter groups conducted by himself, but it is difficult to render such data into a form in which one can estimate either the frequency or the extent of such effects. An attempt to provide a more systematically-constructed psychometric instrument has been made by Shostrom (1966). He devised the Personal Orientation Inventory (POI) which purports to be a measure of self-actualization. This is a self-report questionnaire in which the respondent has to choose between 150 pairs of statements describing oneself. The statements in the inventory are based on the concepts of Maslow and of other humanistic personality theorists as to how one might expect a self-actualized person to behave and feel. The two major scales of the test are termed 'time-competence' and 'inner-directed support'. A time-competent person is one who is engrossed neither in the past nor the future, but who makes choices about what to do on the basis of present experience. A person with inner-directed support is one who decides what to do not on the basis of others' possible demands or reactions, but on the basis of attention to one's own inner feelings, priorities and goals. In evaluating this instrument it is important to note that it no longer treats self-actualization as a variable state, but as an attribute which one has to a greater or lesser degree either got or not got.

The Personal Orientation Inventory has proved immensely attractive to researchers within the field of humanistic psychology. It has been widely used to assess whether or not particular workshops or other personal growth experiences do have an impact in the intended direction. For instance, several dozen studies have been published which test for increased self-actualization after encounter groups. If one considers only studies which included also control groups of those who did not attend groups (Smith, 1980), a substantial number remain and most of these do show increased POI scores after group experience. However, in some studies these increases are also found among the controls. In addition, there is some suggestion from studies with more elaborate designs that the act of completing a POI may in itself induce changes in subsequent responses. Knapp (1976) reviews a larger number of studies using the POI and concludes that POI scores can increase after a wide range of experiences, including taking drugs and studying courses in humanistic psychology.

The readiness with which changes may apparently be induced in POI scores suggests that one should examine more closely just what it is that the test may measure. It is formulated in terms devised by humanistic personality theorists and yet its structure is similar to that espoused by trait-personality theorists. The respondent's answers to the test are evaluated not from the viewpoint of the respondent, as a humanistic-personality theorist would argue that they should be, but in terms of whether they do or do not fall into categories which are pre-established by the researcher. Thus the scores may be expected to tell us not about how the respondent *experiences* particular situations or responses, but about how the respondent *reports* responses to a series of questions about how he or she usually feels or behaves.

My own confidence that such responses might provide a valid measure of self-actualization was strongly affected by taking the test on first encountering it some years ago. My scores indicated that I was on the 99th percentile for self-actualization, at a time in life when I was not aware of being a markedly more fulfilled person than others I associate with. Flattered though I was by the possibility I had all along been self-actualized without being aware of it, I reluctantly reached the conclusion that a simpler explanation for my impressive score was that I had read a good many books on humanistic psychology and knew what the right answers were supposed to be.

In a similar manner one can imagine that the studies showing increased POI scores after various personal growth experiences are just as readily explicable in terms of increased exposure to a new vocabulary as they are in terms of an actual increase in self-actualization. If we wish for greater certainty as to whether or not people's level of experiencing themselves and others does increase after a workshop or therapy, measures which ask more directly about specific experience should provide more valid data. As Wylie's (1974) critique of a wide range of measures of self-concept has shown, the fact that a test is presented in a packaged and readily usable form by no means guarantees that it will be an appropriate measure to use.

The concept of self-actualization has played an important role in the development of humanistic psychology. However this importance has not lain in the provision of a precisely delineated and measurable construct, but rather in helping to define in a more general way the range of experiences which are of interest to humanistic psychologists. The work of the Rogerians has in many ways proved more directly expressible in terms of empirical work and it is to this field which we now turn.

The preconditions for effective therapy

Rogerian theory lays less stress on the state of self-actualization and more on the qualities of experience which are required to enhance it. Researchers in the Rogerian tradition have consequently not employed tests such as the POI as criteria of effective therapy but have relied on measures in more general use in the clinical field such as ratings of improvement by therapists, clients or third parties, more general psychometric tests such as the MMPI (see Chapter 6) and more specific ratings of particular symptoms or problems.

Unsurprisingly, the earliest tests of the Rogerian hypotheses were made by Rogerians and concerned Rogerian therapy. Measures were required of the levels of genuineness, unconditional positive regard and accurate empathy shown by the therapists. In most studies these qualities were assessed by having trained judges rate excerpts from tape-recordings of therapy sessions. Truax and Mitchell (1971) summarize the early studies and conclude that a substantial majority of them do support the view that therapist genuineness, empathy and unconditional positive regard are associated with therapeutic success.

The relationship between the Rogerian triad of variables and positive outcome appeared to hold for both individual and group therapy and for a wide variety of types of clients. Truax and Mitchell indicate that in some studies not only were high scores on the Rogerian triad associated with positive outcome, but low scores were associated with clients who deteriorated.

The optimism of Truax and Mitchell's conclusions has encouraged a good deal of further work in this field. However, before passing to more recent studies it is worthwhile to note that even within the studies reviewed by Truax and Mitchell, the findings are not precisely as Rogers' theory requires. Rogers specified that his triad of variables were *necessary and sufficient* for therapeutic change. However, what Truax and Mitchell reported was that the relationship between therapeutic outcome and the Rogerian triad varied from one study to another. Thus in one study genuineness might be positively associated with outcome while accurate empathy was not, while in another these relationships would be reversed. It is possible that some of this variability is due to the fact that different measures of therapeutic success are employed in the various studies, and that many of these measures do not correlate too well with one another. But Rogers is clear that all the conditions are required, not just some of them.

More recent studies of the Rogerian triad of variables and therapeutic outcome have yielded much more mixed results (Mitchell et al., 1977). Approximately equal numbers of studies which offer some support for the Rogerian hypotheses and those which do not have been reported. Behind this bald summary statement lies a huge amount of variability in the nature of the different studies testing the hypotheses. In order to decide whether or not it is damaging to Rogerian theory that some studies have failed to support it, this variability must be examined. As Keith Oatley (see Chapter 13) makes clear, Rogers does not regard his theory simply as a theory of how to do therapy in the Rogerian manner. It asserts some linkages between the way that one person behaves and the responses to be expected of a second person. If correct, the hypotheses should hold up just as well as a statement about behaviour therapy or about psychoanalysis as they should about client-centred therapy. The most recent studies do indeed span a wider range of types of therapy, but it is not clear that this is why they are less supportive of Rogers.

A more methodologically oriented point is that to enable the hypotheses to be supported there must be within the sample of therapists studied some who score high on the Rogerian variables and others who score low. Where the therapists all score at similar levels it is simply impossible to test the hypotheses in a valid manner. Some of the most frequently discussed 'failures' of the Rogerian hypotheses fall into this category. For instance Sloane et al., (1975) compared the effectiveness of three psychoanalysts and three behaviour therapists. Five of the six therapists scored close to the maximum on the rating scales, so that the low variance in their scores precludes a valid test of Rogers' view. Other studies have included a wider range of therapists but have found that they virtually all scored at the lower end of the scales. In a similar manner one can only test the hypotheses if there is a good degree of variability in the amount of improvement shown by clients in therapy.

Points such as these make it possible to argue that some of the recent failures to support the Rogerian hypotheses may not be too serious for their continuing viability. A more fundamental debate concerns whether or not the studies so far reviewed use research methods which are in fact appropriate to the question at issue. It will be recalled that these studies have for the most part rested on ratings made by judges of excerpts from tape-recordings of therapy. Rappoport and Chinsky (1972) have argued that it is very difficult for judges to make valid judgements of the qualities of the therapists' behaviour when that behaviour is judged out of context and on the basis of only brief samples. They propose that faced with such a difficult task, judges may in fact base their judgements on simpler criteria such as whether they like the therapist or not. If this were shown to be so, it would certainly call into question just what it was which had been established by the findings so far reported which are favourable to the Rogerian hypotheses. More seriously still there can be little confidence that ratings made by trained raters will necessarily match the perceptions of the patients themselves.

It is possible, even likely, that attributes of the therapist's behaviour which seem crucial to the therapist's genuineness from the patient's point of view may be less so from the point of view of the trained raters. Similarly there are likely to be other attributes to which the raters give more weight than the clients. Rogers is clear that his theory has to do with clients' perceptions, not with 'objective' judgements, so a case can only be made out for the use of trained raters if there is a good match between clients' perceptions and the ratings made by raters. This match becomes less and less likely the more the raters differ from the clients. One instance of such divergence is provided by the research which Rogers et al. (1967) undertook with schizophrenics. In this study therapists who saw themselves as being more genuine were perceived by the clients as being less genuine and vice versa. Client improvement was associated with high client-perceived therapist genuineness and therefore with low therapist-perceived therapist genuineness.

Studies such as this indicate that just as there is some difficulty in devising valid measures of self-actualization, so too is caution required in devising measures which do adequately reflect the phenomenological basis of Rogers' hypotheses. Fortunately in this instance we are somewhat better off than in the instance of self-actualization: there is a further set of studies which have attempted to test Rogers' theory using perceptions from clients. Gurman (1977) summarizes the current position. He reviews twenty-two studies of individual therapy in which client perceptions of the therapist were obtained. Of these no less than twenty-one did show a positive relation between perception of the therapist and the outcome criteria employed. This sample of studies was very diverse in terms of type of client, duration of therapy and type of outcome measures employed. In some ways this very diversity lends strength to the conclusion that a relationship does exist between the client's perception of the therapist and therapeutic outcome. It is none the less important to look at these studies somewhat more stringently in order to clarify whether the results might be explained in some manner which does not accord with Rogers' views.

Parloff et al. (1978) provide such a sceptical viewpoint of Gurman's review. They identify three difficulties in accepting Gurman's conclusion. Firstly, some of these twenty-two studies employed measures which do not derive very closely from Rogers' hypotheses. In fact, eleven of them employed the Barrett-Lennard (1962) Relationship Inventory, which is explicitly based on Rogers' work, whereas the remainder used a much more diverse range of ratings of various aspects of the therapist–patient relationship. Parloff et al.'s second criticism is that many of the studies not only asked clients to assess their relationship to the therapist but also to assess their own improvement in therapy. Thus no independent check was available as to improvement as perceived by someone other than the client. There were indeed eight studies in the sample in which the only outcome measure was one completed by the client. The final criticism is that, of the twenty-two studies, only one makes any statistical correction for the fact some clients are inevitably more distressed than others before treatment. Without such a correction it is likely that those who were initially most distressed will subsequently appear most improved. As Gurman acknowledges, the only study in his sample which made this correction was also the only one to fail to find a relationship between perception of the therapist and outcome of therapy.

These criticisms are differentially evaluated by Gurman and by

Parloff et al. For Gurman the probability remains strong that the Rogerian hypotheses are supported. While some studies are problematic it is clear that, with just one exception, the better-designed studies are just as favourable to the hypotheses as the less well-designed. For Parloff et al. the verdict remains an open one. Apart from their emphasis on the methodological weaknesses of the studies, they are sceptical that any one variable could be found which was necessary and sufficient to account for the success or failure of therapy.

In a further section of his review, Gurman examines ten studies of group therapy in which client perceptions of the therapist were obtained. In none of these was there very convincing evidence linking perception of the therapist to outcome. One might presume that this contrast with individual therapy studies occurs simply because therapist–client relationships are less salient in groups. Improvement might turn out instead to be a function of client–client relationships. But the findings have some further implications. At the methodological level the criticism of the individual therapy studies advanced by Parloff et al. should be just as strongly operative in the group therapy studies. And yet here no positive findings are reported. This suggests that although the sources of potential error discussed by Parloff et al. are certain to be present, they do not appear sufficiently potent to guarantee positive findings. One's confidence in Gurman's relatively optimistic conclusions about individual therapy is thus enhanced. A further implication from the studies of group therapy is that Rogers' hypotheses must be slightly amended. It is clearly only sensible to argue that the therapist may provide the necessary and sufficient conditions for change where the therapist is in fact the most salient figure for the client.

The debate concerning the validity of the Rogerian hypotheses is unique in the field of humanistic psychology. Only at this point has a confrontation occurred between hypotheses central to humanistic personality theory and a large and systematically collected body of empirical data. The confrontation has not been a wholly conclusive one, but it none the less serves a number of continuing functions. Chief among these are the assertions that the collection of empirical data concerning humanistically derived hypotheses *is* feasible, and that the demands of empiricism do *not* require that one's hypotheses be trivial ones. A further function of the confrontation is to illuminate the difficulties to be overcome if research in this field is to be more fruitful, and some of these will now be explored.

The search for new research methods

The format of the research studies reviewed in the preceding section accords well with that employed by experimentalists. There is an independent variable, therapist behaviour (which is not actually controlled by the researcher) and a dependent variable. The studies are thus correlational rather than experimental, but they are discussed as though they were true experiments. Researchers frequently refer to 'therapist-offered conditions' (by which they mean levels of congruence, empathy and so forth) and they adhere to the assumption that these conditions *cause* the patient's response, whether it be improvement or deterioration. Very little attention is paid to the possibility that the client's behaviour may be an equally potent cause of what goes on between therapist and client. For instance it is not implausible that if a client for some reason or other starts to improve, the therapist may respond with increased empathy, genuineness or positive regard. Oatley has outlined in Chapter 13 how Laing's ideas come closer to acknowledging the multidirectionality of causation in interpersonal relationships than do those of Rogers. Once one acknowledges that each party in an interpersonal transaction has some potentiality for influencing what happens, then each person's perception of what is going on takes on an equal validity. It is to the credit of the researchers testing the Rogerian hypotheses that they have been able to transcend their own assumptions and show that in therapy the perceptions of the various parties do indeed diverge in the ways that one might predict.

The question to be addressed is whether in letting all the complexity of conflicting perceptions into one's range of valid research data one loses the possibility of drawing coherent or concise conclusions from that research. Two of Laing's books provide a sufficiently detailed basis of empirical data to consider this question. In the first (Laing and Esterson, 1964), a series of case studies is presented of the families of girls and women who had previously been diagnosed as schizophrenic. By the use of extensive interviews with the various family members, both together and apart, Laing and Esterson build up a vivid picture of the conflicting perceptions within each family. By charting the context within which each schizophrenic has been located, it became possible to argue that their perceptions are not intrinsically 'mad' but are comprehensible responses to a chaotic and confusing setting. Esterson (1970) has made a more detailed study of one of these families, and provides a fuller exposition of the methods employed.

These case studies have been much argued over by protagonists and critics of Laing. While they have a compelling vividness they do not lead us clearly toward any new research method. Originally, Laing and Esterson had also planned to undertake studies of a series of 'control' families with no schizophrenic member, but these were never completed. Such studies would certainly have helped to clarify how far the degree of confusion and mystification characterizing these families does or does not overlap the range to be found in 'normal' families. Even supposing that a difference had been found between the two samples of families, we should still be left uncertain as to what might be the cause of the disordered communications of the 'mad' families. Such possible causes could include the whole broad range of explanations currently canvassed for the origins of schizophrenia including both genetic and environmental effects.

The second of Laing's studies provides a more systematic basis for the development of new research methods. Laing et al. (1966) devised a procedure, already touched upon by Oatley in the preceding chapter, for exploring relationships, particularly in dyads and families. The Interpersonal Perceptions Method (IPM) faces each party of a relationship with sixty statements. Each of four relationships is viewed from three perspectives (*direct, meta* and *meta-meta*). Thus: '(1) She depends on me; (2) I depend on her; (3) She depends on herself; (4) I depend on myself' are each answered in terms of the following three questions: 'Is the statement true?' 'How would the other party answer this statement?' and 'How would the other party think that I will answer this statement?' The book describes the development of the IPM technique and its use primarily in the context of marital therapy. Data are presented showing greater agreement of perception in non-disturbed than disturbed couples.

The IPM as presented is exceedingly complex, and it is perhaps for this reason that other researchers appear to have made little subsequent use of it. It is also open to criticism as not taking account of various sources of potential error in the measurement of interpersonal accuracy, which have been extensively explored by social psychologists (e.g. Cook, 1971). Research based on the IPM is thus not so much an achievement as a suggestion for a future direction. It treats conflicting perceptions not as evidence of error but as data for explanation. Whether that exploration should then be designated as therapy or as research is unclear, but the blurring of the two provides some intimation of a new kind of relationship between researcher and 'subject'.

One of the most sustained attempts to develop and use new research methods in this field is that initiated by Harré and Secord (1972) and Harré (1979). These authors undertook an extensive critique of the philosophical assumptions underlying empiricist psychology and found them lacking. They question the use of a framework which construes behaviour in terms of invariant cause-and-effect sequences, noting in particular the divergence between the way psychology experiments are set up and the experience of everyday life. In experiments (and equally in the research into the Rogerian hypotheses) persons are considered as entities to whom things are done or to whom events occur. In life, according to Harré and Secord, we rather frequently experience 'agency' or the use of personal powers; in other words we make active choices about how to behave. These are not seen as unconstrained but as regulated by a rule structure which governs the range of our choices. This rule structure is not fixed and immutable but evolves over time. It is both a cause and an effect of social history.

Harré and Secord propose that we explore the interface between personal agency and the rule structure through a new approach which they term ethogeny or ethogenics. The essence of this approach is that the researcher asks people for 'accounts' of what they are doing in a particular circumstance. It is expected that such accounts will enable preliminary assignment of events to three types of episode, known as formal, causal and enigmatic. In formal episodes people account for their behaviour entirely in terms of rules which apply to that setting. Examples would be a wedding or being introduced to a stranger. In causal episodes people account for their behaviour in terms of some external imperative, perhaps physical or chemical in nature. Examples would be pregnancy or drunkenness.

Harré and Secord argue further that the huge majority of episodes fall into neither of these categories and as a consequence are what they term 'enigmatic'. The essence of an enigmatic episode is that neither of the more simple types of account will encompass it. One should expect that by asking different parties to the episode for their accounts of what was happening one will reveal differences and contradictions. This brings us back to the position argued by Laing. Harré and Secord assert that after the taking of accounts, the next and crucial stage is what they term the 'negotiation of accounts'. Any enigmatic episode under study must generate at least three accounts, one each from the two parties and a third from bystander(s), who will include the researcher.

To describe this stage in the research as the negotiation of accounts has a rather different emphasis than is found in other approaches. Essentially Harré and Secord agree with the behaviourist view that particular accounts will be biased and subjective. However they reject the view that the way out of this dilemma is to accept one particular 'objective' account as the correct one and all others as wrong. They propose instead a process of 'negotiation' which is initiated by the researcher but which gives all accounts equal validity as data bearing on what is happening. The process of negotiation starts to sound rather like Laing and his colleagues going through the IPM with their disturbed couples.

The test of the usefulness of Harré's approach must not rest solely on the persuasiveness of his rhetoric, which is considerable, but also on whether it leads to new and different types of research. The principal empirical studies generated by this approach so far are those reported in Marsh et al. (1977). This book reports two projects, both concerned with unruly behaviour. The first study reports accounts collected from school children concerning their misbehaviour in school. The descriptions are vivid and interesting and show that the children had a sharp understanding of how they differentiated their behaviour as between teachers of various kinds. However, no accounts were taken from teachers and no report is made of attempts to negotiate different accounts. The second study examines the behaviour of fans watching the Oxford United football team. A wider range of accounts was collected here, including the 'objective' one of video recordings of the crowd. The main emphasis of the report is on how the supposedly chaotic behaviour of football crowds is actually regulated by a rather precise rule structure. These rules are widely diffused and include procedures for regulating aggressive encounters as well as for reinterpreting them after they are over in the most aggressive manner possible. The negotiation of accounts in this study is not systematically described, but appears to have included playing back videos to fans, playing bacd tapes of interviews to fans, and trying out the researchers' own conclusions on fans. In this situation then the 'negotiation' of accounts appears a little unilateral, no doubt reflecting the very different bases for involvement of the researchers and the fans.

The search for new methods of research which adequately express the emphasis of humanistic personality theory has reached an interesting stage. From the time when humanistic psychologists simply asserted the value of studying subjective experience in face of the behaviourists' dismissal of it, there has been a movement to locate that subjective experience in a context. The formulations of both Laing and of Harré currently offer more hope and aspiration than achievement and substance. There is none the less some agreement between them as to what is required. The metaphor of 'negotiating' accounts may prove to be illuminating. Negotiations can only take place when all parties wish to enter into them, and the instance of the football study suggests that in some settings negotiations will need to be quick and to the point. Other settings, of which therapy is an obvious instance, sanction a far more profound process of negotiation, partly no doubt because there is a potentially more equal sharing of the benefits. There are certainly further settings which will accept such research methods and if the researchers into the Rogerian hypotheses are right, these will be settings where the parties experience the genuineness, empathy and positive regard of one another.

Bibliography

Abraham, K. (1927) The influence of oral eroticism on character formation. In *Selected Papers*. London: Hogarth Press.

Adams-Webber, J. (1969) Cognitive complexity and sociality. *British Journal of Social and Clinical Psychology 8*: 211-16.

Adams-Webber, J. (1970) Actual structure and potential chaos. In D. Bannister (ed.) *Perspectives in Personal Construct Theory*. London: Academic Press.

Adams-Webber, J. (1978) A further test of the golden section hypothesis. *British Journal of Psychology 69*: 439-42.

Adams-Webber, J. (1979) *Personal Construct Theory: Concepts and Applications*. New York: Wiley.

Adams-Webber, J. and Davidson, D. (1979) Maximum contrast between self and others. *British Journal of Psychology 70*: 517-18.

Adams-Webber, J. and Mirc, E. (1976) Assessing the development of student teachers' role conceptions. *British Journal of Educational Psychology 46*: 338-40.

Adorno, T.W., Frenkel-Brunswik, E., Levinson, D.J. and Sanford, R.N. (1950) *The Authoritarian Personality*. New York: Harper & Row.

Alcock, T. (1963) *The Rorschach in Practice*. London: Tavistock.

Allport, G.W. (1937) *Personality: A Psychological Interpretation*. New York: Holt.

Ames, L.B. and Ilg, F.L. (1962) *Mosaic Patterns of American Children*. New York: Harper & Row.

Arnold, M.B. (1962) *Story Sequence Analysis: A New Method of Measuring Motivation and Predicting Achievement*. New York: Columbia University Press.

Aronow, E. and Reznikoff, M. (1976) *Rorschach Content Interpretation*. New York: Grune & Stratton.

Bakan, D. (1966) *The Duality of Human Existence.* Chicago: Rand McNally.

Bandura, A. (1969) *Principles of Behavior Modification.* New York: Holt, Rinehart & Winston.

Bannister, D. (1959) An application of personal construct theory (Kelly) to schizoid thinking. Unpublished Ph.D. thesis, University of London.

Bannister, D. (1962) The nature and measurement of schizophrenic thought disorder. *Journal of Mental Science 108*: 825-42.

Bannister, D. (1963) The genesis of schizophrenic thought disorder: a serial invalidation hypothesis. *British Journal of Psychiatry 109*: 680-8.

Bannister, D. (1965) The genesis of schizophrenic thought disorder: a retest of the serial invalidation hypothesis. *British Journal of Psychiatry 111*: 377-82.

Bannister, D. (1977) The logic of passion. In D. Bannister (ed.) *New Perspectives in Personal Construct Theory.* London: Academic Press.

Bannister, D. (ed.) (1977a) *New Perspectives in Personal Construct Theory.* London: Academic Press.

Bannister, D. and Agnew, J. (1977) The child's construing of self. In J.K. Cole and A.W. Landfield (eds) *1976 Nebraska Symposium on Motivation.* Lincoln, Nebraska: University of Nebraska Press.

Bannister, D. and Fransella, F. (1966) A grid test of schizophrenic thought disorder. *British Journal of Social and Clinical Psychology 5*: 95-102.

Bannister, D. and Fransella, F. (1967) *A grid test of schizophrenic thought disorder.* Barnstaple: Psychological Test Publications.

Bannister, D. and Fransella, F. (1980) *Inquiring Man: The Psychology of Personal Constructs* (2nd edn). London: Penguin.

Bannister, D., Fransella, F. and Agnew, J. (1971) Characteristics and validity of the grid test of thought disorder. *British Journal of Social and Clinical Psychology 10*: 144-51.

Bannister, D. and Mair, J.M.M. (1968) *The Evaluation of Personal Constructs.* London: Academic Press.

Bannister, D. and Salmon, P. (1966) Schizophrenic thought disorder: specific or diffuse. *British Journal of Medical Psychology 39*: 215-19.

Banta, T.J. (1970) Tests for the evaluation of early childhood education: The Cincinnati Autonomy Test Battery (CATB).

Bargman, G. (1953) *The Statistical Significance of Simple Structure in Factor Analysis.* Frankfurt: HFITS.

Baron, R.A., Byrne, D. and Kantowitz, B.H. (1977) *Psychology: Understanding Behaviour.* Philadelphia and London: Saunders.

Barrett, P. and Kline, P. (1980) Effects on factor structure in items of varying the ratio of subjects to variables. *Journals of Personality and Individual Differences* (in press).

Barrett-Lennard, G.T. (1962) Dimensions of therapist response as causal factors in therapeutic change. *Psychological Monographs 76*: 43 (whole no. 5629).

Barton, K. (1973) *The Relative Validities of the CTS, the EPI and the Comrey Scales as Measures of Second-order Personality Source Traits by Questionnaire.* Boulder: IRMA.

Basch, M.F. (1976) Psychoanalysis and communication science. *Annual of Psychoanalysis 4:* 355-421.

Beck, A.T. (1962) Reliability of psychiatric diagnoses: a critique of systematic studies. *American Journal of Psychiatry 11*: 210-15.

Beck, S.J. (1960) *The Rorschach Experiment: Ventures in Blind Diagnosis.* New York: Grune & Stratton.

Beck, S.J. (1978) *Rorschach's Test. II Gradients in Mental Disorder.* New York: Grune & Stratton.

Becker, H. and Barnes, H.E. (1952) *Social Thought from Lore to Science* (2 vols). Washington, D.C.: Harren Press.

Bellak, L. (1954) *The Thematic Apperception Test and the Children's Apperception Test in Clinical Use.* New York: Grune & Stratton.

Bellak, L. and Adelman, C. (1960) The Children's Apperception Test (CAT). In A.I. Rabin and M.R. Haworth (eds). *Projective Techniques with Children.* New York and London: Grune & Stratton.

Bellak, L. and Hurvich, M.S. (1966) A human modification of the Children's Apperception Test (CAT-H). *Journal of Projective Techniques and Personality Assessment 30*: 228-42

Beloff, H. (1957) The structure and origin of the anal character. *Genetic Psychological Monographs 55*: 141-72.

Benjafield, J. and Adams-Webber, J. (1975) Assimilative projection and construct balance. *British Journal of Psychology 66*: 169-73.

Benjafield, J. and Adams-Webber, J. (1976) The golden section hypothesis. *British Journal of Psychology 67*: 11-15.

Berlyne, D.E. (1971) *Aesthetics and Psychobiology.* New York: Appleton-Century-Crofts.

Berne, E. (1961) *Transactional Analysis in Psychotherapy: A Systematic Individual and Social Psychiatry.* New York: Grove Press.

Bieri, J. et al. (1966) *Clinical and Social Judgment: The Discrimination of Behavioral Information.* New York: Wiley.

Bieri, J., Atkins, A.L., Briar, S., Leaman, R.L., Miller, H. and Tripodi, T. (1955) Cognitive complexity – simplicity and predictive behavior. *Journal of Abnormal and Social Psychology 51*: 263-8.

Blatt, S.J. (1975) The validity of projective techniques and their research and clinical contribution. *Journal of Personality Assessment 39*: 327-43.

Block, J. and Block, J.H. (1951) An investigation of the relationship between intolerance of ambiguity and ethnocentrism. *Journal of Personality 19*: 303-11.

Block, J., Block, J.H. and Harrington, D.M. (1974) Some misgivings about the Matching Familiar Figures Test as a measure of reflection – impulsivity. *Developmental Psychology 10*: 611-32.

Bogen, J. (1969) The other side of the brain II. An appositional mind. *Bulletin of the Los Angeles Neurological Society 37*: 135-62.

Boring, E.G. (1950) *A History of Experimental Psychology* (2nd edn). New York: Appleton-Century-Crofts.

Bowlby, J. (1969) *Attachment and Loss.* Vol. 1: Attachment. London: Hogarth Press and Institute of Psychoanalysis.

Bowlby, J. (1973) *Attachment and Loss*. Vol. 2: *Separation, Anxiety and Anger*. London: Hogarth Press.

Bowlby, J. (1980) *Attachment and Loss*. Vol. 3: *Loss, Sadness and Depression*. London: Hogarth Press.

Bowyer, L.R. (1970) *The Lowenfeld World Technique*. Oxford and London: Pergamon.

Boxer, P. (1980) Supporting reflective learning: towards a reflexive theory of form. *Human Relations* (in press).

Breuer, J. and Freud, S. (1895) Studies on hysteria. In *Standard Edition of the Complete Psychological Works of S. Freud*. Vol. 2. London: Hogarth Press.

Briggs, K.C. and Myers, B.B. (1962) *The Myers-Briggs Type Indicator*. Princeton Educational Testing Service.

Broadhurst, P.L. (1975) The Maudsley reactive and non-reactive strains of rats – a survey. *Behavioural Genetics 5*: 299-319.

Brown, R.W. (1958) Is a boulder sweet or sour? *Contemporary Psychology 3*: 1139.

Browne, J.A. and Howarth, E. (1977) A comprehensive factor analysis of personality questionnaire items: a test of twenty putative factor hypotheses. *Multivariate Behavioural Research 12*: 399-427.

Buros, O.K. (ed.) (1970) *Personality Tests and Reviews*. Highland Park: Gryphon Press.

Buros, O.K. (ed.) (1978) *The VIIIth Mental Measurements Year Book*. New Jersey: Gryphon Press.

Burt, C. (1921) *Mental and Scholastic Tests*. London: King.

Button, E. and Fransella, F. (1980) Changes in construing during treatment for anorexia nervosa. Unpublished manuscript.

Cattell, R.B. (1964) *Description and Measurement of Personality*. London: Harrap.

Cattell, R.B. (1957) *Personality and Motivation: Structure and Measurement*. Chicago: World Book Co.

Cattell, R.B. (1966) *Handbook of Multivariate Experimental Psychology*. Chicago: Rand McNally.

Cattell, R.B. (1966a) The Scree test for the number of factors. *Multivariate Behavioural Research 1*: 140-61.

Cattell, R.B. (1971) *Abilities: Their Structure Growth and Action*. New York: Houghton Mifflin.

Cattell, R.B. (1973) *Personality and Mood by Questionnaire*. New York: Jossey-Bass.

Cattell, R.B. (1978) *Personality and Learning Theory*. New York: Springer.

Cattell, R.B. and Butcher, H.J. (1968) *The Prediction of Achievement and Creativity*. New York: Bobbs Merrill.

Cattell, R.B. and Child, D. (1975) *Motivation and Dynamic Structure*. London: Holt-Blond.

Cattell, R.B. and Gibbons, B.D. (1968) Personality factor structure of the combined Guilford and Cattell personality questionnaires. *Personality and Social Psychology 9*: 107-20.

Cattell, R.B. and Kline, P. (1977) *The Scientific Analysis of Personality and Motivation*. London: Academic Press.

Cattell, R.B., Pierson, G. and Finkbeiner, C. (1976) Alignment of personality source trait factors from questionnaires and observer ratings: the theory of instrument-free patterns. *Multivariate Experimental Clinical Research 2*: 63-88.

Cattell, R.B. and Vaughan, D.S. (1974) A large sample cross-check on the factor structure of the 16PF by item and by parcel factoring. Boulder: IRMA.

Chamone, A.S., Eysenck, H.J. and Harlow, H.F. (1972) Personality in monkeys: factor analysis of Rhesus social behaviour. *Quarterly Journal of Experimental Psychology 24*: 496-504.

Chein, I. (1972) *The Science of Human Behaviour and the Image of Man*. New York: Basic Books.

Claxton, G. (1979) Individual relativity: the model of man in modern physics. *Bulletin of the British Psychological Society 32*: 415-18.

Coates, S.W. (1972) *The Preschool Embedded Figures Test Manual*. Palo Alto: Consulting Psychologists Press.

Cochran, L.R. (1977) Inconsistency and change in conceptual organization. *British Journal of Medical Psychology 50*: 319-28.

Comrey, A.L. (1970) *The Comrey Personality Scales*. San Diego: Educational and Industrial Testing Service.

Comrey, A.L. and Duffy, K.E. (1968) Cattell and Eysenck Factor scores related to Comrey Personality factors. *Multivariate Behavioural Research 3*: 379-92.

Cook, M. (1971) *Interpersonal Perception*. Harmondsworth: Penguin.

Cornford, F.M. (1912) *From Religion to Philosophy*. London: Arnold.

Crockett, W.H. (1965) Cognitive complexity and impression formation. In B.A. Maher (ed.) *Progress in Experimental Personality Research*. Vol. 2. New York: Academic Press.

Crockett, W.H. and Meisel, P. (1974) Construct connectedness, strength of disconfirmation and impression change. *Journal of Personality 42*: 290-9.

Cronbach, L.J. (1946) Response sets and test validity. *Educational and Psychological Measurement 6*: 475-94.

Cronbach, L.J. (1950) Further evidence on response sets and test validity. *Educational and Psychological Measurement 10*: 3-31.

Cronbach, L.J. and Meehl, P.E. (1955) Construct validity in psychological tests. *Psychological Bulletin 52*: 177-94.

Czikszentmihalyi, M. (1975) Play and intrinsic rewards. *Journal of Humanistic Psychology 15*: 41-63.

Dahlstrom, W.G. and Welsh, G.S. (1960) *An MMPI Handbook*. London: Oxford University Press.

Davidoff, L.L. (1976) *Introduction to Psychology*. New York and London: McGraw-Hill.

Delia, J.G. and Crockett, W.H. (1973) Social schemes, cognitive complexity and the learning of social structures. *Journal of Personality 41*: 413-29.

Denckla, W.D. (1974) Role of the pituitary and thyroid glands in the decline of minimal oxygen consumation with age. *Journal of Clinical Investigation 53*: 572-81.

Denckla, W.D. (1975) Pituitary inhibitor of thyrotoxine. *Federation Proceedings* *37*: 96.

Denckla, W.D. (1975a) A time to die. *Life Sciences 16*: 31-44.

Denckla, W.D. (1977) Systems analysis of possible mechanisms of mammalian aging. *Mechanisms of Aging and Development 6*: 143-52.

Deri, S. (1949) *Introduction to the Szondi Test: Theory and Practice.* New York: Grune & Stratton.

Dimond, S. (1979) Symmetry and asymmetry in the vertebrate brain. In D.A. Oakley and H.C. Plotkin (eds) *Brain, Behaviour and Evolution.* Methuen: London.

Dixon, N.F. (1971) *Subliminal Perception: The Nature of a Controversy.* London: McGraw-Hill.

Dixon, N.F. and Haider, M. (1961) Changes in the visual threshold as a function of subception. *Quarterly Journal of Experimental Psychology 13*: 229-35.

Duck, S.W. (1979) The personal and the interpersonal in construct theory: social and individual aspects of relationships. In P. Stringer and D. Bannister (eds) *Constructs of Sociality and Individuality.* London: Academic Press.

Eccles, J.C. (1979) The creation of the self. *Bulletin of the Menninger Clinic 43*: 3-19.

Edwards, A.L. (1957) *The Social Desirability Variable in Personality Research.* New York: Dryden Press.

Edwards, A.L. (1959) *The Edwards Personal Preference Schedule.* New York: Psychological Corporation.

Elkisch, P. (1960) Free art expression. In A.I. Rabin and M.R. Haworth (eds) *Projective Techniques with Children.* New York and London: Grune & Stratton.

Ellis, A. (1962) *Reason and Emotion in Psychotherapy.* New York: Lyle Stuart.

Ellis, A. E. (1963) An introduction to the principles of scientific psychoanalysis. In S. Rachman (ed.) *Critical Essays on Psychoanalysis.* New York: Pergamon.

English, H.B. and English, C.A. (1958) *A Comprehensive Dictionary of Psychological and Psychoanalytical Terms.* New York and London: Longmans Green.

Erikson, E.H. (1950) *Childhood and Society.* New York: Norton.

Erikson, E.H. (1959) *Identity and the Life Cycle.* New York: International Universities Press.

Esterson, A. (1970) *The Leaves of Spring: A Study in the Dialectics of Madness.* London: Penguin.

Exner, J.E. (1974) *The Rorschach: A Comprehensive System.* New York and London: Wiley.

Eysenck, H.J. (1944) Types of personality – a factorial study of 700 neurotics. *Journal of Mental Science 90*: 851-961.

Eysenck, H.J. (1947) *Dimensions of Personality.* London: Routledge.

Eysenck, H.J. (1953) The logical basis of factor analysis. In D.N. Jackson and S. Messick (eds) *Problems in Human Assessment.* New York: McGraw-Hill.

Eysenck, H.J. (1957) *Sense and Nonsense in Psychology*. Harmondsworth: Penguin.

Eysenck, H.J. (1965) *Fact and Fiction in Psychology*. Harmondsworth: Penguin.

Eysenck, H.J. (1967) *The Biological Bases of Personality*. Springfield, Ill.: C.C. Thomas.

Eysenck, H.J. (1976) Genetic factors in personality development. In A.R. Kaplan (ed.) *Human Behaviour Genetics*. Springfield, Ill.: C.C. Thomas.

Eysenck, H.J. (1976a) The learning theory model of neurosis – a new approach. *Behaviour Research and Therapy 14*: 251-68.

Eysenck, H.J. (1977) *Crime and Personality*. London: Routledge & Kegan Paul.

Eysenck, H.J. (1978) Superfactors, P, E and N in a comprehensive factor space. *Multivariate Behavioural Research 13*: 475-81.

Eysenck, H.J. (1980) The bio-social model of man and the unification of psychology. In A.J. Chapman and D. Jones (eds) *Models of Man*. London: British Psychological Society.

Eysenck, H.J. and Eysenck, S.B.G. (1969) *Personality Structure and Measurement*. London: Routledge & Kegan Paul.

Eysenck, H.J. and Eysenck, S.B.G. (1976) *Psychoticism as a Dimension of Personality*. London: Hodder & Stoughton.

Eysenck, H.J. and Wilson, G.D. (1973) *Experimental Studies of Freudian Theories*. London: Methuen.

Fairbairn, W.R.D. (1952) *Psycho-analytic Studies of Personality*. London: Tavistock.

Ferguson, G.A. (1949) On the theory of test development. *Psychometrika 14*: 61-8.

Fernald, L.D. and Fernald, P.S. (1978) *Introduction to Psychology* (4th edn). Boston: Houghton Mifflin.

Fingarette, H. (1974) Self deception and the 'splitting of the ego'. In R. Woolheim (ed.) *Freud: A Collection of Critical Essays*. New York: Doubleday.

Finney, J.C. (1963) Maternal influences on anal or compulsive character in children. *Journal of Genetic Psychology 103*: 351-67.

Fisher, S. (1973) *The Female Orgasm*. New York: Basic Books.

Fisher, S. (1978) Dirt-anality and attitudes toward negroes. A test of Kubie's hypothesis. *The Journal of Nervous and Mental Disease 166*: 280-91.

Fisher, S. and Greenberg, R. (1977) *The Scientific Credibility of Freud's Theories and Therapy*. Brighton: Harvester Press.

Fjeld, S.P. and Landfield, A.W. (1961) *Psychological Reports 8*: 127-9.

Francis-Williams, J. (1968) *Rorschach with Children: A Comparative Study of the Contribution made by the Rorschach and Other Projective Techniques to Clinical Diagnosis with Children*. Oxford: Pergamon.

Frank, A. (1979) Two theories or one? or none? *Journal of the American Psychoanalytical Association 27*: 169-207.

Frank, L.K. (1939) Projective methods for the study of personality. *Journal of Psychology 8*: 389-413.

Fransella, F. (1970) ...and then there was one. In D. Bannister (ed.) *Perspectives in Personal Construct Theory*. London: Academic Press.

Fransella, F. (1972) *Personal Change and Reconstruction: Research on a Treatment of Stuttering.* London: Academic Press.

Fransella, F. (1977) The self and the stereotype. In D. Bannister (ed.) *New Perspectives in Personal Construct Theory.* London: Academic Press.

Fransella, F. (1980) Man-as-scientist. In A.J. Chapman and D. Jones (eds) *Models of Man.* London: The British Psychological Society.

Fransella, F. (1980a) Nature babbling to herself: the self characterisation as a therapeutic tool. In H. Bonarius, R. Holland and S. Rosenberg (eds) *Recent Advances in the Theory and Practice of Personal Construct Psychology.* London: Macmillan.

Fransella, F. and Bannister, D. (1967) A validation of repertory grid technique as a measure of political construing. *Acta Psychologica 26.* 97-106.

Fransella, F. and Bannister, D. (1977) *A Manual for Repertory Grid Technique.* London: Academic Press.

Fransella, F. and Crisp, A.H. (1979) Comparisons of weight concepts in groups of neurotic, normal and anorexic females. *British Journal of Psychiatry 134*: 79-86.

Freedman, D.A. (1977) Studies in sensory deprivation. *Annual of Psychoanalysis 5*: 195-215.

Freedman, D.A. (1979) The sensory deprivations: an approach to the study of the emergence of affects and the capacity for object relations. *Bulletin of the Menninger Clinic 43*: 29-68.

Frenkel-Brunswik, E. (1948) A study of prejudice in children. *Human Relations 1*: 295-306.

Freud, S. (1900) The interpretation of dreams. In *Standard Edition of the Complete Psychological Works of S. Freud.* Vols. 4-5. London: Hogarth Press.

Freud, S. (1905) Three essays on the theory of sexuality. In *Standard Edition of the Complete Psychological Works of S. Freud.* Vol. 7. London: Hogarth Press and Institute of Psychoanalysis.

Freud, S. (1908) Character and anal eroticism. In *Standard Edition of the Complete Psychological Works of S. Freud.* Vol. 9. London: Hogarth Press.

Freud, S. (1911) Psychoanalytic notes upon an autobiographical account of a case of paranoia (dementia paranoides). In *Collected Papers.* Vol. 3. London: Hogarth Press.

Freud, S. (1914) On narcissism: an introduction. In *Standard Edition of the Complete Psychological Works of S. Freud.* Vol. 14. London: Hogarth Press.

Freud, S. (1917) Mourning and melancholia. In *Standard Edition of the Complete Psychological Works of S. Freud.* Vol. 14. London: Hogarth Press.

Freud, S. (1920) Beyond the pleasure principle. In *Standard Edition of the Complete Psychological Works of S. Freud.* Vol. 18. London: Hogarth Press and Institute of Psychoanalysis.

Freud, S. (1923) The ego and the id. In *Standard Edition of the Complete Psychological Works of S. Freud.* Vol. 19. London: Hogarth Press.

Freud, S. (1925) An autobiographical study. In *Standard Edition of the Complete Psychological Works of S. Freud.* Vol. 20. London: Hogarth Press.

Freud, S. (1937) Construction in analysis. In *Standard Edition of the Complete Psychological Works of S. Freud.* Vol. 23. London: Hogarth Press.

Galin, D. (1974) Implications for psychiatry of left and right cerebral specialization. *Archives of General Psychiatry 31*: 572-83.

Galin, D., Dimond, R. and Braff, D. (1977) Lateralization of conversion symptoms: more frequent on the left. *American Journal of Psychiatry 134*: 578-80.

Gedo, J.E. and Goldberg, A. (1973) *Models of the Mind.* Chicago: University of Chicago Press.

Gill, M.M. (1976) Metapsychology is not psychology. *Psychological Issues 9*: 4, monograph 36.

Glover, E. (1924) Notes on oral character formation. In E. Glover (1956). *On the Oral Development of the Mind.* London: Mayo Publishing.

Goffman, E. (1961) *Encounters: Two Studies in the Sociology of Interaction.* London: Allen Lane.

Goldfried, M.R., Stricker, G. and Weiner, I.B. (1971) *Rorschach Handbook of Clinical and Research Applications.* Englewood Cliffs, NJ: Prentice-Hall.

Goldman-Eisler, F. (1948) Breast feeding and character formation. *Journal of Personality 17*: 83-103.

Goldman-Eisler, F. (1951) The problem of 'orality' and its origin in early childhood. *Journal of Mental Science 97*: 765-82.

Goldstein, K.M. and Blackman, S. (1978) *Cognitive Style: Five Approaches and Relevant Research.* New York: Wiley.

Goodenough, F.L. (1926) *Measurement of Intelligence by Drawings.* New York: Harcourt Brace.

Goodge, P. (1979) Problems of repertory grid analysis and a cluster analysis solution. *British Journal of Psychiatry 134*: 516-21.

Gough, H.G. (1957) *The Californian Psychological Inventory.* Palo Alto: Consulting Psychology Press.

Grygier, T.G. (1961) *The Dynamic Personality Inventory.* Windsor: National Foundation for Educational Research.

Guilford, J.P. (1956) *Psychometric Methods.* New York: McGraw-Hill.

Guilford, J.P. (1959) *Personality.* New York: McGraw-Hill.

Guilford, J.P. and Guilford, R.B. (1934) An analysis of the factors in a typical test of introversion–extraversion. *Journal of Abnormal Psychology 28*: 377-99.

Guilford, J.S., Zimmerman, W.S. and Guilford, J.P. (eds) (1976) *The Guilford Zimmerman Temperament Survey Handbook.* San Diego: Stendon.

Gurman, A.S. (1977) The patient's perception of the therapeutic relationship. In A.S. Gurman and A.M. Razin (eds) *Effective Psychotherapy: A Handbook of Research.* Oxford: Pergamon.

Haber, R.N. and Fried, A.H. (1975) *An Introduction to Psychology.* New York: Holt, Rinehart & Winston.

Halpern, J. (1977) Projection: a test of the psychoanalytic hypothesis. *Journal of Abnormal Psychology 86*: 536-42.

Hamilton, V. (1970) Non-cognitive factors in university students' performance. *British Journal of Psychology 61*: 229-41.

Harman, H.H. (1976) *Modern Factor Analysis.* Chicago: University of Chicago Press.

Harré, R. (1979) *Social Being.* Oxford: Blackwell.

232   Personality

Harré, R. and Secord, P.F. (1972) *The Explanation of Social Behaviour.* Oxford: Blackwell.

Harris, D.B. (1963) *Children's Drawings as Measures of Intellectual Maturity.* London: Harrap.

Hartman, A.A. (1970) A basic TAT set. *Journal of Projective Techniques and Personality Assessment 34:* 391-6.

Harvey, O.J. (1964) Some cognitive determinants of influencibility. *Sociometry 27:* 208-21.

Harvey, O.J., Hunt, D.E. and Schroder, H.M. (1961) *Conceptual Systems and Personality Organization.* New York: Wiley.

Hathaway, S.R. and McKinley, J.C. (1951) *The Minnesota Multiphasic Personality Inventory and Manual.* New York: The Psychological Corporation.

Hathaway, S.R. and Meehl, P.E. (1951) *An Atlas for the Clinical Use of the MMPI.* Minneapolis: University of Minnesota Press.

Hayslip, B. and Derbes, A. (1974) Intrasubject response consistency in the Holtzman Inkblot Technique. *Journal of Personality Assessment 38:* 149-53.

Heather, B.B. (1976) The specificity of schizophrenic thought disorder: a replication and extension of previous findings. *British Journal of Social and Clinical Psychology 15:* 131-7.

Heilbrunn, G. (1979) Biologic correlates of psychoanalytic concepts. *Journal of American Psychoanalytical Association 27:* 597-626.

Heim, A.W. (1975) *Psychological Testing.* London: Oxford University Press.

Hernstein, M.I. (1963) Behavioural correlates of breast – bottle regimes under varying parent – infant relationships. *Monographs of the Society for Research in Child Development 28:* 4.

Hertz, M.R. (1934) The reliability of the Rorschach ink-blot test. *Journal of Applied Psychology 18:* 461-77.

Hetherington, E.M. and Brackbill, Y. (1963) Etiology and covariation of obstinacy, orderliness and parsimony in young children. *Child Development 34:* 919-43.

Higgins, K. and Schwarz, J.C. (1976) Use of reinforcement to produce loose construing. *Psychological Reports 38:* 799-806.

Hilgard, E.R. (1980) Consciousness in contemporary psychology. *Annual Review of Psychology 31:* 1-26.

Hill, A.B. (1976) Methodological problems in the use of factor analysis: a critical review of the experimental evidence for the anal character. *British Journal of Medical Psychology 49:* 145-59.

Hill, E.F. (1972) *The Holtzman Inkblot Technique.* San Francisco: Jossey-Bass.

Hinkle, D.E. (1965) The change of personal constructs from the viewpoint of a theory of implications. Unpublished Ph.D. thesis, Ohio State University.

Holland, R. (1977) *Self and Social Context.* London: Macmillan.

Holtzman, W.H., Thorpe, J.S., Swartz, J.D. and Herron, E.W. (1961) *Inkblot Perception and Personality: Holtzman Inkblot Technique.* Austin, Texas: University of Texas Press.

Home, H.J. (1966) The concept of mind. *International Journal of Psychoanalysis 47:* 43-9.

Hoppe, K.D. (1977) Split brains and psychoanalysis. *Psychoanalytic Quarterly* 46: 223-44.

Howarth-Williams, M. (1977) *R.D. Laing: His Work and its Relevance for Sociology*. London: Routledge & Kegan Paul.

Howells, J.G. and Lickorish, J.R. (1967) *Family Relation Indicator*. Revised and enlarged edition: manual. Edinburgh and London: Oliver & Boyd.

Hoyt, C. (1941) Test reliability estimated by analyses of variance. *Psychometrika* 6: 153-60.

Jackson, D.N. (1956) A short form of Witkin's Embedded Figures Test. *Journal of Abnormal and Social Psychology* 53: 254-5.

Jackson, L. (1950) Emotional attitudes towards the family in normal, neurotic and delinquent children. *British Journal of Psychology* 41: 35-51; 173-85.

Jackson, L. (1966) *Family Attitudes Test*. Brussels: Editest.

Jahoda, M. (1977) *Freud and the Dilemmas of Psychology*. London: Hogarth Press.

John, E.R. (1976) A model of consciousness. In G.E. Schwartz and D. Shapiro (eds) *Consciousness and Self-Regulation 1*. London: Wiley.

Jung, C.G. (1910) The association method. *American Journal of Psychology* 21: 219-69.

Jurjevich, R.R.M. (1974) *The Hoax of Freudism*. Ardmore, Pa: Dorrance.

Kagan, J. and Lemkin, J. (1960) The child's differential perception of parental attributes. *Journal of Abnormal and Social Psychology* 61: 440-7.

Kagan, J. and Moss, H.A. (1962) *Birth to Maturity: A Study in Psychological Development*. New York: Wiley.

Kagan, J., Moss, H.A. and Sigel, I.E. (1964) Psychological significance of styles of conceptualization. In J.C. Wright and J. Kagan (eds) Basic cognitive process in children. *Monographs of the Society for Research in Child Development* 28: 2(86).

Kagan, J., Pearson, L. and Welch, L. (1966) Conceptual impulsivity and inductive reasoning. *Child Development* 37: 583-94.

Kagan, J., Rosman, B., Day, D., Albert, J. and Phillips, W. (1964) Information processing in the child: significance of analytic and reflective attitudes. *Psychological Monographs* 78: 1 (whole no. 578).

Karp, S.A. (1963) Field dependence and overcoming embeddedness. *Journal of Consulting Psychology* 27: 294-302.

Karst, T.O. and Groutt, J.W. (1977) Inside mystical minds in D. Bannister (ed.) *New Perspectives in Personal Construct Theory*. London: Academic Press.

Kelly, G.A. (1930) The social inheritance. In P. Stringer and D. Bannister (eds) *Concepts of Individuality and Sociality*. London: Academic Press (1979).

Kelly, G.A. (1955) *The Psychology of Personal Constructs*. Vols 1 and 2. New York: Norton.

Kelly, G.A. (1962) Europe's matrix of decision. In M.R. Jones (ed.) *Nebraska Symposium on Motivation*. Lincoln: University of Nebraska Press.

Kelly, G.A. (1960) The language of hypothesis: man's psychological instrument. In B. Maher (ed.) *Clinical Psychology and Personality: The Selected Papers of George Kelly*. New York: Wiley.

Kelly, G.A. (1969a) Ontological acceleration. In B.A. Maher (ed.) *Clinical*

Psychology and Personality: The Selected Papers of George Kelly. New York: Wiley.

Kelly, G.A. (1969b) Man's construction of his alternatives. In B. Maher (ed.) *Clinical Psychology and Personality: The Selected Papers of George Kelly.* New York: Wiley.

Kelly, G.A. (1969c) Humanistic methodology in psychological research. In B. Maher (ed.) *Clinical Psychology and Personality: The Selected Papers of George Kelly.* New York: Wiley.

Kelly, G.A. (1969d) Non-parametric factor analysis of personality theories. In B. Maher (ed.) *Clinical Psychology and Personality: The Selected Papers of George Kelly.* New York: Wiley.

Kent, G.H. and Rosanoff, A.J. (1910) A study of association in insanity. *American Journal of Insanity 67*: 37-96; 317-90.

Kenyon, F.E. (1976) Hypochondriacal states. *British Journal of Psychiatry 129*: 1-14.

Kerlinger, F. and Rokeach, M. (1966) The factorial nature of the F and D scales. *Journal of Personality and Social Psychology 4*: 391-9.

Kirscht, J.P. and Dillehay, R.C. (1967) *Dimensions of Authoritarianism.* Lexington, Ky: University of Kentucky Press.

Klein, G.S. (1954) Need and regulation. In M.R. Jones (ed.) *Nebraska Symposium on Motivation.* Lincoln, Nebraska: University of Nebraska Press.

Klein, G.S. (1973) Is psychoanalysis relevant? *Psychoanalysis and Contemporary Science 2:* 3-21.

Klein, G.S. (1976) Freud's two theories of sexuality. *Psychological Issues 9*: monograph 36, 14-70.

Kline, P. (1968) The validity of the Dynamic Personality Inventory. *British Journal of Medical Psychology 41*: 307-11.

Kline, P. (1971) *Ai3Q Test.* Windsor: National Foundation for Educational Research.

Kline, P. (1972) *Fact and Fantasy in Freudian Theory.* London: Methuen.

Kline, P. (1973) *New Approaches in Psychological Assessment.* New York and London: Wiley.

Kline, P. (1979) *Psychometrics and Psychology.* London: Academic Press.

Kline, P. (1980) *The Construction of Psychological Tests.* London: Batsford.

Kline, P. and Storey, R. (1977) A factor analytic study of the oral character. *British Journal of Social and Clinical Psychology 16*: 317-28.

Kline, P. and Storey, R. (1978) The Dynamic Personality Inventory: what does it measure? *British Journal of Psychology 69*: 375-83.

Klopfer, B., Ainsworth, M.D., Klopfer, W.G. and Holt, R.R. (1954) *Developments in the Rorschach Technique.* Vol. 1: *Technique and Theory.* Chicago: World Book Co.; London: Harrap.

Klopfer, W.G. and Taulbee, E.S. (1976) Projective tests. *Annual Review of Psychology 27*: 543-67.

Knapp, R.R. (1976) *Handbook for the POI.* San Diego: Educational and Industrial Testing Service.

Kogan, N. (1973) Creativity and cognitive style: a life span perspective. In P. Baltesand and K.W. Schaie (eds) *Life Span Developmental Psychology: Personality and Socialization.* New York: Academic Press.

Kogan, N. (1976) *Cognitive Styles in Infancy and Early Childhood.* Hillsdale, NJ: Lawrence Erlbaum Associates.

Krug, R.E. (1961) An analysis of the F Scale: 1. Item factor analysis. *Journal of Social Psychology 53*: 285-91.

Krug, S.E. (1978) Reliability and scope in personality assessment: a comparison of the Cattell and Eysenck inventories. *Multivariate Experimental Clinical Research 3*: 195-204.

Krug, S.E. and Laughlin, J.E. (1977) Second-order factors among normal and pathological primary personality traits. *Journal of Consulting and Clinical Psychology 45*: 575-82.

Kuhn, T.S. (1970) *The Structure of Scientific Revolutions (2nd edn).* Chicago: University of Chicago Press.

Laing, R.D. (1960) *The Divided Self.* London: Penguin.

Laing, R.D. (1967) *The Politics of Experience and The Bird of Paradise.* London: Penguin.

Laing, R.D. (1976) *The Facts of Life.* London: Penguin.

Laing, R.D. and Cooper, D.G. (1964) *Reason and Violence.* London: Tavistock.

Laing, R.D. and Esterson, A. (1964) *Sanity, Madness and the Family.* London: Penguin.

Laing, R.D., Phillipson, H. and Lee, A.R. (1966) *Interpersonal Perception: A Theory and a Method of Research.* London: Tavistock.

Landfield, A.W. (1954) A movement interpretation of threat. *Journal of Abnormal and Social Psychology 49*: 539-42.

Landfield, A.W. (1971) *Personal Construct Systems in Psychotherapy.* Chicago: Rand McNally.

Langer, S.K. (1948) *Philosophy in a New Key.* New York: Penguin.

Langley, C.W. (1971) Differentiation and integration of systems of personal constructs. *Journal of Personality 39*: 10-25.

Lazare, A., Klerman, G.I. and Armor, D.J. (1966) Oral, obsessive and hysterical personality patterns: an investigation of psychoanalytic concepts by means of factor analysis. *Archives of General Psychiatry 14*: 624-30.

Leitner, L.M. Landfield, A.W. and Barr, M.A. (1974) Cognitive complexity: a review and elaboration within personal construct theory. Unpublished manuscript, University of Nebraska.

Lemon, N. (1975) Linguistic development and conceptualisation: a bilingual study. *Journal of Cross-cultural Psychology 6*: 173-88.

Lemon, N. and Warren, N. (1974) Salience, centrality and self-relevance of traits in construing others. *British Journal of Social and Clinical Psychology 13*: 119-24.

Levi-Strauss, C. (1963) *Structural Anthropology.* New York: Basic Books.

Levinger, G. and Clark, J. (1961) Emotional factors in the forgetting of word associations. *Journal of Abnormal and Social Psychology 62*: 99-105.

Lowenfeld, M. (1939) The world pictures of children: a method of recording and studying them. *British Journal of Medical Psychology 18*: 65-101.

Lowenfeld, M. (1954) *The Lowenfeld Mosaic Test.* London: Newman Neame.

Luborsky, L. (1973) Forgetting and remembering during psychotherapy. *Psychological Issues 8*: 29-55.

Lüscher, M. (1969) *Lüscher-Test* (10th edn). Basel: Test-Verlag.

Lüscher, M. (trans. and ed. I.A. Scott) (1970) *The Lüscher Colour Test.* London: Cape.

McClelland, D., Atkinson, J.W., Clark, R.A. and Lowell, E.L. (1953) *The Achievement Motive.* New York: Appleton-Century-Crofts.

McCoy, M. (1977) A reconstruction of emotion. In D. Bannister (ed.) *New Perspectives in Personal Construct Theory.* London: Academic Press.

McDougal, W. (1932) *The Energies of Men.* London: Methuen.

McGaughran, L.S. and Moran, L.J. (1956) 'Conceptual levels' versus 'conceptual area', analysis of object sorting behaviour of schizophrenic and neuropsychiatric groups. *Journal of Abnormal Social Psychology 52*: 43-50.

McGuire, W. (ed) (1974) *The Freud/Jung letters.* (Translated by R. Manheim and R.F.C. Hull.) Princeton, NJ: Princeton University Press.

McIntosh, D. (1979) The empirical bearing of psychoanalytic theory. *International Journal of Psychoanalysis 60*: 405-32.

McKinnon, J.A. (1979) Two semantic forms: neuro-psychological and psychoanalytic descriptions. *Psychoanalysis and Contemporary Thought 2*: 25-76.

McLaughlin, J.T. (1978) Primary and secondary process in the context of cerebral hemispheric specialization. *Psychoanalytic Quarterly 47*: 237-66.

McPherson, F.M., Armstrong, J. and Heather, B.B. (1978) Psychological construing and thought disorder: another test of the difficulty hypothesis. *British Journal of Medical Psychology 51*: 319-24.

McPherson, F.M., Blackburn, I.M., Draffan, J.W. and McFayden, M. (1973) A further study of the grid test of thought disorder. *British Journal of Social and Clinical Psychology 12*: 420-7.

McWilliams, S. (1980) Personal communication.

Maher, B. (ed.) (1969) *Clinical Psychology and Personality: The Selected Papers of George Kelly.* New York: Wiley.

Mahmood, Z. (1978) An objective application of the Lowenfeld Mosaic Test in work rehabilitation of psychiatric patients. *British Journal of Projective Psychology and Personality Study 23* (2): 31-7.

Mair, J.M.M. (1970) Psychologists are human too. In D. Bannister (ed.) *Perspectives in Personal Construct Theory.* London: Academic Press.

Mair, J.M.M. and Boyd P. (1967) A comparison of two grid forms. *British Journal of Social and Clinical Psychology 6*: 220.

Makhlouf-Norris, F., Jones, G. and Norris, H. (1970) Articulation of the Conceptual structure in obsessional neurosis. *British Journal of Social and Clinical Psychology 9*: 264-74.

Marcel, T. and Patterson, K. (1978) Word recognition and production. In J. Requin (ed.) *Attention and Performance 7.* Hillside, NJ: Lawrence Erlbaum Associates.

Marsh, P., Rosser, E. and Harré, R. (1977) *The Rules of Disorder.* London: Routledge & Kegan Paul.

Marx, M.H. (1976) *Introduction to Psychology: Problems, Procedures and Principles.* New York and London: Macmillan.

Maslow, A.H. (1962) *Toward a Psychology of Being.* Princeton, NJ: Van Nostrand.

Maslow, A.H. (1954) *Motivation and Personality*. New York: Harper & Row.

Medawar, P.B. (1967) *The Art of the Soluble*. London: Methuen.

Meissner, W.W. (1979) Critique of concepts and therapy in the action language approach to psychoanalysis. *International Journal of Psychoanalysis* 60: 291-310.

Messer, S.B. (1976) Reflection – impulsivity: a review. *Psychological Bulletin* 83: 1026-52.

Messick, S. (1970) The criterion problem in the evaluation of instruction: assessing possible, not just intended, outcomes. In M.C. Wittrock and D. Wiley (eds). *The Evaluation of Instruction: Issues and Problems*. New York: Holt, Rinehart & Winston.

Messick, S. (1976) Personality consistencies in cognition and creativity. In S. Messick and Associates, *Individuality in Learning*. San Francisco: Jossey-Bass.

Messick, S. and Fredericksen, N. (1958) Ability, acquiescence and authoritarianism. *Psychological Reports 4*: 687-97.

Miller, C.A., Galanter, E. and Pribram, K.H. (1960) *Plans and the Structure of Behaviour*. New York: Holt, Rinehart & Winston.

Miller, N.E. and Bugelski, R. (1948) Minor studies of aggression II. The influence of frustrations imposed by the in-group on attitudes expressed towards out-groups. *Journal of Psychology 25*: 437-42.

Mitchell, K.M., Bozarth, J.D. and Krauft, C.C. (1977) A reappraisal of the therapeutic effectiveness of accurate empathy, nonpossessive warmth, and genuineness. In A.S. Gurman and A.M. Razin (eds) *Effective Psychotherapy: A Handbook of Research*. Oxford: Pergamon.

Mitchison G.J. (1977) Phyllotaxis and the Fibonacci series. *Science 196*: 270-5.

Morgan, C.D. and Murray, H.A. (1935) A method for investigating phantasies. *Archives of Neurological Psychiatry 34*: 289-306.

Murray, H.A. (1938) *Exploration in Personality: A Clinical and Experimental Study of Fifty Men of College Age*. New York: Oxford University Press.

Murray, H.A. (1943) *Thematic Apperception Test Manual*. Cambridge, Mass: Harvard University Press.

Murstein, B.L. (1963) *Theory and Research in Projective Techniques (emphasizing the TAT)*. New York and London: Wiley.

Nidorff, L.J. and Crockett, W.H. (1965) Cognitive complexity and the integration of conflicting information in written impressions. *Journal of Social Psychology 66*: 165-9.

Noblin, C.D., Timmons, E.O. and Kael, H.C. (1966) Differential effects of positive and negative verbal reinforcement on psychoanalytic character types. *Journal of Personality and Social Psychology 4*: 224-8.

Noy, P. (1973) Symbolism and mental representation. *Annual of Psychoanalysis 1*: 125-58.

Nunnally, J. (1978) *Psychometric Theory* (2nd edn). New York: McGraw-Hill.

Oakley, D.A. (1979) Cerebral cortex and adaptive behaviour. In D.A. Oakley and H.C. Plotkin (eds) *Brain, Behaviour and Evolution*. London: Methuen.

O'Grady, M. (1977) Effect of subliminal pictorial stimulation on skin resistence. *Perceptual and Motor Skills 44*: 1051-6.

238   Personality

Osgood, C.E., Suci, G.J. and Tannenbaum, P.H. (1957) *The Measurement of Meaning*. Urbana, Ill.: University of Illinois Press.

Parloff, M.B., Waskow, I.E. and Wolfe, B.E. (1978) Research on therapist variables in relation to process and outcome. In Garfield, S.L. and Bergin, A.E. (eds) *Handbook of Psychotherapy and Behaviour Change*. (2nd edn) New York: Wiley.

Peck, D. and Whitlow, D. (1975) *Approaches to Personality Theory*. London: Methuen.

Pedhazur, E.J. (1971) Factor structure of the Dogmatism Scale. *Psychological Reports 28*: 735-40.

Penfield, W. (1958) The role of the temporal cortex in recall of past experiences and interpretation of the present. In *Neurological Bases of Behaviour*. Boston: Little, Brown.

Perls, F., Hefferline, R. and Goodman, P. (1965) *Gestalt Therapy*. New York: Dell Publishing.

Peterfreund, E. (1971) Information systems and psychoanalysis. *Psychological Issues 7*: monograph 25/26.

Peterfreund, E. (1975) The need for a new general theoretical frame of reference for psychoanalysis. *Psychoanalytic Quarterly 44*: 534-49.

Peterson, C.H. and Spano, F. (1941) Breast feeding, maternal rejection and child personality. *Character and Personality 10*: 62-6.

Pettigrew, T.F. (1958) The measurement of correlates of category width as a cognitive variable. *Journal of Personality 26*: 532-44.

Phillipson, H. (1955) *The Object Relations Technique*. London: Tavistock.

Phillipson, H. (1973) *A Short Introduction to the Object Relations Technique* (2nd edn). London: Tavistock Institute of Human Relations.

Piaget, J. (1967) *Six Psychological Studies*. New York: Random House.

Pickford, R.W. (1963) *Pickford Projective Pictures*. London: Tavistock.

Piotrowski, Z.A. (1937) The Rorschach ink blot method in organic disturbances of the central nervous system. *Journal of Nervous and Mental Diseases 86*: 525-37.

Pitcher, E.G. and Prelinger, E. (1963) *Children Tell Stories: An Analysis of Fantasy*. New York: International Universities Press.

Plato, Gorgias (1952). In R.M. Hutchins (ed.) *Great Books of the Western World*. Vol 7. Chicago: Encyclopedia Britannica.

Pollak, J.M. (1979) Obsessive–compulsive personality: a review. *Psychological Bulletin 86*: 225-41.

Procter, H.G. (1978) Personal construct theory and the family: a theoretical and methodological study. Unpublished Ph.D. thesis, University of Bristol.

Rabin, A.I. (ed.) (1968) *Projective Techniques in Personality Assessment*. New York: Springer.

Rabin, A.I. and Haworth, M.R. (eds) *Projective Techniques with Children*. New York and London: Grune & Stratton.

Radley, A.R. (1974) Schizophrenic thought disorder and the nature of personal constructs. *British Journal of Social and Clinical Psychology 13*: 315-27.

Rappoport, J. and Chinsky, J.M. (1972) Accurate empathy: confusion of a construct. *Psychological Bulletin 77*: 400-04.

Rawn, M.L. (1979) Schafer's 'Action Language': a questionable alternative to metapsychology. *International Journal of Psychoanalysis 60*: 455-65.

Rickers-Ovsiankina, M.A. (ed.) (1963) *Rorschach Psychology*. New York: Wiley.

Ricoeur, P. (1970) *Freud and Philosophy: An Essay in Interpretation*. New Haven, Conn.: Yale University Press.

Rogers, C.R. (1951) *Client-centred Therapy*. Boston: Houghton Mifflin.

Rogers, C.R. (1959) A theory of therapy, personality, and interpersonal relationships as developed in the client-centred framework. In S. Koch (ed.) *Psychology: A Study of a Science*. Vol. 3. New York: McGraw-Hill.

Rogers, C.R. (1961) *On Becoming a Person: A Psychotherapist's View of Psychotherapy*. London: Constable.

Rogers, C.R. (1970) *Encounter Groups*. New York: Harper & Row.

Rogers, C.R. (1973) *Becoming Partners: Marriage and Its Alternatives*. London: Constable.

Rogers, C.R. (1974) In retrospect: forty-six years. *American Psychologist 29*: 115-23.

Rogers, C.R. (1977) *Carl Rogers on Personal Power*. London: Constable.

Rogers, C.R., Gendlin, E.T., Kiesler, D.V. and Truax, C.B. (1967) *The Therapeutic Relationship and its Impact*. Madison, Wisconsin: University of Wisconsin Press.

Rokeach, M. (1948) Generalized mental rigidity as a factor in ethnocentrism. *Journal of Abnormal and Social Psychology 43*: 259-78.

Rokeach, M. (1960) *The Open and Closed Mind*. New York: Basic Books.

Rokeach, M., McGovney, W.C. and Denny, M.R. (1955) A distinction between dogmatic and rigid thinking. *Journal of Abnormal and Social Psychology 51*: 87-93.

Rorschach, H. (1921) *Psychodiagnostics: A diagnostic Test Based on Perception* (2nd edn 1942) Bern: Huber.

Rosanoff, A.J. (ed.) (1927) *Manual of Psychiatry*. New York: Wiley.

Rosenblatt, A.D. and Thickstun, J.T. (1977) Modern psychoanalytic concepts in a general psychology. *Psychological Issues 11*: 2/3 monograph 42/3.

Rosenwald, G.C. (1972) Effectiveness of defences against anal impulse arousal. *Journal of Consulting and Clinical Psychology 39*: 292-8.

Royce, J.R. (1963) Factors as theoretical constructs. In D.N. Jackson and S. Messick (eds) *Problems in Human Assessment*. New York: McGraw-Hill.

Rychlak, J.F. (1977) *The Psychology of Rigorous Humanism*. New York: Wiley.

Rycroft, C. (1966) Introduction: causes and meaning. In C. Rycroft (ed.) *Psychoanalysis Observed*. London: Constable.

Rycroft, C. (1968) *A Critical Dictionary of Psychoanalysis*. Harmondsworth: Penguin.

Ryle, A. (1975) *Frames and Cages*. Edinburgh: Sussex University Press.

Ryle, A. and Lunghi, M. (1970) The dyad grid: a modification of repertory grid technique. *British Journal of Psychiatry 117*: 323-7.

Sackheim, H.A. and Gur, R.C. (1978) Lateral asymmetry in intensity of emotional expression. *Neuropsychologia 16*: 473-81.

Salmon, P. (1976) Grid measures with child subjects. In P. Slater (ed.) *Explorations of Intrapersonal Space.* Vol 1. London: Wiley.

Salmon, P. (1978) Doing psychological research. In F. Fransella (ed.) *Personal Construct Psychology 1977.* London: Academic Press.

Sandler, J. (1969) *On the Communication of Psychoanalytic Thought.* Leiden: University Press.

Sandler, J., Dare, C. and Holder, A. (1972) Frames of reference in psychoanalytic psychology: IV. The affect-trauma frame of reference. *British Journal of Medical Psychology 45*: 265-72.

Sandler, J., Dare, C. and Holder, A. (1972a) Frames of reference in psychoanalytic psychology: I. Introduction. *British Journal of Medical Psychology 45*: 127-31.

Sandler, J., Dare, C. and Holder, A. (1972b) Frames of reference in psychoanalytic psychology: II. The historical context and phases in the development of psychoanalysis. *British Journal of Medical Psychology 45*: 133-42.

Sandler, J., Dare, C. and Holder, A. (1972c) Frames of reference in psychoanalytic psychology: III. A note on the basic assumptions. *British Journal of Medical Psychology 45*: 143-7.

Sandler, J., Dare, C. and Holder, A. (1973a) Frames of reference in psychoanalytic psychology: V. The topographical frame of reference: the organization of the mental apparatus. *British Journal of Medical Psychology 46*: 29-36.

Sandler, J., Dare, C. and Holder, A. (1973b) Frames of reference in psychoanalytic psychology: VI. The topographical frame of reference: the Unconscious. *British Journal of Medical Psychology 46*: 37-43.

Sandler, J., Dare, C. and Holder, A. (1973c) Frames of reference in psychoanalytic psychology: VII. The topographical frame of reference: the Preconscious and the Conscious. *British Journal of Medical Psychology 46*: 143-53.

Sandler, J., Dare, C. and Holder, A. (1974) Frames of reference in psychoanalytic psychology: VIII. The topographical frame of reference: transference as an illustration of the functioning of the mental apparatus. *British Journal of Medical Psychology 47*: 43-51.

Sandler, J., Dare, C. and Holder, A. (1975) Frames of reference in psychoanalytic psychology: IX. Dream processes in the topographical frame of reference. *British Journal of Medical Psychology 48*: 161-74.

Sandler, J., Dare, C. and Holder, A. (1976) Frames of reference in psychoanalytic psychology: X. Narcissism and object-love in the second phase of psychoanalysis. *British Journal of Medical Psychology 49*: 267-74.

Sandler, J., Dare, C. and Holder, A. (1978) Frames of reference in psychoanalytic psychology: XI. Limitations of the topographical model. *British Journal of Medical Psychology 51*: 61-5.

Sandler, J. and Joffe, W.G. (1966) On skill and sublimation. *Journal of American Psychoanalytic Association 14*: 335.

Santostefano, S. (1978) *A Biodevelopmental Approach to Clinical Child-Psychology*: *Cognitive Controls and Cognitive Control Therapy*. New York: Wiley.

Sarnoff, I. and Corwin, S.M. (1959) Castration anxiety and the fear of death. *Journal of Personality 27*: 374-85.

Sarnoff, I. and Zimbardo, P.G. (1961) Anxiety, fear and social affiliation. *Journal of Abnormal and Social Psychology 62*: 356-63.

Sartre, J.P. (1960) *Critique de la raison dialectique*. Paris: Gallimard.

Saville, P. and Blinkhorn, S. (1976) *Undergraduate Personality by Factored Scales*. Windsor: National Foundation for Educational Research.

Scarlett, H.H., Press, A.N. and Crockett, W.H. (1971) Children's descriptions of their peers. *Child Development 42*: 439-53.

Schachtel, E.G. (1967) *Experiential Foundations of Rorschach's Test*. London: Tavistock.

Schafer, R. (1976) *A New Language for Psychoanalysis*. New Haven and London: Yale University Press.

Schafer, R. (1979) Character, ego-syntonicity and character change. *Journal of the American Psychoanalytic Association 27*: 785-802.

Schaie, K.W. and Heiss, R. (1964) *Colour and Personality*. Bern and Stuttgart: Huber.

Schmidl, F. (1955) The problem of scientific validation in psychoanalytic interpretation. *International Journal of Psychoanalysis 36*: 127-45.

Schroder, H.M., Driver, M.J. and Streufert, S. (1967) *Human Information Processing*. New York: Holt, Rinehart & Winston.

Schwartz, E.K., Riess, B.F. and Cottingham, A. (1951) Further critical evaluation of the negro version of the TAT. *Journal of Projective Techniques 15*: 394-400.

Schwartz, F. and Lazar, Z. (1979) The scientific status of the Rorschach. *Journal of Personality Assessment 43*: 3-11.

Sears, R.R., Rau, L. and Alpert, R. (1965) *Identification and Child Training*. Stanford, Ca: Stanford University Press.

Sears, R.R., Whiting, J.W.M., Nowlis, V. and Sears, P.S. (1953) Some child-rearing antecedents of aggression and dependency in young children. *Genetic Psychology Monographs 47*: 135-234.

Sells, S.B., Demaree, R.G. and Will, D.P. (1970) Dimensions of personality 1: congent factor structure of Guilford and Cattell trait markers. *Multivariate Behavioural Research 5*: 391-422.

Semeonoff, B. (1958) Projective techniques in selection for counselling. *Human Relations 11*: 113-22.

Semeonoff, B. (1968) The equivalence of Rorschach and Zulliger's test in a selection context. *British Journal of Projective Psychology and Personality Study 13* (2): 11-12.

Semeonoff, B. (1971) Rorschach and the development of projective psychology: a personal view. *British Journal of Projective Psychology and Personality Study 16* (2): 5-10.

Semeonoff, B. (1973) New developments in projective testing. In P. Kline (ed.) *New Approaches in Psychological Assessment*. New York and London: Wiley.

Semeonoff, B. (1976) *Projective Techniques*. London and New York: Wiley.

Semeonoff, B. (1976a) The effect of colour on TAT response. *British Journal of Projective Psychology and Personality Study 21* (1): 31-8.

Semeonoff, B. (1980) The Colour Pyramid Test: some considerations of scope and validity. *British Journal of Projective Psychology and Personality Study 25* (1) (in press).

Shevrin, H. (1973) Brain wave correlates of subliminal stimulation in psychoanalytic research. *Psychological Issues 8*: monograph 30.

Shevrin, H. (1973) Brain wave correlates of subliminal stimulation on psychoanalytic research. *Psychological Issues 8*: 2 monograph 30.

Shostrom, E.L. (1966) *The Personal Orientation Inventory: An Inventory for the Measurement of Self-actualisation*. San Diego: Educational and Industrial Testing Service.

Silverman, L.H., Bronstein, A. and Mendelsohn, E. (1976) The further use of the subliminal psychodynamic activation method for the experimental study of the clinical theory of psychoanalysis. *Psychotherapy: Theory, Research and Practice 13*: 2-16.

Silverman, L.H. Ross, D.L., Adler, J.M. and Lustig, D.A. (1978) Simple research paradigm for demonstrating subliminal psychodynamic activation: effects of Oedipal stimuli on dart-throwing accuracy in college males. *Journal of Abnormal Psychology 87*: 341-57.

Skinner, B.F. (1971) *Beyond Freedom and Dignity*. New York: Knopf.

Slater, P. (1976) *The Measurement of Intrapersonal Space by Grid Technique*. Vol. 1: *Explorations of Intrapersonal Space*. Chichester: Wiley.

Slater, P. (1977) *The Measurement of Intrapersonal Space by Grid Technique*. Vol. 2: *Dimensions of Intrapersonal Space*. Chichester: Wiley.

Sloane, R.B., Staples, F.R., Cristol, A.H., Yorkston, N.J. and Whipple, K. (1975) *Psychotherapy versus Behaviour Therapy*. Cambridge, Mass: Harvard University Press.

Smith, P.B. (1980) An attributional analysis of personal learning. In C.P. Aldorfer and C.L. Cooper (eds) *Advances in Experiential Processes*. Vol. 2. Chichester: Wiley.

Smith, P.B. (1980a) *Group Processes and Personal Change*. London: Harper & Row.

Sneddon, P.M. (1971) A study of the principles underlying the TAT, with special reference to the development of a technique for use in counsellor selection. Unpublished Ph.D. thesis, University of Edinburgh.

Space, L.G. and Cromwell, R.L. (1978) Personal constructs among schizophrenic patients. In S. Schwartz (ed.) *Language and Cognition in Schizophrenia*. New York: Halsted Press.

Spiro, A.M. (1979) A philosophical appraisal of Roy Schafer's 'A New Language for Psychoanalysis'. *Psychoanalysis and Contemporary Thought 2*: 253-91.

Steele, R. (1979) Psychoanalysis and Hermenentics. *The International Review of Psycho-Analysis 6*: 4, 389-412.

Streufert, S. and Driver, M.J. (1965) Conceptual structure, information load and perceptual complexity. *Psychonomic Science 3*: 249-50.

Stringer, P. (1967) A comparison of the self-images of art and architecture students. *Studies in Art Education 9*: 33-49.

Stringer, P. (1970) A note on the factorial structure of the Dynamic Personality Inventory. *British Journal of Medical Psychology 43*: 95-103.

Stringer, P. and Bannister, D. (eds) (1979) *Constructs of Sociality and Individuality.* London: Academic Press.

Stroop, J.R. (1935) Studies of interference in serial verbal reactions. *Journal of Experimental Psychology 18*: 643-62.

Sullivan, H.S. (1947) *Conceptions of Modern Psychiatry.* New York: Norton.

Thomas, L. (1978) A personal construct approach to learning in education, training and therapy. In F. Fransella (ed.) *Personal Construct Psychology 1977.* London: Academic Press.

Thurstone, J.R. and Mussen, P.H. (1951) Infant feeding gratification and adult personality. *Journal of Personality 19*: 449-58.

Thurstone, L.L. (1944) A factorial study of perception. *Psychometric Monographs 4.* Chicago: University of Chicago Press.

Thurstone, L.L. (1947) *Multiple Factor Analysis: A Development and Expansion of the Mind.* Chicago: University of Chicago Press.

Timmons, E.O. and Noblin, C.D. (1963) The differential performance of orals and anals in a verbal conditioning paradigm. *Journal of Consulting Psychology 27*: 383-6.

Tribich, D. and Messer, S. (1974) Psychoanalytic type and status of authority as determiners of suggestibility. *Journal of Consulting and Clinical Psychology 42*: 842-8.

Truax, C.B. and Mitchell, K.M. (1971) Research on certain therapist interpersonal skills in relation to process and outcome. In A.E. Bergin and S.L. Garfield (eds) *Handbook of Psychotherapy and Behaviour Change.* New York: Wiley.

Tuckman, B.W. (1966) Integrative complexity: its measurement and relation to creativity. *Educational and Psychological Measurement 26*: 369-82.

Tyler, L. (1978) *Individuality: Human Possibilities and Personal Choice in the Psychological Development of Men and Women.* San Francisco: Jossey-Bass.

Tyrer, P., Lewis, P. and Lee, J. (1978) Effects of subliminal and supraliminal stress on symptoms of anxiety. *Journal of Nervous and Mental Disease 168*: 88-95.

Vacchiano, R.B., Strauss, P.S. and Hochman, L. (1969) The open and closed mind: a review of dogmatism. *Psychological Bulletin 71*: 261-73.

Vagg, P.R. and Hammond, S.B. (1976) The number and kind of invariant personality Q factors: a partial replication of Eysenck and Eysenck. *British Journal of Social and Clinical Psychology 15*: 121-30.

Vaihinger, H. (1924) *The Philosophy of 'As If': A System of the Theoretical, Practical and Religious Fictions of Mankind* (translated by C.K. Ogden). London: Routledge & Kegan Paul.

Vaughan, D.S. (1973) The relative methodological soundness of several major personality factor analyses. *Journal of Behavioural Science 1*: 305-13.

Wallach, M.A. and Greenberg, C. (1960) Personality functions of symbolic sexual arousal to music. *Psychological Monographs 74*: 494.

Watson, J. B. (1913) Psychology as a behaviourist views it. *Psychological Review 20*: 158-77.

Watson, J. P., Gunn, J. C. and Gristwood, J. (1976) A grid investigation of long-term prisoners. In P. Slater (ed.) *The Measurement of Intrapersonal Space by Grid Technique*. London: Wiley.

Weiskrantz, L. (1977) Trying to bridge some neuropsychological gaps between money and man. *British Journal of Psychology 68*: 431-45.

Weiskrantz, L. (1980) Varieties of residual experience. The Eighth Bartlett Lecture, presented at University College, London.

Weiskrantz, L. and Warrington, E. K. (1979) Conditioning in amnesic patients. *Neuropsychologia 17*: 187-94.

Wheeler, L., Goodale, R. and Deese, J. (1974) *General Psychology*. Boston: Allyn & Bacon.

Whiting, J. W. and Child, I. L. (1953) *Child Training and Personality: A Cross-Cultural Study*. New Haven, Conn: Yale University Press.

Wilkinson, F. R. and Cargill, D. W. (1955) Repression elicited by story material based on the oedipus complex. *Journal of Social Psychology 42*: 209-14.

Windelband, W. (1904) *Geschichte und Naturwissenschaft* (3rd edn). Strasburg, Germany: Heitz.

Winnicott, D. W. (1957) *The Child and the Family*. London: Tavistock.

Winnicott, D. W. (1958) *Collected Papers: Through Paediatrics to Psycho-Analysis*. London: Tavistock.

Winnicott, D. W. (1965) *Maturational Processes and the Facilitating Environment*. London: Hogarth Press.

Witkin, H. A., Dyk, R. B., Faterson, H. F., Goodenough, D. R. and Karp, S. A. (1962) *Psychological Differentiation*. New York: Wiley.

Witkin, H. A., Oltman, P. K., Raskin, E. and Karp, S. A. (1971) *A Manual for the Embedded Figures Tests*. Palo Alto: Consulting Psychologists Press.

Wolpe, J. and Rachman, S. (1963) Psychoanalytic evidence: a critique based on Freud's case of Little Hans. In S. Rachman (ed.) *Critical Essays on Psychoanalysis*. New York: Pergamon.

Worthington, A. G. (1964) Differential rates of dark adaptation to 'taboo' and 'neutral' stimuli. *Canadian Journal of Psychology 18*: 257-68.

Wright, J. C. (1973) *A User's Manual for the KRISP*. St Louis, Missouri: CEMREL, Inc.

Wurmser, L. (1977) A defense of the use of metaphor in analytic theory formation. *Psychoanalytic Quarterly 46*: 466-98.

Wylie, R. C. (1974) *The Self Concept*. Lincoln, Nebraska: University of Nebraska Press.

Wylie, R. C. and Mitchell, K. M. (1971) Research on certain therapist interpersonal skills in relation to process and outcome. In A. E. Bergin and S. L. Garfield (eds) *Handbook of Psychotherapy and Behaviour Change*. New York: Wiley.

Zaidel, E. (1978) Auditory language comprehension in the right hemisphere following cerebral commissurotomy and hemispherectomy. In A. Caramazza and E. Zuriff (eds) *Acquisition and Language Breakdown: Parallels and Divergences*. Baltimore, Md: John Hopkins University Press.

Zalot, G. and Adams-Webber, J. (1977) Cognitive complexity in the perception of neighbours. *Social Behavior and Personality* 5: 281-3.

Zubin, J., Eron, L. D. and Schumer, F. (1965) *An Experimental Approach to Projective Techniques.* New York: Wiley.

Zulliger, H. (1956) The Behn – Rorschach Test. Bern: Huber.

Zulliger, H. (1962) *Der Zulliger – Tafeln – Test* (2nd edn). Bern and Stuttgart: Huber.

Zulliger, H. (1969) *The Zulliger Individual and Group Test* (ed.) F. Salomon. New York: International Universities Press.

Name index

Subject index